Running Mad for Kentucky

Running Mad
for Kentucky

FRONTIER
TRAVEL
ACCOUNTS

Edited by Ellen Eslinger

THE UNIVERSITY PRESS OF KENTUCKY

Publication of this volume was made possible in part by a grant from the National Endowment for the Humanities.

Editorial and Sales Offices: The University Press of Kentucky
663 South Limestone Street, Lexington, Kentucky 40508-4008
www.kentuckypress.com

Library of Congress Cataloging-in-Publication Data

Running mad for Kentucky : frontier travel accounts
/ Ellen Eslinger.
p. cm.
Includes bibliographical references and index.
ISBN 0-8131-2313-5 (hardcover : alk. paper)
1. Kentucky—History—To 1792. 2. Frontier and pioneer
life—Kentucky. 3. Kentucky—Description and travel.
4. Pioneers—Kentucky—Diaries. I. Eslinger, Ellen, 1956- II. Title.
F454.R86 2004
976.9'02—dc22   2003020884
ISBN 978-0-8131-2313-4
ISBN 978-0-8131-3379-9 (pbk. : alk. paper)

This book is printed on acid-free recycled paper meeting
the requirements of the American National Standard
for Permanence in Paper for Printed Library Materials.

Manufactured in the United States of America.

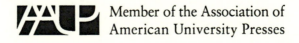   Member of the Association of
American University Presses

To my mother and father

Contents

Illustrations

Preface

This project was undertaken from a realization that the crossing of America's first divide, the Appalachian Mountains, has long been underappreciated in the general story of westward expansion. The existing works, written more than half a century ago, are technical. They seek to detail the route and give much less attention to the actual experience of the migrants. Compared with the mighty effort demanded by the Overland Trail to California, the near-dismissal of the Appalachian crossing is understandable. This imbalance has grown stronger in recent years with the publication of several compelling works on the Overland Trail.[1] The pioneers who ventured into Kentucky and adjacent regions of Ohio and Tennessee faced lower heights and a shorter trek. In terms of the eighteenth century, however, the venture across the Appalachians, whether overland or by river, was nonetheless a huge undertaking and fraught with danger—even by modern standards.

The most significant reason for the discrepancy in historical recognition is probably the few personal accounts of what the early trans-Appalachian crossing entailed. While diaries from the Overland Trail number in the several hundreds, those that survive from the trans-Appalachian crossing number only a few dozen. Yet, at least 100,000 adults, plus innumerable children, undertook this journey by 1800. The dearth of personal accounts therefore cannot readily be attributed to a lack of potential authors. The more likely reason is a lower level of literacy in the eighteenth century. This was especially the case for southern regions, where many of the early westerners originated, as well as among women and the poorer ranks of society. Among the thousands of slaves who were taken, literacy was practically nonexistent.[2] Most of the personal accounts of travel to Kentucky and the Ohio Valley were therefore written by white males, usually of privileged background. Yet even these are few in number. Those that do exist, however, reveal that status and wealth offered little protection from the danger and discomfort of travel through an extended mountain wilderness during a period when government aid was weak and Indian resistance was strong.

The lack of documentation notwithstanding, surviving records indicate that the experience of crossing the Appalachians merits a place in the nation's historical memory on par with that of crossing the Rockies. In the imaginations of the people who lived in the eighteenth century, traversing several hundred miles of uninhabited wilderness might as well have been a thousand miles. Kentucky was the first major attempt at noncontiguous American settlement since the European arrival in the seventeenth century. For the participants, no less than for the later gold rushers to California, it was an unprecedented and daunting experience. Although crossing the Appalachians presented fewer difficulties than did the heights of the Rocky Mountains, those difficulties were nonetheless often extremely costly, both personally and materially. Whether migrants came via the Ohio River or the Wilderness Road, they encountered life-threatening natural obstacles. And, to a much greater degree than on the Overland Trail, they faced a formidable danger of Indian attack. Also overlooked is the scale of relocation on a national level, for both black and white. The appetite for Bluegrass land in Kentucky was as powerful as that for California gold. Indeed, within twenty years of initial settlement, a greater proportion of the national population had crossed the Appalachians (7.8 percent by 1800) than had followed the prospect of gold in California and land beyond the Rockies (2.6 percent by 1870).[3] The effect upon the new American republic was enormous.

The way to Kentucky and neighboring regions, by land or by water, therefore requires no apologies. It is the dearth of documentation rather than the scale of enterprise that has prevented its proper acknowledgment. As the following firsthand accounts attempt to demonstrate, the trans-Appalachian crossing can stand sufficiently on its own merits, well bracketing the Overland Trail in the story of continental expansion.

The travel accounts selected for this volume are presented as closely to the originals as possible. Some punctuation has been added or altered for the sake of clarity and the daily entries are each presented as indented paragraphs. Spelling in the eighteenth century was fluid but has been left in the original form where the meaning seemed clear. Some of the selections have been previously published in their entirety or as part of a biography, and although accessible to scholars, few have been read by the modern public. Moreover, when read together rather than individually, they yield a deeper appreciation for the range of experiences, as well as for how those experiences have changed over the years.

The travel accounts collected for this volume were selected according to several criteria. Those that were terse, recording only the covered mileage or weather, were eliminated. Also omitted were those in readily available publications, although many of these were consulted and used to enrich the introductory essay. All of the selected journals had to document the journey as experienced rather than as remembered later. In addition, I wanted to show as much breadth as possible. Journals written by people of little means—women, slaves, and ethnic minorities—are rare, but every effort was made to include people of different backgrounds. The date of travel was also taken into consideration so that the eighteenth-century time period would receive balanced coverage. Another goal was to balance travel experiences on the Wilderness Road and the Ohio River routes. The final selections seek to represent what it was like to cross the Appalachian Mountains in the early period as fully as possible, although, of course, they cannot capture this story in its entirety.

Acknowledgments

I owe thanks first of all to the ongoing support of my family, who are too numerous to name individually; but in my heart their many acts of love, from both young and old, cannot be condensed to fit in this limited space.

I am also heavily indebted to several professional staffs who went beyond the call of duty to help bring this work together. Among these are Lisa McCoun at Washington and Lee University, the fabulous staffs at the Filson Historical Society and the Virginia Historical Society, and Denise Rogers at DePaul University. The American Antiquarian Society, the Colonial Williamsburg Foundation, the Massachusetts Historical Society, and the University of Chicago granted kind permission to reproduce extensively from works in their collections and to provide appropriate illustrations. DePaul University provided valuable financial support for summer research and writing.

I owe further debt to Tracy Roberts, Joe and Kathleen Herring, Owan Pursell, Fred and Barbara Giloth, Charles Goldstein, Judith Gillard-Kaufman, David and Laurie Carroll, Dick Goldberg, and Tom Mockaitis. John Zeigler at The University Press of Kentucky was unflagging in his support and enthusiasm, as were all the other staff members.

As any author, or in this case, editor, will readily admit, our name may be on a book's cover, but it is the product of many people who cared. The shortcomings are due to me alone.

Introduction

Early Explorations

A number of Spanish, French, and English explorers and traders infiltrated the North American interior in the latter part of the seventeenth century. Perhaps the most important was Robert Cavalier Sieur de la Salle in 1669, who established the claim of France from the headwaters of the Ohio River down to the falls at the present site of Louisville. This expedition was followed by Father [Jacques] Marquette's journey from Lake Michigan to the Mississippi and in 1682, a second journey by la Salle from the Illinois River to the Gulf of Mexico. A chain of French military outposts, trading houses, and missions soon connected the Canadian provinces through the Mississippi Valley to New Orleans.

Some English exploration of the trans-Allegheny region was undertaken by a small number of private hunters and traders, but the first organized interest in colonization did not surface until the middle of the eighteenth century. The Loyal Land Company received a royal charter in 1748 for 800,000 acres in a region now embraced by Kentucky. The Ohio Company received a charter for 200,000 acres between the Kanawha and Monongahela rivers on the south side of the Ohio River, plus 300,000 acres lower down the Ohio River on whichever shore the company selected.[1] Dr. Thomas Walker of Virginia, as an agent for the Loyal Land Company (and one of its major investors), led an important scouting expedition across the Alleghenies in early 1750, found Cumberland

Gap, giving it that name, and traveled through what is now eastern Kentucky northward to the Ohio. Christopher Gist, an agent for the Ohio Company, passed just a few months later through Ohio westward to the Great Miami River, thence from the mouth of the Scioto River southward into Kentucky. Both men wrote journals of their experience, the earliest such records known, and stimulated interest in the trans-Allegheny region. Neither man, however, went far enough west to discover the lush region in central Kentucky called the Great Meadow in the eighteenth century but later better known as the Bluegrass. This region would soon become a magnet pulling thousands of people across the Alleghenies, a "land rush" nearly as powerful as the discovery of gold in California decades later.

Walker and Gist were followed by other explorers in the next few years. Most of these men went west on their own initiative, usually to hunt or trade with the Indians, inevitably noting the fine quality of western lands. Among these was a trader named John Finley (sometimes spelled Findley), who made two trading expeditions down the Ohio River, one in 1752 and a second in 1767. Finley seems to have been the source of earliest colonial knowledge of Kentucky's Bluegrass region. The greater number of western adventurers, however, were commercial hunters who worked for many months at a stretch and collected hundreds of hides for eventual export to Europe. The most famous of these was Daniel Boone.[2] As early as 1767, Boone had begun undertaking extended hunts up and down the Holston and Clinch river valleys. Boone and five other men, including John Finley, headed west again for an extended hunt in 1769, seeking an overland approach to the Great Meadow that Finley insisted lay south of the Ohio River. When they reached it, they discovered that Finley's praise for the land had not been an exaggeration.[3]

The American frontier is often portrayed in popular historical literature as a zone of ambiguous wilderness where settlers of European descent encountered and ultimately displaced the native occupants. Kentucky presented a slightly different situation. By the late eighteenth century, no Indian group actually inhabited the area, although this huge territory served as a shared hunting ground. Several native groups, particularly the Shawnees to the north and the Cherokees to the south, attentively guarded this strategic region. Daniel Boone discovered this firsthand in late 1769 when a group of Shawnees confiscated his large accumulation of furs because he had, as they viewed the situation, poached on their land.[4] The beginning of Kentucky settlement is also unusual because it did not proceed from east to west: American settlers had their sights on the Great Meadow. Settlement began there and with few exceptions expanded its way outward, like concentric circles, from what is now the vicinity of Lexington, in Central Kentucky's Blugrass region, timed mostly by the fear of Indian attack. Also worth noting is that, unlike frontier expansion later in United States history, Kentucky settlement began during an ambiguous political period. The lush soil lured hundreds of people westward just at the moment that their communities of origin were launching a challenge for independence from the Western world's greatest military power. Modern Americans often forget this was a long war, suffered over the course of nearly a decade, sometimes fought to the death very close to home. In isolated frontier areas such as Kentucky, civilians had to primarily rely upon their own resources.

Despite his substantial loss of furs in 1769, Boone's infatuation with Kentucky did not diminish. In 1773, he joined with an intrepid Virginian named William Russell who was equally determined to be among the first settlers. Russell and Boone acted on their own initiative, without official sanction, anticipating that settlement would continue to infiltrate the interior continent as it had been gradually doing for many decades. The group was small. The Russell and Boone families, some additional relatives, and their slaves were joined by only about two dozen hired men. The venture, however, ended in disaster. While Boone and the main party proceeded quickly ahead, a second group was sent back for additional supplies. The eldest sons of Boone and Russell were part of this group, which was intercepted on their return by a party of Indians angered by this intrusion into their hunting ground. The initial attack wounded both youths, who were then subjected to protracted and excruciating deaths. Distraught by the loss of their sons and fearful of further attack, Russell and Boone abandoned their enterprise and retraced their route back to the settlements.[5]

By this time a number of other British colonists began acting on their curiosity about the region. They did not go with an intention to settle, for that was too dangerous, but to hunt and inspect the region for its future potential. Some may have found their way overland like Boone, but the greater number apparently followed Finley's original route down the Ohio River. These individuals tended to be from the western settlement regions of Pennsylvania, Virginia, and North Carolina, an area often referred to as the colonial "backcountry." They had good skills as hunters and woodsmen as well as firsthand experience in creating a farmstead from wilderness. Robert McAfee of western Virginia, one of these adventurers, recalled having been "informed by the report of some hunters and Indians that there was a rich and delightful tract of country to the west, on the waters of the Ohio River, which at that time opened a large field to enterprising individuals."[6]

In addition, wealthy land speculators similar to those who had backed the explorations of Walker and Gist were also alert to western prospects. Although British policy after the French and Indian War rendered prospects for official Kentucky settlement uncertain, it also seemed inevitable before long. The challenge was to beat the competition in finding the best tracts of land. The royal government of Virginia was not eager to take on the innumerable obligations of a new and distant settlement on her "western waters." Yet Kentucky was drawing so much interest, and the informal practice of laying claim was increasing so quickly, that John Murray, Lord Dunmore and governor of Virginia, found it prudent to send an official surveying party on behalf of influential friends such as George Washington without waiting for British authorization in 1774. This group, led by a deputy surveyor named John Floyd, encountered a number of other adventurers already marking unofficial claims. Some of Floyd's own men used the occasion to do likewise for themselves. Whether Virginia would honor these homestead claims was uncertain, but it did not hurt to prepare, just in case.[7]

These activities, as well as several acts of vigilantism on the upper Ohio, generated an acute tension between Virginia and the Shawnee Indians. That summer, as the prospect of war became imminent, John Floyd and his aides were in great danger of being cut off. Governor Dunmore commissioned Daniel Boone and another renowned woodsman named Michael Stoner to hasten to Kentucky to warn Floyd and help him back. However, Floyd and the others had already sensed the danger and begun their return.[8] All exploration of Kentucky came to an abrupt halt. Yet the effect of Lord Dunmore's War was but momentary. Virginia and the Shawnees met in battle at Point Pleasant on the Ohio River in October and in this single battle the conflict was decided in favor of Virginia. Although the Shawnees lost their claims to Kentucky at Point Pleasant, they would remain deeply resentful of American incursions into the Ohio Valley, harboring special resentment toward Virginians.[9]

Western explorations resumed almost immediately. Some of these undertakings were by small parties of friends and kin intent upon little more than an opportunity to satisfy their curiosity and enjoy some good hunting. But others were already entertaining more ambitious plans. The spring of 1775 witnessed the founding of two permanent settlements in Kentucky, as well as plans laid for others. None had authorization from the government of Virginia, but the fantastic quality of Kentucky's Bluegrass soil was too compelling to risk further delay. In the words of one early settler, which was echoed by countless others, the land was "delightful beyond conception."[10] The rush to claim a personal piece of North America's best real estate had begun.

The impending break with Britain also contributed to the American infiltration of Kentucky. Governor Dunmore was in no position to prevent settlement and soon abdicated office. The Virginia authorities who filled the void of leadership also had their attention on more immediate concerns. Facing a war with Britain, they had little desire to have potential soldiers disappear across the mountains. Furthermore, they justly feared provoking Indians eager to avenge Dunmore's War and thereby opening a second warfront. But they also lacked the means to obstruct Kentucky settlement. Thus, the opportunity created by the political void rendered those who did venture west responsible for their own safety. Settlers were forced to build their cabins within stockades, known as stations, and remain there for most of the war years. The British garrisons around the Great Lakes found ready allies among the Shawnees and other Ohio Indians, arming and provisioning several large campaigns into Kentucky. Wartime Kentucky became a very dangerous place. Even more vulnerable were the intrepid souls en route on the Ohio River and Wilderness Road.[11]

The first permanent settlements began almost simultaneously in early 1775. Harrodsburg, founded by James Harrod, holds the honor of being Kentucky's first settlement.[12] In 1774, Harrod, who hailed from western Pennsylvania, had led about fifty men down the Ohio River, but their plans for settlement were disrupted by the outbreak of Dunmore's War. Although they—and other prospective settlers—had been forced to abandon their site, winter was barely over before Harrod returned to Kentucky, this time for good. Harrodsburg's permanent occupation dates mere weeks before that of the better-known settlement of Boonesborough. Named after Daniel Boone, Boonesborough served as headquarters for the Transylvania Company, a group of private investors centered in North Carolina. The idea was to obtain a large tract of land south of the Kentucky River from the primary Indian claimants, the Cherokees, and then establish an independent colony.[13] Although private purchases of this sort were prohibited, the Transylvania proprietors believed that, once the company was a reality, it would receive legal recognition.

Because of his extensive knowledge of the trans-Appalachian South, Daniel Boone was hired by the Transylvania proprietors, first to help negotiate for land with the Cherokees in March 1775 at Sycamore Shoals and then to mark out a route across the mountains to the company's new territory.[14] Boone's route was merely a pathway, becoming known as the Wilderness Road only toward the close of the century when it was widened for wagons. One of the men with Boone, Felix Walker, remembered years later that about thirty men joined Boone in blazing the trail. "About the 10th of March we put off from the Long Island [on Holston River], marked out our track with our hatchets." Boone took advantage of preexisting pathways whenever possible, but no natural track led directly to Kentucky's Bluegrass region. According to Walker, after leaving the Rockcastle River, the men had to "cut our way through a country of about twenty miles, entirely covered with dead brush, which we found a difficult and laborious task." This was followed by hacking through some thirty miles more of dense groves of native bamboo, commonly called cane.[15] Hard work was only part of the challenge. One dawn, just as the group was nearing its destination, Indians attacked the camp and killed two men. The rest of the trail was completed as best as circumstances allowed. According to Walker, Boone conducted his men through the wilderness "with great propriety, intrepidity and courage."

Although the Wilderness Road's original terminus was the Transylvania Company's headquarters at Boonesborough, the company's questionable legitimacy, as well as excellent land beyond the company's territory, limited its authority. A fork at a point known as the Hazel Patch headed toward the alternative settlement at Harrodsburg developed early on. According to Humphrey Marshall, one of Kentucky's early historians, this western spur off Boone's original path was blazed by a prominent settler named Benjamin Logan following a heated disagreement with the Transylvania Company's leader, Richard Henderson, in 1775. This explanation has dominated the historical literature. Logan's biographer, however, believes that the contingent of early emigrants chose this western fork (known as Skagg's Trace) probably to accompany John Floyd's fresh group of Virginia surveyors. Given the disputable legitimacy of Henderson's Transylvania colony and its oppressive land policy, Logan's small contingent probably felt that Floyd's group of Virginia surveyors offered a superior potential for legal land title. Logan therefore joined Floyd's main camp at a place called St. Asaph's. Logan later helped establish a fortified settlement or "station," at this site, and St. Asaph's eventually became better known as Logan's Station.[16] This western spur of the Wilderness Road soon extended onward to the larger settlement growing at Harrodsburg and its vicinity, superseding the original path to Boonesborough, particularly after Virginia declared the Transylvania colony illegal in 1778.[17]

Whether immigrants to Kentucky took the Wilderness Road or descended the Ohio was determined by two primary factors. "Travellers or emigrants take different methods of transporting their baggage, goods, or furniture, from the places they may be at to the Ohio, according to the circumstances, or their object in coming to the country," explained Gilbert Imlay in a promotional treatise. "For instance, if a man is travelling only for curiosity, or has no family or goods to remove, his best way would be to purchase horses, and take his route through the Wilderness; but provided he has a family or goods of any sort to remove, his best way, then, would be to . . . carry his property to Redstone Old Fort [on the Monongahela River], or to Pittsburgh, according as he may come from the northern or southern States."[18] As the nearly simultaneous founding of Harrodsburg and Boonesborough suggests, the Ohio River and the Wilderness Road were both important routes from the very beginning of Kentucky settlement. Over time, the Ohio route came to supersede the Wilderness Road because, though longer, it was judged cheaper for settlers bringing household property.

The Wilderness Road

The original Wilderness Road, the sole track across the Alleghenies through Cumberland Gap, involved a distance of about 200 rugged miles devoid of settlement. Until the closing years of the eighteenth century when government funding made improvements possible, it was more of a packhorse trail than a road. Although portions had to be freshly opened, Boone took advantage of pre-existing paths whenever possible. Travel through the mountain gaps had originated in ancient times. Herds of bison and smaller animals had trodden a maze of trails, or traces. Humans had also left their mark. One of the primary routes between northern and southern Indian groups, the "Warriors' Path," stretched from Ohio, across Cumberland Gap, through Tennessee. Following these preexisting pathways whenever possible not only reduced the labor of clearing brush but also permitted crossing elevations with the least change in grade and crossing waterways near the best possible fords. The preexisting pathways, however, did not lead to Kentucky's Great Meadow of bluegrass land. Significant sections had to be freshly cut through thick underbrush and then be kept clear, particularly during the early years of low traffic.

Boone's trail was not an easy journey. The gap across Cumberland Mountain has garnered the greatest fame, but reaching Kentucky required several other challenging ascents as well. Five major river crossings as well as innumerable smaller streams also posed troublesome natural obstacles. Each ford raised the

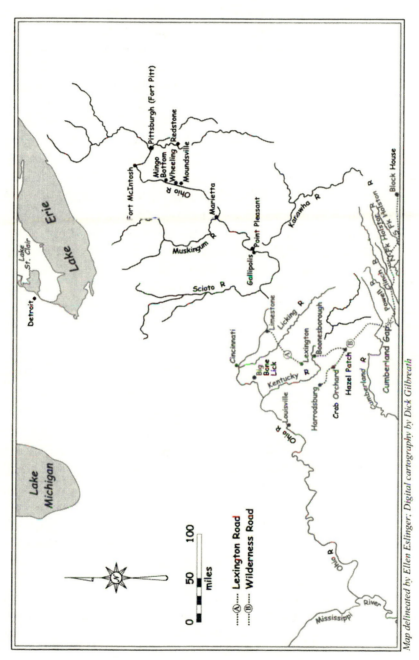

Map delineated by Ellen Eslinger; Digital cartography by Dick Gilbreath

Routes to Kentucky and the Ohio Valley in the eighteenth century.

chance of injury, loss, or even death. Boone's trail challenged the most intrepid traveler and wore down many a beast.

The Wilderness Road began in far western Virginia at a point simply known as the Block House, located about one mile north of the modern North Carolina and Tennessee border, in present Washington County. In the late eighteenth century, this was Virginia's frontier.[19] The Block House was built in 1777 by Captain John Anderson and, as its name suggests, incorporated defensive features in its design. From Anderson's Block House, the Wilderness Road proceeded northwesterly. The first challenge lay only two miles away, the ford of the North Branch of the Holston River. The road then resumed its northwestward path toward Clinch Mountain, the first of two major ascents. Moccasin Gap was the only practical crossing of Clinch Mountain, a long, forbidding range extending for miles in both directions. The descent from Moccasin Gap followed the narrow gorge created by aptly named Troublesome Creek. The trail proceeded westward between Clinch Mountain and Moccasin Ridge, following narrow gorges up Little Moccasin Creek and then down Troublesome Creek to the ford at Clinch River, where the water passed over a firm yet often slippery shelf of rock. As with every unfamiliar river crossing, potential disaster lurked its entire width.

The Wilderness Road then followed the easy grade of the river northward to Stock Creek, at modern Clinchport. Crossing at the mouth, where the creek emptied into Clinch River, was dangerous, but a ford existed a small distance upstream. The trail then continued along the steep and narrow banks of Stock Creek. The next forty-five miles involved a difficult ascent over Purchase Ridge. The next landmark was near the present town of Duffield, a salt spring known as Little Flat Lick. (At this point a very steep shortcut known as the Devil's Race Path, between Stock Creek to Little Flat Lick across Purchase Ridge, saved about two miles of travel.) Boone's route headed north at this point. About one mile past Flat Lick Creek came the ford across the North Fork of the Clinch River. Then began the steep four miles of switchbacks up Powell Mountain, crossing at Kane's Gap, then an equally difficult descent. The road then made the steep climb over Wallen Ridge.

After this series of tiring climbs and descents, the trail proceeded through the rolling terrain of Powells Valley. Here was the important outpost operated by Capt. Joseph Martin, Virginia's agent for Indian affairs during the Revolutionary War. Martin occupied this site for most of the war, shifting his operations in 1782 to Long Island on the South Fork of the Holston River. Near the Wilderness Road's midpoint and only about twenty miles east of Cumberland Gap, Martin's Station was one of the very few places where travelers could rest in safety and regroup. In addition, Martin kept both settlers and the government well informed about western conditions. Its isolation, however, forced Martin to evacuate more than once.[20]

The Wilderness Road then proceeded along Indian Creek toward Cumberland Gap. As travelers crossed at the top of the gap, Pinnacle Mountain rose about 900 feet on the right, with a lesser rise on the gap's southern side. The gap, "the most lofty of all the Aleganies," stated traveler John Smyth in 1775, "is near a mile wide, and consists of excellent strong rich land." The descent, however, was "exceedingly steep."[21] The pathway joined the ancient Warriors' Path along the Cumberland River for a short distance to Pine Mountain Gap (modern Pineville). Although less famous than Cumberland Gap, Pine Mountain Gap was of nearly equal importance for reaching Kentucky. The long mountain ridges offered no alternative crossing point for many miles. Although not as high as Cumberland Gap, Pine Mountain Gap was choked with dense thickets of laurel, a native variety of rhododendron, which travelers often had to hack back in order to pass through.

The major mountain crossings were now completed, but many miles of rough and rolling terrain lay ahead, as well as countless stream crossings. From Pine Mountain Gap, the Wilderness Road followed the Cumberland River for about seven miles, then turned north for a short distance to Flat Lick. The next section followed a series of streams, most of them of modest size. This minimized variations in elevation but required numerous stream crossings, many of which had steep and slippery embankments. Several streams had to be forded more than once. Travelers complained of being continually soaked.

The final leg of the journey went from Raccoon Spring on Robinson Creek to a point called Hazel Patch on Rockcastle River.

From this point the road forked. Boone's original route went north to the site of Boonesborough on the southern shore of the Kentucky River. Yet almost immediately settlers who did not wish to take land on the Transylvania Company's terms parted at the Hazel Patch, following Skagg's Trace to Harrodsburg, and soon superseded Boone's original trail to Boonesborough. The Wilderness Road proper was generally regarded as ending at a point on Skagg's Trace known as the Crab Orchard, so-called for a group of wild crab apple trees there. Here the Bluegrass meadows began. Here, also, travelers returning to the seaboard states (what Kentuckians called "the settlements") would organize groups and travel together for mutual assistance and safety.

The Ohio River Voyage

Despite Pittsburgh's later prominence, "Redstone was the general place to take water to descend the Ohio." Located about ten miles upstream from Pittsburgh on the Monongahela River, Red Stone or Redstone Old Fort (modern Brownsville) marked the beginning of navigability to the Ohio Valley. Emigrant David Barrow, a Baptist minister, observed in 1795 that Redstone had good land, and the inhabitants "appear to make a great deal of money from Emigrants of the Eastern states, from boat making and furnishing provisions." And, as emigrants often remarked, prices at Redstone were generally cheaper than in Pittsburgh.[22] A short distance down the Monongahela, Elizabethtown (modern Elizabeth) developed into a rival point of departure. In addition, early Pittsburgh offered few attractions. When Congressman Arthur Lee visited in 1784, he thought future prospects were dubious, observing that most of the settlers were Scots Irish, content to "live in paltry loghouses" and filth. Most of the inhabitants were transients or connected in some way with the Indian trade. Traveler John Pope observed in 1790 that Pittsburgh "is inhabited with only some few Eceptions, by Mortals who act as if possessed of a Charter of Privileges to filch from, annoy and harrass her Fellow Creatures, particularly the incautious and necessitous; many who have emigrated from various Parts to *Kentucky* can verify this Charge—Goods of every Description are dearer in *Pittsburg* than in *Kentuckey*."[23]

Although avoided by westward emigrants when possible, Pittsburgh's commercial importance continued to grow. French botanist Andre Michaux, passing through in 1793 reported, "The number of houses is about 250 and it increases considerably every year. The ditches are still to be seen that served as the entrenchment of the Fort built by the French and called Fort Duquesne [built 1754]. The English, since that time, had built another almost beside it at the angle formed by the junction of the two rivers. It was built of brick and the Americans are demolishing it to use the bricks in building the houses that are being erected every day at Fort Pitt." The 1790s witnessed considerable growth, and by 1800 the federal census counted 1,565 inhabitants. Michaux's son revisited Pittburgh in 1802 and estimated some 400 houses, built principally of brick. Pittsburgh "serves as a staple for the different sorts of merchandise that Philadelphia and Baltimore send, in the beginning of spring and autumn, for supplying the states of Ohio, Kentucky, and the settlement of Natches," he explained in his travel journal. As the region of Ohio Valley settlement expanded, Pittsburgh's role as the commercial linchpin with eastern port cities fueled continued growth. This was readily apparent by 1799, when a western merchant named Louis Tarascon predicted, "This town will one day become very important because of its location, . . . at the *confluence* of two beautiful rivers, both of which can bring there from about 200 miles away products from inland, and also because it is located at the head of the Ohio which offers an outlet more than sufficient for everything that agricultural and manufacturing will one day be able to furnish in this part of the United States."[24] Westward emigrants in the eighteenth century, however, preferred to embark at Redstone or Elizabethtown on the Monongahela because they were closer and cheaper.

The boats used by westward emigrants, being intended for only a single voyage, were cumbersome, crudely constructed vessels. "On the banks of this river [the Monongahela] is built the greater part of the flat-bottomed boats which convey the emigrant to Kentucky, and also the boats with keels for the Mississipi; the first called Kentucky boats, have the form of a great oblong, varying in its proportions from thirty to fifty feet in length, and from twelve to twenty in width, but never less than four in depth," reported Victor Collot, a French visitor who made the voyage in 1794. The sides were often higher than four feet. The Froman family's boat was lined in the cabin area with extra plank "to prevent the Indians from penetrating through with their balls, should they attack us." Collot noted that, being constructed without nails, flatboats were also rather fragile. And, given their boxy shape and flat bottom, were difficult to steer around obstacles in the water (a mere plank attached to a long pole in the stern served as the main directional tool). Francois A. Michaux commented upon the distinctive boat design as well, stating, "The amazing rapidity of the Ohio has an influence on the shape of the boats that navigate upon it, and that shape is not calculated to accelerate their progress, but to stem the current of the stream." Michaux continued, "They are of a square form, some longer than others; their sides are raised four and a half feet above the water; their length is from fifteen to fifty feet; the two extremities are square, upon one of which is a kind of awning, under which the passengers shelter themselves when it rains." From shore, "I could not conceive what these great square boxes were, which, left to the stream, presented alternated their ends, sides and even their angles." Only from a higher riverbank might an observer see over the high wooden sides to view the contents within. Another observer said the boats, especially when they had a roofed shelter, looked like "floating houses."[25]

Migrant needs varied according to family structure, wealth, the number of livestock, and similar factors, and this meant that boats tended to be commissioned on site. According to emigrant Thomas Rogers, "Two families generally joined and purchased a boat. They got them made to suit the size or number of families that would occupy them." Moving a large household often required more than a single vessel. Settler James Hedge "came down on two boats. One a family boat, and one a horse boat." Similarly, Benjamin Van Cleve explained in his memoir, "I engaged some boat-builders to build a small Kentucky flat-boat, sufficient to take the four families down to Marietta." The custom construction usually caused some delay. The families of James Hedge and Benjamin Allen waited at Redstone two weeks for their boats. A woman who traveled the Ohio as a girl recalled that "6 or 7 families came down when we did, and had about 40 head of horses, also of cattle

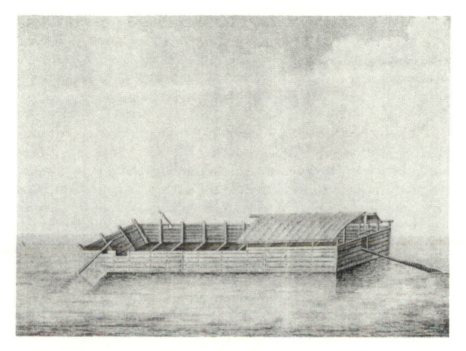

Engraving of a Kentucky-style flatboat. A shelter for the family and perishable goods, as in this example, became a standard feature. Source: Georges-Henri-Victor Collot, *A Journey in North America* (Paris: Printed for Arthus Bertrand, Bookseller, 1826).

& sheep." It took, she claimed, about six weeks to build the boats. Laurence Butler, on the other hand, wrote that his boat, forty feet long and fourteen feet wide, was finished in a mere two days.[26]

Despite the custom specifications, it is probable that, as the volume of westward emigration increased, the boatbuilders at Redstone and neighboring Monongahela towns adopted some modes of efficiency or standardization. The demand for boats was highly seasonal, governed by the Ohio River's water levels. In winter when the river was obstructed by ice and in summer when water levels were low, boatbuilders probably kept busy preparing lumber or even doing some basic assembly in anticipation of the spring surge of emigration. By 1787, a few entrepreneurs had established sawmills and boatyards to cater to the western-bound migrants. The mercantile firm of Stephen Bayard and Samuel

McKay advertised their boatyard at Elizabethtown, located on the Monongahela between Redstone and Pittsburgh. They offered "boats of every dimension at a short notice on reasonable terms." The Pittsburgh firm of Turnbull, Marmie and Company advertised that "several Kentucke Boats Will be here for sale in the course of next month."[27]

The price of boats was determined primarily by size. According to Gilbert Imlay, writing around 1790, emigrants "can either buy a boat, which will cost them about 5 s[hillings] per ton, or freight their goods to Kentucky for about 1 s[hilling] per cwt [hundred pounds]." William M. Kenton got a large boat made for £30 (for 41 people). In general, prices ran between a $1.00 and $1.25 per running foot. The general lack of comment in contemporary records implies in its silence that the cost was perceived as reasonable or at least unavoidable.[28] As the number of boatyards multiplied, prices may have become more competitive.

Emigrants traveling alone, with a small household, or with few possessions might join a boat having extra room. Reported one man, "We took water at Redstone, and from want of a better opening, I paid for a passage in a lonely, ill-fixed boat of strangers." Another traveler recalled, "On the 25 of December 1789 We sailed from Crawfords ferry our boat carrying the families of my father & uncle Richard Benham & some passengers one of whom was a Jacob Tappan from New Jersey." Sometimes people paid for their passage but often they contributed labor instead. This practice worked to mutual advantage. According to Gilbert Imlay, "Frequently when there is boat room to spare, it is given to such as are not able to purchase a boat, or have not a knowledge of the navigation." Fortunately, "that is a business which requires no skill, and there are always numbers of people coming down, who will readily conduct a boat for the sake of a passage." One western merchant, for example, took on board his boat "5 passengers going to Limestone who, in return for food, enlisted to row and to do on board whatever the circumstances required."[29]

Always interested in taking shortcuts whenever practical, emigrants embarking from the Monongahela with horses and other livestock often split company, with one part driving the livestock overland from Redstone to Wheeling, thereby lightening the boats through the shallow upper section of river. The Monongahela and upper Ohio rivers followed a circuitous path, and water levels were frequently shallow. "The trip by land is about 30 miles longer," explained a western merchant, "but you avoid about 100 miles of navigation which is often dangerous and always difficult." Coordinating a reunion of the two parties, however, could be tricky. When William Sudduth's family emigrated in 1783, the group included four families and twenty horses. "Thomas Brown, myself & some others took the horses across to Wheeling where we arrived some days before the boat." Wheeling, just a small settlement at this time, offered little protection, so Sudduth's group decided to proceed down along the riverbank until their boats loomed into sight. Unfortunately for Sudduth, the rivers emptying into the Ohio were very high and could be forded only several miles upstream "& when we returned to the river the boat had passed unseen by us." He added, "The danger of Indians was so great that the boatmen thought [it] imprudent to wait for us." A few years later when John Graves emigrated from Virginia, a slightly different problem arose. He recalled, "The river was low, and our horses had been sent across the country to Wheeling from Red Stone Old Fort and had gotten there a day before us." The Graves boat hove into sight at Wheeling just as a group of Indians were mounting an attack, but all escaped unharmed.[30] Such experiences as these were probably rare, given that driving livestock to Wheeling was such a common practice, but they show how unpredictable problems could befall emigrants.

Wheeling existed as the sole settlement from Pittsburgh to Kentucky for years. Isolated by distance on the Ohio River, its exposed location deterred early settlement. Settlement at Wheeling was begun by Ebenezer Zane during Dunmore's War in 1774 at Fort Fincastle (during the Revolution the fort was renamed for Patrick Henry). Fort Henry experienced numerous Indian raids during the Revolution, plus major sieges in 1777, 1781, and 1782. French visitor Andre Michaux noted about twelve families there in 1793. Western merchants in the 1790s often preferred to embark down the Ohio at Wheeling, instead of Pittsburgh, in order to avoid the unpredictable and tricky waters of the upper river. The commercial activity fostered town growth. By 1802 Wheeling had about seventy houses and twenty stores and served as a prominent river port.[31]

Herding the larger animals overland from Redstone to Wheeling not only lightened the boats through a shallow part of the river system, but reduced the need to carry fodder and deal with nervous livestock, particularly horses. As might be expected, livestock disliked the Ohio voyage even more than did their owners. Larger families, or families that combined their endeavor, often relegated livestock to a separate boat. Some travel accounts describe how the livestock boats put to shore, when possible, to allow the animals to graze. According to a settler who journeyed in 1780 from Maryland with six families in four boats, "One of the 4 boats contained the stock." The animals might be landed periodically for a chance to graze, but before the 1790s, this was avoided when possible because of the danger. "It was intended not to go on shore between Wheeling and the Falls [Louisville], except occasionally to take on fuel for cooking, etc., and cane for the cattle," recalled John Rowan. "We seldom ventured on land on our journey," recalled Samuel Forman, "for fear of lurking Indians." Most emigrants hoped to make the voyage without interruption.[32]

The great majority of Ohio River emigrants to Kentucky disembarked at Limestone (modern Maysville). This was the first place along the Kentucky shore that offered any sort of protection or harbor from the river's current. Limestone was not an easy harbor, having a steep bluff (estimated by one traveler at thirty feet) close to the shore. Benjamin Hardesty, who arrived there in 1784, recalled that the bluff was "so bad, we had to take our wagons to pieces, piece by piece, and pack them up." As a settlement, Limestone grew slowly, despite being a major entrepôt, because its location on the Ohio River placed it on the frontier and therefore vulnerable to Indian raids. Settler Jeptha Kemper, who arrived in late 1785, recalled years later, "When we got to Limestone, most of the houses were new, and the people hadn't gotten into them yet." Army paymaster Erkuries Beatty arrived the following year and noted that Limestone had perhaps twelve dwellings. When Benjamin Allen's family arrived in early 1789, he recalled only "two or three houses, cabins." A visitor a few years later wrote, "In this harbour are seen a few Kentucky boats, generally laying near the mouth [of the creek], many of which have been broken up to form those straggling houses which are perceived on the bank." He described Limestone derogatorily as "the fag end of Kentuckey."[33]

Limestone's reputation improved little over time. James Taylor, the son of a Virginia planter, landed there in 1792 and commented disparagingly that Limestone was "a muddy hole of a place with two or three log houses and a tavern kept by M. Kenny." As the main port for Kentucky, however, it did a brisk business. Boats often crowded the shore, and up on the bluff enterprising Kentuckians waited with wagons to carry immigrants and their goods into the settlements. Isolated from the interior, however, Limestone also remained exposed to attack. As late as 1793 an emigrant remarked, "When we landed, we were surprised to see all under arms. Every man to be seen about the streets had his gun." Frenchman Victor Collot, passing through in 1794, left a slightly more detailed description. "Limestone is a very small town on the left of the Ohio, at the foot of a steep mountain, and which, from the narrow space between the hill and the banks of the river, can never be very populous; it is, nevertheless, the depot of whatever goods pass from Baltimore and Philadelphia to Kentucky, as well as the halting place of all travellers who visit these countries." Traveler Lewis Condict, passing through in 1795, estimated only about thirty houses. Despite Limestone's key location, Condict reported that "few resources are to be found; the inns are wretched public houses without provisions, and the little that can be obtained is procured with difficulty and at exorbitant price."[34] Other eighteenth-century commentators usually agreed. Most Kentucky emigrants were as eager to leave Limestone as they had been to reach it.

Although they were now in Kentucky, one last leg of the journey remained. Most emigrants proceeded overland about sixty-five miles toward Lexington in the heart of the Bluegrass region. Not only was the land there superior to that around Limestone, but the concentration of settlements in central Kentucky offered protection from Indian raids. So many emigrants, however, had underfinanced their trip that they settled temporarily as "cabineers" on leased land, making Mason County one of Kentucky's most populous regions. By 1800, Mason County had 12,182 inhabitants (a number exceeded only by Fayette County, distinguished by the attractions of Lexington and Bluegrass soil). Some of these poor emigrants eventually gained a better foothold in Kentucky, but many probably continued on to Ohio as land there came on the market. Tenancy arrangements were generous for most of the eighteenth century, but the counties along the Ohio were the most exposed to Indian raids as long as that danger remained.[35]

Those emigrants who proceeded to the Kentucky interior were not yet beyond danger. The last stage of the journey went through fairly level terrain, but it was sparsely settled and could be treacherous, particularly during the early years. Pioneer Spencer Records recalled that when his family landed at Limestone in late 1783, there was still no settlement and they searched in vain for the head of the road into Kentucky. Records's group therefore continued down the Ohio River to the mouth of the Licking River and set up that river, "sometimes wading and pulling our periogue and canoe over the ripples." It was four days of hard work. Finally, recalled Records, "we came to three families encamped. They had landed at Limestone, but finding no road, they wandered through the woods, crossed Licking [River], and happening to find the road, took it, the night before we came to them." This group had stopped when one of the women went into labor. "They were poor people, and had not so much as a spare blanket to stretch over her, but were obliged to put up forks & poles, and place brush thereon for a kind of shelter." Records noted that snow covered the ground and "She had no necessaries of any kind, not even bread, nothing but venison and turkey." By 1784, the trees on the road from Limestone had been freshly blazed with tomahawks, but that was the only guidance, easy to miss amid the underbrush. Benjamin Hardesty's group got lost, finally reaching Bryant's Station two weeks later (a trip that should have taken only a couple of days). Ned Danaby arrived at Limestone and recalled, "there was no road, only a blazed way up the hill." One year later, settler Jeptha Kemper noted, "There was no place [no settlement] from Limestone to Blue Licks, and the path, that far, was fresh."[36]

The village of Washington, established on this road in late 1785 about four miles from Limestone, offered a cheaper and more pleasant resting place than Limestone, but the territory from there to the Blue Licks remained very thinly settled for most of the period. According to Ned Danaby, from Washington to the town of Paris, in Bourbon County, there was nothing but a "tolerable cart road" in 1787. From Washington, "we cut the road broad and open. But the farther [toward Paris] they went the more careless they were, till they at last just blazed the way, and threw the bushes out of the road." By the time the crew reached Paris, Danaby noted, "When I passed at *Paris*, they were just gathering the brush and piling it." A frontier "road" obviously encompassed quite a range of definitions. Getting lost prolonged not only the ordeal of the trip but the exposure to attack as well.[37]

The journey from Limestone to Lexington, once the road existed, normally took from three to five days for most emigrants. The danger of Indian attack remained high, particularly between Limestone and the Lower Blue Licks on the Licking River. According to Benjamin Allen, the steady stream of weary and encumbered travelers presented easy prey for Indians. In 1789, "It was told to us, before we left Limestone, that it was sort of dangerous." Few Indian attacks had occurred recently, however, and the Allens were impatient to get to their destination. They decided not to "wait for any guard or company. Just went by ourselves." A fresh grave by the roadside, however, reminded them of the risk they were taking.[38] Less fortunate was a family that landed at Limestone in 1794 with smallpox, which was terrifying and highly contagious in the eighteenth century. Forced to move on, they had reached Licking River's ford at the Lower Blue Licks, where a fortified station had recently been built. But because of the smallpox, they were not allowed entrance and therefore camped nearby. During the night, as the family was attacked by Indians and all were killed, their cries for help were audible to everyone in the fort. In 1784, "The evening before we got there 2 young women & a ½ grown boy were tomahawked & scalped just below the ford of the Blue Licks. It was not more than 300 or 400 yards from the Fort to the ford," recalled Ben Guthrie. Fortunately, "The Indians were in such a hurry they did not stop to kill those they got to attack." Samuel Potts Pointer traveled this road alone in 1788 and had a very close call. The morning sun revealed three gun barrels behind a log on the side of the roadway, but fortunately their owners were busy fixing breakfast, and Pointer passed by as quietly as possible, unmolested.[39] As Kentucky settlement grew and spread, the danger from Indians significantly diminished, but the road from Limestone did not become completely safe until well into the 1790s.

The next point on the Kentucky side of the Ohio River where emigrants could put to shore was several days farther downstream, at Louisville. Few emigrants seeking a home in the Bluegrass settlements, however, chose this port because it added several days of river travel with little advantage. Louisville lay a substantial distance from the main settlements in the interior, and the town seemed to hold little appeal. Although protected by Fort Nelson (built in 1782), its swampy location was regarded as unhealthy. In 1799, a merchant commented, "Its population, instead of increasing, seems on the contrary to be decreasing each day."[40] Those who landed at Louisville usually had business there; the remainder headed promptly for the central Kentucky settlements.

Despite the establishment of the Northwest Territory in 1787, settlement on the Ohio side of the river began later because the northern shore remained largely Indian territory and was fiercely defended. Military efforts were only partially successful, and Gen. Josiah Harmar's defeat in 1790, and especially Gen. Arthur St. Clair's defeat the following year, delivered costly and embarrassing setbacks for the United States. Indian raids on Ohio boats and outlying Kentucky settlements therefore remained as bold as before, if not more so. These did not entirely deter Ohio settlement, but it remained dangerous until the victory of Gen. Anthony Wayne in 1794 and the ensuing Treaty of Fort Greenville in 1795. Settlements prior to this time hugged the Ohio River, and either they had their own fortifications or they clustered around those of the federal army.[41]

After Wheeling, the first settlement of note was the town of Marietta, founded by the Ohio Company in 1788 at the mouth of the Muskingum River just across from Fort Harmar. Most of the early inhabitants, like the company's leaders, were from New England. By 1790, the town numbered about 2,400 inhabitants. Arriving in 1795, Ephriam Cutler observed that the settlement was dominated by three forts—Fort Harmar and two forts erected by the Ohio Company of Associates—and that the early settlers oriented themselves close to these garrisons. But already Marietta was viewed as "a flourishing settlement." The Ohio Company soon founded smaller settlements on the Ohio, also garrisoned, in 1789 at Belpre and Belleville.[42] The next early Ohio settlement was nearly 100 miles farther downriver at Gallipolis, founded as a French colony in 1789. Although the land was good, few people were prepared for the danger from Indians. In 1792, approximately 100 Indians besieged the shrinking French settlement. "Out of the 600 persons who came there to settle," reported a traveler the following year, "only about 150 remain." In 1799, a western merchant described it as "the saddest picture of poverty and disorder."[43] However small or weak, Gallipolis and the other settlements constituted important milestones for Ohio River emigrants and a refuge for those in trouble.

The most successful of the early Ohio towns was farther downriver, at Cincinnati (initially called Losantiville), and was founded in late 1788 across from the mouth of Kentucky's Licking River. The vulnerability to Indian raids hindered the town's early development, but this problem diminished after construction of Fort Washington in 1792. As the primary outpost for the federal army in the Ohio Valley, Fort Washington brought the town not only security but also much business. A garrison town was not without drawbacks, however, as New Jersey emigrant Lewis Condict observed in 1795: "It appears to be the most debauched place I ever saw." Cincinnati's advantageous location nonetheless led to rapid growth, especially after it was selected as the governmental seat for the Northwest Territory. Condict noted that it "has flourished with more rapidity that any town in the western Country beside." A western merchant in 1799 described Cincinnati as "a town already of considerable size," predicting "its pleasant and advantageous location seem to make it destined to be one day one of the most flourishing towns of the interior."[44] By the end of the century, a small but increasing proportion of river travelers were making Ohio their destination, although Kentucky still drew the great majority.

Although the Ohio voyage usually took less than two weeks, unfavorable weather conditions, particularly winds and water levels, could make it take much longer. Benjamin Van Cleve started his voyage on Christmas Day, 1789, from a point on the Monongahela near Pittsburgh called Crawford's Ferry and made it to Cincinnati on January 2. Later that year, John Pope made the slightly shorter distance from Pittsburgh to Limestone in five days and nights, while William Brown struggled thirty-five days on the nearly 500 miles of river from Redstone to Limestone. When Van Cleve again descended the Ohio in 1792, his luck was poor. "The river being so low we often run on shoals & sand bars," he wrote in his diary. The boat only averaged about fifteen miles a day. Ephriam Cutler, traveling in 1795, recalled, "After passing Pittsburgh . . . we made exceedingly slow progress, sometimes not more than three or four miles a day." James Hedge remembered that the descent of the Ohio took his family eighteen days. In 1785, William Sudduth's family took twenty days to descend the river in late winter. Another family took 21 days to reach Kentucky from Redstone. Benjamin Allen's family, however, made the voyage in a mere seven days. A Baptist preacher named John Gregg came down the next year and reported, "This passage has been ten days and a few hours long, still we have left other boats that were set out before us, and many are much longer." His Baptist colleague John Taylor took nearly seven weeks from Redstone to Louisville due to extremely low water levels.[45]

Whereas weather conditions governed the speed of river travel, fear of Indian attacks on the Wilderness Road pushed emigrants up mountains and across fords as quickly as they could manage. A land speculator from Virginia named John May completed the Wilderness Road in ten days in 1780. William Brown, traveling as a single man to investigate the land before settling, took only seven days to cover the 200 miles between settlements in 1782. Emigrants with young families, however, who were often burdened with livestock and tools, could not proceed so quickly. The Trimble family, part of a large group slowed by a measles outbreak and constant rain, took twenty days to get through the wilderness.[46]

The actual trip to Kentucky was longer than it might first appear, because by the time emigrants set out from Redstone or the Block House, many had already spent considerable time on the road. A young lawyer who went to Kentucky in 1784 left Orange County, Virginia, on September 27, 1784, and reached the Block House on October 10. For Baptist preacher John Taylor, whose voyage was severely hampered by low water levels, the trip from his home in Virginia to Louisville took about three months.[47] Emigrant William Lytle's father left Cumberland County, Pennsylvania, in late 1779, but the severe and prolonged winter prevented the family from descending the river until April 1 the next year. Ephriam Cutler spent thirty-one days on the river before reaching the Ohio town of Marietta, some three months after leaving home. The Sudduth family left their home in Fauquier County, Virginia, on September 4, reached Redstone on September 20, and arrived at Bryant's Station in Kentucky on October 28. William Brown left Hanover County in Virginia on May 27, 1782, but did not reach the Block House until the first week of July. It took Major Samuel S. Foreman three weeks to travel from Monmouth, New Jersey, to Pittsburgh. In 1785, Laurence Butler took thirteen days to get from Westmoreland County, Virginia, to the Monongahela River, traversing snow three feet deep at the top of the Blue Ridge Mountains. Baptist preacher John Gregg traveled 300 miles to reach Redstone from his Virginia home, struggling with cold winds and icy roads.[48] Whether the point of departure was Redstone or the Block House, often emigrants had already contended with rough roads, bad weather, and considerable mountain crossings.

Despite the relative brevity of the migration to Kentucky, food shortages were not uncommon. In the early years, many migrants mistakenly believed that they could hunt their way to Kentucky. "We understood a little provision would Do as we could kill a plenty on the way," explained Daniel Trabue, traveling in 1778 on the Wilderness Road. They prepared by bringing good rifles and plenty of ammunition. Even had game been more available, however, the danger of Indian attack made hunting perilous. Consequently, "Our provision Give out. We could not kill any thing to eat. Thirsday morning about Day light we ate the last of our provisions, which was one Rasher of hog bacon to each man. And not a nother mouthfull Did we git until sunday (which was easter sunday) about 2 o'clock when we got to Boonsborough on the Kentucky River."[49] Later migrants also sought to supplement their diet with game, but few relied entirely upon hunting their way west. The sheer volume of emigration tended to drive off the game, and fear of hostile Indians tended to keep people from going too far from their group. Emigrants supplemented their provisions with fish and the occasional turkey, whose placid nature made it easy prey, but seldom with larger game.

Pioneer memoirs often complain of a poor diet, and sometimes of actual hunger. Herman Bowman's group was out of flour almost before they had started the Wilderness Road because the wartime military had commandeered local supplies. John Hedge, who came to Kentucky in 1789 via the Ohio River, complained that the "Wind was a great-deal against us, and we had turkey-pot-pie till I got so tired I never wanted to eat any more as long as I lived." A diet of meat with little bread was a common experience. William Sudduth, who drove horses from Redstone to Wheeling and, missing his boat, had to finish the whole trip along the Ohio shore, wrote that his party quickly ran low on ammunition and therefore resolved to kill only one turkey a day "for five men, & that roasted, without bread or salt." They lived that way for eleven days before encountering larger game. Mrs. Sarah Graham, who came via the Wilderness Road in 1780 as a seven-year-old girl, recalled, "The first man I met was old Col. [Benjamin] Logan. Met us just above the Crab Orchard, where he lived, and gave us a pumpkin loaf. His wife did not do anything else but bake in the ashes what he ground on the hand-mill, and give it to the people moving out; he was so glad they were coming." Young Spencer Records recalled that, upon arriving in Kentucky in 1783, the people gave him a small wheat cake, "and as I was not well and had not seen bread for more than two weeks, I thought it was the best bread that I had ever tasted."[50] Although malnutrition produced by an unbalanced diet caused discomfort, actual starvation was rare.

The overwhelmingly westward direction of population movement has tended to overshadow a substantial volume of travel going in the reverse direction. Prospective settlers commonly made an initial visit to scout land, mark a claim, and perhaps prepare a rough cabin before bringing their families. During the Revolutionary War years, it was a common practice to visit Kentucky and prepare a homestead but return east in spring, before the northern snows melted and Indian attacks from Ohio resumed. Complained an early settler in 1783, "our Winter inhabitants are flying for fear of the hard frost of Summer." Another person recalled, "Vas. [Virginians], & land jobbers, used to come out & spend the winter at the [Kentucky] Stations, and go back again before the dangerous times commenced." They would "Crowd the fort, & eat the provisions, & in the spring go back." Others found pioneering in Kentucky too dangerous and returned to their old homes to await safer times. After the decisive Indian victory at the Lower Blue Licks in 1782, where Kentucky casualties were devastating, Sarah Graham recalled that one man offered her father "the whole 1,400 acres of his preemption, . . . for one little black horse to carry his family back to Virginia." A small number of other eastbound travelers were engaged in government business. Emigrants headed for Kentucky in spring often encountered these returning settlers, who provided valuable information on trail conditions ahead as well as in Kentucky. In 1784, a young man traveling by way of the Wilderness Road noted, "The next day after crossing the mountain, I met a company from Kentucky, who confirmed the accounts I had before heard that the Indians were growing very troublesome in the wilderness."[51]

People returning east sought to join a group for mutual protection, just as they had in coming west. The common meeting place in Kentucky was the Crab Orchard on Skagg's Trace, where a fort offered some protection. As one Kentucky settler explained, "At the Crab Orchard, to go through the wilderness, it was usual for notices to be set up at Court Houses, Mills, and public places, giving notice of the time of meeting at that place." Kentucky's only newspaper, established in 1787, carried announcements regularly. For example, the November 1, 1788, issue of the *Kentucky Gazette* noted, "A large company will meet at the Crab-Orchard on the 19th. of November in order to start the next day through the Wilderness. As it is very dangerous on account of the Indians, it is hoped each person will go well armed." The regular appearance of such notices attests to a steady stream of return traffic. Some returning travelers had come west via the Ohio but chose not to fight the river's current in returning east. Laurence Butler, for example, went to Kentucky in 1784 by the Ohio River and returned through the Wilderness Road with a group of 100 armed men and about as many packhorses loaded with furs.[52]

Returning up the Ohio, however, was not impossible. William

Sudduth returned to Virginia by joining a large canoe, one of sixteen men. "We worked eight oars. The weather was very hot & the labour exceedingly hard. We went about thirty miles per day." As Benjamin Van Cleve's group descended the river in 1792, they encountered "a number of canoes from Kentucky." In 1793, Kentuckian Jacob Meyers announced that he was constructing an armed sailing packet that would ply the Ohio between Cincinnati, stopping at Limestone and Pittsburgh, carrying letters and passengers and departing every other Saturday.[53] The majority of travelers returning east, however, chose an overland route; most often the Wilderness Road route. After 1796, eastbound travelers also could take Zane's Road from Limestone to Wheeling.

The Challenges of Nature

Although the trans-Appalachian crossing did not involve massive natural obstacles like the Rocky Mountains or Death Valley, it presented some significant challenges. Firsthand accounts of the Wilderness Road contain numerous references to the journey's difficulty. The Block House was barely out of sight before one emigrant began complaining about "rugged ascents and desents, which seemed wordlessly impossible." Half a century later, Jane Stevenson recalled her fear descending from Cumberland Gap in 1779 because it was extremely "narrow and rocky." The rocks "stood up," she remembered, "on either side, not broader than a horse." William Hickman's large family "had to travel a small and miserable track, over mud and logs and high waters." Emigrant Lewis Condict complained, "Nothing can exceed the road for badness in some particular places, the mud being belly deep to our horses, & the banks of the Creeks almost insurmountable, from their steepness & slippery nature." Such conditions took their toll on both man and beast. Condict noted that numerous dead horses lay by the wayside, "killed by the badness of the roads." The ground was drier in summer, but the narrow pathway through the mountains could quickly become choked with undergrowth. F.F. Jackson, who was about ten years old when his family came in 1785, recalled, "Neither cane, saplings, nor anything else had been cut out of the way." At places the trail was perilous. "As we came

along Rock-castle [river], the path was narrow, and along a precipice. The clothes were in a bag, and the bag fastened across the
horse." Unfortunately for the Jacksons, "The horse rubbed against
a sapling, and the bag thrown across his back, pitched him over
the precipice into the river. The clothes were lost." This sort of
accident could have just as easily happened to a rider.[54]

One of the earlier travelers, a British visitor writing in 1775,
although young, unencumbered by numerous possessions, and
without family responsibilities, frequently found the journey challenging. "These vast ridges of mountains which we crossed rendered this day's journey extremely severe and fatiguing both for
ourselves and our horses, although we did not travel more than
about thirty miles," he wrote. "In the morning we undertook the
hazardous task of fording Clinch's River, and accomplished it after several plunges, as usual, over our heads." His party prudently
waited until the next day to climb Cumberland Gap in order to get
some rest, "for we always alighted and led our horses up these
prodigious steep, and perilous ascents." The descent of Cumberland
Gap, also steep, presented a different set of difficulties: "This northwest side was almost bare of soil; . . . and quite incumbered with
rocks and loose stones, which exceedingly impeded our way, and
retarded our progress." Pine Mountain Gap was "almost entirely
covered with universal and impenetrable thickets of laurel." Getting past the mountains did not put an end to the hard work of
travel, for although "all this country to the westward . . . appeared
as a beautiful level extended far beyond the view, and all the hori-
zon was as straight and even as a line, or as the ocean itself, yet
now we had descended into it we found it extremely broken, with
abundance of rocks, and thickly intersected with water-courses."
No man, woman, child, or beast could escape these difficulties.[55]

Seven years later, in the summer of 1782, Virginian William
Brown complained of similar problems. Brown noted that from
the Block House to Wallen Ridge the road "generally is bad, some
part very much so, particularly about Stock Creek and Stock Creek
Ridge." Likewise, "The fords of Holstein [Holston] and Clinch
are both good in dry weather, but in rainy season you are often
obliged to raft over." But, "From then along down Powell's Valley
until you get to Cumberland Gap is pretty good." Brown thought

the land was generally poor from the gap to the Rockcastle River. "This tract of country is very mountainous, and badly watered along the trace, especially for springs." Except for a few large hills, the remainder of the journey was judged "tolerable good."[56]

The Wilderness Road's river crossings, even more than the steepness of the mountain terrain, posed the greatest hazard to emigrants. A simple misstep could result in death. Allen Trimble, who made the trek as a boy, recalled many years later how his mother narrowly escaped disaster at the ford of Clinch River. Trimble wrote, "The ford was a difficult one, running up near the shore, which was rock bound 150 yards, and then forming the segment of a circle, reaching the western bank some distance, say 50 yards higher than the entrance on the east shore." The emigrants in front paused to consider how best to proceed, but the long line behind on the narrow path kept coming. Trimble's mother was one of those in the front, riding with an infant on her lap and a three-year-old holding on from the rear. Her horse, upset by all the shoving and noise, bolted and then plunged into the water only to land in quicksand. The horse panicked in its trap, bucking wildly in an effort to escape. Mrs. Trimble immediately gave her horse its reins and pulled her toddler around from her back and held him in front with the infant. With the other hand, Mrs. Trimble grasped the horse's mane as it wheeled and bucked. The horse finally extracted itself and stumbled across some 300 yards of water "and arrived safely with her precious charges on the opposite bank, amid palpitating hearts." Meanwhile, the horse carrying another woman had likewise leapt off the bank, plunging into a section of deep water. With her were two small black children, riding in a pair of saddle bags. As the horse went down, the saddlebags floated off downstream. Fortunately one of the men ran downstream and into the water and "as it passed a bend in the river, he caught it and brought the little fellows safely to shore."[57]

The greater ease of floating down the Ohio River was somewhat offset by the greater risk posed by natural obstacles. Sandbars and buried logs lurked all along the shores, shifting location after every flood. The river's water level, moreover, could change drastically in the space of a few hours. Emigrants had no experience maneuvering the bulky and heavily laden boats. When water levels were low, few escaped at least one snag on a submerged limb. "This river runs so extremely serpentine, that in going down it, you appear following a track directly opposite to the one you mean to take. Its breadth varies from two hundred to a thousand fathoms," explained Francois A. Michaux. "The islands that are met with in its current are very numerous. We counted upward of fifty in the space of three hundred and eighty miles. . . . These islands are a great impediment to the navigation in summer . . . the few boats, even of a middling size, that venture to go down, are frequently run aground."[58]

The beginning of the voyage, where the Monongahela and Ohio were shallower, presented the greatest problem. "The Monongahela was very much obstructed by rocks, the water being low," recalled Jeptha Kemper. "After that we had a ride—but when we got to the junction forming the Ohio, the other rivers were low and the freshet could not be perceived." The family of Ephriam Cutler headed to Marietta in 1795 but made slow progress because "the river had fallen, and we were often aground." Cutler "was much of the time in the river lifting at the boat to get it over the sand-bars and shallows." In 1784, Nathan Ewing, age fourteen, accompanied a trading expedition with whiskey, salt, and flour to Vincennes when the boat snagged just thirty miles below Pittsburgh. The expedition was marooned on the island for the entire winter.[59]

Running aground on submerged tree limbs or sandbars was possible even well down the Ohio. Just thirteen miles above Limestone, Jeptha Kemper recalled, "we heared a great roaring. . . . [We] had been on the rocks so much above Red-Stone, where we had to get into the water and shore our boats off, that we very much dreaded [similar problems] there." The right of the island ahead seemed smoother and therefore it was chosen over the left. But even so, "at the lower end of the island we found it clogged with drift and brush—and impassable." The men got out on shore and with ropes dragged the boats back to the head of the island, preferring to run the rapids. This arduous labor was undertaken amid signs of Indians in the vicinity. Rarely were migrants as fortunate as Benjamin Van Cleve, who encountered only a minor delay on his first western voyage in 1789. "Our boat proved staunch

& we met with no accident except running on a sandbar in the middle of the Ohio a little below Pittsburgh," he recalled, "where we lay about 20 hours when the waters rising carried us off."[60]

Even worse than delays and dangerous work, running aground could damage the boat. Waterlogged possessions plagued many voyagers. In extreme circumstances, a family could lose everything they owned as well as their lives. This was nearly the fate of Alexander Martin and his family in late 1790. When the Martin boat hit the Red House Shoals at dusk one day near the mouth of the Great Kanawha River, water began pouring in and "all like to have been lost." Martin and another man grabbed buckets and began bailing water as fast as possible. The two men hoped to keep the boat afloat long enough to reach Point Pleasant, another twenty-five miles or so downstream. The alternative, to go ashore, unload the boat, and make repairs on an isolated shore, risked exposure to Indian attack. "In this Situation we Stood, in water nearly to our knees till next day about three o'clock in the afternoon when we Landed at the Often and Sincere Wish'd for Spot." They were alive, but "wet, Cold, and hungry, our Goods lying on the Bank exposed to the Weather, and our Boat sunk to the Bottom." They faced two choices: winter where they had landed or replace the boat. Four miles further downstream was a settlement where Martin heard he could probably get what he needed. But unable to bring the cumbersome vessel upstream, he found it necessary to rent canoes to ferry his family and goods to the new boat—all of which was expensive. Finally underway again, Martin joined four other boats headed for Kentucky. "We made a Promissory Agreement to waite on one another as we thought it would be for our Safety." But more misfortune was yet to come. One of the boats sank during the first night together, drowning three horses. Martin and the others spent the next day helping to get this boat off the bottom, repaired, and reloaded. Yet, when the Martin boat encountered further trouble, the "promissory agreement" proved a dead letter. Martin bitterly finished the voyage alone, with four other men and only three guns, his wife, and two children, one of whom was deathly ill. The migration to Kentucky had been "a long and Fatigueing Journey accompanied with both Great Danger and Loss."[61]

Ohio River travelers avoided stopping on shore once under-way because to do so invited attack and risked damage to the boat, although landing became safer once settlements began to appear. Yet the alternative, floating through the night, could be tricky. William Brown explained, "Some of the Is[lands] . . . lie low and when-ever the river is above a common height will be covered with water." The deeper channels lay toward the shores. "However in the day-time the current of water and your eye must direct you in a great measure, and in the night if it be dark and you must let the current carry you, but keep a good look out to avoid running upon the trees that are stuck about in the river and the rocks of which there is not many—but a number of old trees." Brown advised, "To avoid running upon these if it be dark you must listen very attentively to hear the riffling of the water, and when you draw near if you find the boat getting on it, you must steer off. In a general way endeav-our to keep your boat in the middle of the river with her head right down stream, and the watchman standing right in the head." Brown offered one final piece of advice. "Avoid rowing at night unless necessity requires—the noise of the oars will prevent you from hearing the riffling of the water occasioned by the rocks and old trees." The ability to make progress almost twenty-four hours a day gave the Ohio River a great advantage over the Wilderness Road, but nighttime sailing was not always possible. Benjamin Van Cleve made poor time in 1792, explaining, "The river was very low & we were unable to drift at night so that we made [only] about 15 miles a day."[62]

Whether by Wilderness Road or the Ohio, bad weather could turn the trip into a painful, even perilous, ordeal. The Trimble family's group suffered nearly constant rain, and the misery was compounded by an outbreak of measles. A man traveling in the same group complained, "From the rugged ascents and descents, which seemed absolutely impassable; and from the mire, which was every step up to my horses knees, occasioned by heavy rains, . . . I had hard work to go a mile in an hour." As for those suffering with measles, "To go back with them was out of the question, to leave them behind certain death: we agreed to keep with them and move on slowly." This decision not only brought greater ex-posure to Indian attack, but also to the raw elements, for "Out of 22 days we had only 4 in which it did not rain and thunder most excessively."[63]

The personal discomfort must have been considerable, but the constant rain caused other problems as well. Preventing the packhorses from slipping on slick wet rocks or bolting when alarmed by lightning on the narrow track was not easy. Recalled Allen Trimble, "One of my father's pack horses, loaded with two pine boxes, packed with axes, drawing chains, iron wedges, etc., weighted about 200 pounds, were crowded off the road at a turn of a point of the Cumberland Mountain, and thrown over a precipice of fearful height, and tearing in its descent the limbs of pine trees." Although the tree boughs had miraculously cushioned the animal from death, when the men later found the horse and recovered the precious tools, they could not find a way back up the sheer slope to the main trail. They were forced to bivouac alone overnight, vulnerable to attack.[64]

Bad weather could produce danger for river travelers as well. Many voyagers found that the wind, which blew primarily eastward, hindered progress. "All this day," complained one man, blew "a high wind, which retarded us very much." Contrary winds were frustrating, but the region's thunderstorms presented actual danger. An emigrant on the Ohio in 1790 recalled that the boats both before and following his sank in a storm. In the havoc of thunder and lightning, all the cattle had pushed together in panic on one side, and the people and cargo on the opposite side were not heavy enough to provide a counterbalance. One woman survived by using a trunk for flotation. The others all drowned.[65]

Cold temperatures also posed a hazard, especially because the peak periods for migration were fall and early spring, between agricultural seasons and when roads were often drier. Settler Patrick Mahon started for Kentucky with his family from western Virginia in October 1779 but, due to early winter conditions, they did not reach their destination until after the new year. William Lytle's father set out from Cumberland County, Pennsylvania, about the same time but, by the time he reached the Monongahela, the early cold made navigation impossible. Water levels remained low well into spring, shutting down sawmill operations and delaying boat construction. In early 1789, an Ohio pioneer noted that, despite numerous ice floes floating down the river, about a dozen boats had passed by the previous week. "Most of them had been frozen in the ice this side of Wheeling these few days past." This had happened to the Rowan family in 1782. They brought provisions expecting only a weeklong voyage, but "the river had fallen and become sluggish, and our progress somewhat retarded by floating ice, and by the time we had descended to the mouth of the Great Kanawha [River] was entirely arrested by the frozen condition of the river." John Rowan, a child at the time, recalled that his family "encamped as comfortable as possible on the margin of the river . . . and remained until the breaking up of the ice in Spring." The Rowans survived, but suffered great hunger that winter. Sharp ice floes also stranded merchant John Wallace. "In December 1793 we started from Pittsburgh and in about four or five days after we got wrecked below [the] Muskingham among the ice on a sandbar in the middle of the River," he recalled. "We suffered much cold."[66] Food shortages combined with frigid temperatures posed not only unimaginable misery but also life-threatening conditions.

The winter of 1779–1780 was exceptionally harsh. The early pioneers called it the "Hard Winter." A resident at Boonesborough noted in his journal, "People hourly arrived with accounts of the distresses of Families on the road." Emigrant Herman Bowman recalled two substantial snows while en route, one at the Cumberland River and the other toward the end at the Rockcastle River. Unlike some others, Bowman had at least a tent. "Had no fear of Indians," he recalled, "it was so cold." Settler John Masterson's brother-in-law got caught in the early snows. "He was detained in the wilderness all winter, w. a parcel of negroes, some of them small," recalled Masterson. "The horses all died for cold & want of salt, but one." The suffering was tremendous. Masterson recalled that hunger drove the stranded party to eat one of their dogs. As one Kentuckian wrote to a kinsman in Virginia, "This world never new human nature so defased as the unhappy settlers that set out late for this place maney of them still remaining in the Wilderness haveing lost every horse & Cow they were possessed of. & hole Families have perished on the [Wilderness] rode whilst others escapeing with the loss of their hands & feet & all the skin & Flesh taken off their face by the excessive Cold."[67] The

Hard Winter was exceptionally brutal, but cold temperatures were probably experienced by many people traveling in the late autumn and early spring.

Very few of the families headed for Kentucky had ever experienced a trip of such magnitude. Ann Christian, who traveled the Wilderness Road in the wet summer of 1785, complained in a letter to her sister-in-law about the heat, lack of water, and fatigue. "Had I any Idea of its being half as bad as I found it no inducement on this earth, would have encouraged me to attempt it, so that my advice . . . is never to think of coming thro' the wilderness to this country." The Ohio route, she thought, was unquestionably preferable. Yet that too could entail much suffering. The Cutler family spent more than a month on the river in 1795, detained by low water levels and illness. They lost an infant son and then their eldest daughter. "To add to our distress," wrote Ephriam Cutler, "we had no alternative but to commit her to the earth in the dreary wilderness, far from the habitation of any civilized being." In addition, Mrs. Cutler broke several ribs while disembarking, and Ephriam suffered debilitating dysentery.[68]

A significant number of Kentucky pioneers, the slaves, faced their hardships with little choice and few opportunities for personal betterment. Kentucky would eventually emerge as a major producer of hemp and tobacco, both crops associated with slave labor. The pioneer generation, however, needed laborers for the huge challenge of clearing land, building fences, and making homesteads. Settler John Graves reported that in 1786, "Father, Mother and myself came out with 30 blacks." John Breckinridge sent some of his slaves a year in advance to begin establishing his family's new homestead. According to John Thompson, who conducted the Breckinridge slaves to Kentucky, the trip to Redstone was miserable. "We had Snow or Rain Every day Except two. . . . Our Negroes [were] Every day out of heart & Sick," Thompson reported. "When the Negroes were wet & almost ready to give out, then I came forward with my good friend whiskey & Once every hour unless they were a Sleep I was Oblige[d] to give them whiskey." The trip from Fluvanna County in Virginia to Redstone took nearly a month, and they reached their Kentucky destination about two weeks later. Daniel Drake, whose family lived at May's Lick on the road from Limestone to Lexington in the 1790s, recalled seeing "the caravans of travelers, mounted on horseback, and the gangs of negroes on foot."

A few blacks resisted by running away before departure or during the journey. One newspaper advertisement was for a slave named Nelson, who "ran away from the subscriber [owner], at Redstone, on his way to Kentucky." Another advertisement sought a man named Tom, who had been given a pass to say good-bye to his wife, whose owner was embarking for Kentucky. Tom's owner stated, "I very much suspect that he intends pursuing his rout to Kentucky." Slaveowners migrating to Kentucky broke up many black families. Furthermore, slave prices were higher in Kentucky than in Virginia, which encouraged bringing slaves for resale. Tax records indicate that about one quarter of Kentuckians owned slaves, usually only one or two, suggesting that the trans-Appalachian migration affected many black families. By 1800, there were 41,084 slaves in Kentucky, 18.6 percent of the state's population.[69]

Many women, although free, were also reluctant pioneers. A Virginia Baptist preacher with nine children, William Hickman, dreaded telling his wife that he had decided the family would fare better in Kentucky. "I knew it would be a killing stroke to my wife," he wrote later, "for she was much attached to the church and neighbors." When he finally told her, "she burst into tears and begged me to decline." Samuel Meredith revealed in a letter, "My Wife being adverse to going Makes me feel very sensible." When they finally set off in 1790, she expressed her feelings in a family letter, writing, "I have just departed with my poor Dear Mother in great dell of distress about my going to Kentucky. . . . I suppose there never wase a person [who] whent to that Country with more reluctance than I shall do." Her brother John Breckinridge encountered similar resistance. He had long entertained ideas of taking his family to Kentucky, where a brother had already settled, and he sent most of his slaves ahead to prepare a home in 1793. Breckinridge's wife, Polly, however, remained unreconciled to the move and accompanied her husband and family reluctantly. John Breckinridge remarked to a fellow traveler that she "has not even smiled since we set out on our journey."[70]

Not all women, however, were so despondent at the prospect

of a western move. A French traveler met a young family that came from Philadelphia. The young couple and their infant had nothing but a horse for the wife, who was only twenty years old, to ride with her baby. "I doubted not but she was in despair at the sacrifice she had made," wrote the Frenchman, but "I saw, not without astonishment, that her natural charmes were even embellished by the serenity of her mind."

Other women displayed remarkable bravery when faced with challenges. A small group recently landed at Limestone was encamped on the road to Lexington when attacked by Indians. "The heroic presence of mind of a woman saved the party," recalled a neighborhood resident. "She broke open a chest in one of the wagons with an axe, got at the ammunition, gave it to the men, and called upon them to fight." One man died in the encounter, but this anonymous female played an instrumental role in saving the others. In other cases, women are described as preparing bullets for male defenders and a few could handle rifles quite well. When the Rowan family's boat was attacked by a number of Indians in canoes one night, "my mother arose from her seat, and without saying a word even in a whisper, . . . collected all the axes and placed one by the side of each man, . . . and then sat down in quiet composure, retaining an axe for herself." The other women, however, "had lain down in despair and pulled their beds over their faces and heads." Unfortunately, attempting to generalize about female emigrants is virtually impossible except to say that their responses were probably conditioned by age, wealth, and temperament.[71]

The Indian Danger

Despite the difficulty and danger posed by natural obstacles, western emigrants were much more concerned about hostile Indians. Virginia land speculator John May, having taken the Wilderness Road in 1780, reported in a letter that he had arrived safely in Kentucky "through an uninhabited County the most rugged and dismal I have ever passed through, there being thousands of dead Horses & Cattle on the Road Side which occasioned a continual Stench; and one Half the way there were no Springs." Yet, "what made the Journey still more disagreeable was the continual apprehension we were under, of an Attack from the Indians, there not being one Day after we left Holston [Valley], but News was brought us of some Murders being committed by those Savages." Emigrant William Hickman took the Wilderness Road and recalled that when sleeping at night "we had our guns under our heads." For emigrants on the Ohio River, worries of attack were also constant. When Rev. John Taylor came in 1783, "Not a soul was then settled on the Ohio between Wheeling and Louisville, a space of five hundred miles or six hundred miles, and not one hour, day or night, in safety." As late as 1795, Lewis Condict noted, "Every person we saw, confirmed the evil tidings of the Indians."[72] The enemy might be lurking behind every mossy log on shore and every craggy ridge overhead.

These fears had a sound basis in reality. The British colonies had long pressed aggressively for native land concessions, often in a manner that would seem ruthless by modern standards. Most Indian groups therefore opposed further colonial infiltration into the North American mainland. British officials, as long as they could retain their authority, sought appeasement. They sincerely wished to avoid conflict that would inevitably be costly and they were unsympathetic to colonial greed for "wilderness" land. But there was little that they could do as news spread of Kentucky's rich land. Diplomatic relations between colonies having western territory and the Indian occupants deteriorated rapidly and set the stage for conflict. The tension caused the Shawnees and most of the other Ohio Valley natives to ally with the British during the revolution. The British garrisons around the Great Lakes became a reliable source of arms and ammunition, making a formidable western foe. American relations with the Cherokees, Creeks, and other southern Indian groups were also unstable. Emigrants strung out in a long thin line along the Wilderness Road made easy targets. Defense was also difficult on the Ohio River, where the difficulty of maneuvering a cumbersome boat without getting snared on a buried obstacle left fewer men to offer resistance.

The danger of Indian attack continued after the war. Although the British had been forced to admit defeat in 1781, the western Indians remained strong and united. They did not regard themselves as part of their ally's capitulation. After a brief season of inactivity immediately following the end of British hostilities, northern and southern Indians both resumed raiding with highly effective results. Yet, as the tide of emigrants swelled, the prospect of expelling western settlers diminished. The focus of Indian attacks shifted accordingly. Whereas western Americans had suffered tremendous civilian losses during the Revolution, postwar hostilities tended to target horses and other personal property. Travelers, disoriented and loaded down with goods, therefore remained vulnerable to raids. Loss of life was a common result.

The threat of attack compelled emigrants to band together, whether traveling by land or water. Thomas Rogers explained in a memoir, "And as it was always considered a very dangerous voyage down the Ohio they commonly went down in companies of three or four boats and at night would tie all together and float as near the middle of the river as possible for fear of an attack of the Indians on the shore." Emigrant James Taylor recalled, "At Redstone we engaged the building of our boats and lay there two weeks to get a strong fleet to descend the river in safety." Recalled William Lytle, "By advertisements all the adventurers in that part of the country who were bound for Kentucky were requested to assemble on a large island in the Ohio a few miles below Pittsburgh." Lytle's family decided to "remain here until a sufficient force should have assembled to pass with safety amidst the country of savage hostility which lay between them and Kentucky." Young Allen Trimble's family took the Wilderness Road in late 1784. He recalled, "Notice had been given of the time of starting and also the place of rendezvous, and when they arrived at Beans Station and Holston river, the frontier fort and place of meeting, near five hundred persons, men, women and children, were assembled." Keeping up with the group, moreover, was essential because stragglers were more likely to suffer attack. The rigors of mountain travel sometimes made this difficult. Kentuckian Daniel Deron recalled that in his company "5 or 6 horses gave out on the road. The riders just got down, and left them stand, with their bridles & saddles, and hastened to keep up with the others."[73]

Some of these companies were quite large. A member of the Trimble group stated that of the 500 or more people, "134 were active men, well armed; the rest were old men, women, children

Portrait of a Shawnee warrior. Source: Georges-Henri-Victor Collot, *A Journey in North America* (Paris: Printed for Arthus Bertrand, Bookseller, 1826).

and negroes." Mrs. Sarah Graham, who was just seven years old at the time, recalled that her father, Charles Spillman, came to Kentucky with some 300 other settlers in 1780. James Wade's family came on the Wilderness Road in 1784 with "375 souls and 60 guns." William Hickman's family, taking the Wilderness Road the same year, traveled with a company of 500. Likewise, "There were 300 in our company," recalled a Virginia woman who came to Kentucky with her husband via the Wilderness Road in 1785, "Started out in September. Had to wait a while till our company collected." One woman recalled that her group was "sometimes in a string of three miles." The Lytle family joined a convoy of sixty-two other boats down the Ohio in 1780. James Taylor, emigrating in 1792, noted, "We set out with a fleet of 25 boats, principally family boats." In Taylor's case, efforts were nearly carried too far. Because "Our boats floated unequally, some faster and some slower, our commander linked us two and two abreast, so the whole flotilla formed one mass of 12 deep." This arrangement worked satisfactorily "till we came to a short bend in the river when we narrowly escaped being crushed against a rocky shore and with great difficulty saved our boat which was the left hand one and in front, [from] being crushed, but chopping our coupling ropes and all, separated." From then on, the boats were kept reasonably together because "some would pull the oars while others would back water and so managed to all arrive in Limestone."[74]

Banding together for mutual protection on a large scale raised a need for some form of leadership or coordination. The persons selected usually lacked any official governing authority, but their good judgment, military experience, and other personal attributes granted important authority. When Thomas Jones descended the Ohio River in 1780, he noted that the twenty-seven family boats put themselves under the leadership of Jacob Van Meter, a prominent man from the western county of Monongahela and a person familiar with modes of Indian warfare. Recalled another settler, "In the spring of 1793, 60 of us went through the wilderness, chosing Capt. Blueford as our leader." Pioneer John McKinney, who brought his family overland to Kentucky with a group of about 300 people in 1785, "was called Captain because the choosing of the lodging place to camp in, at night, was committed to him most of the way."[75]

When the Trimble family joined their about 500 other emigrants on the Wilderness Road in 1784, a rough democratic process prior to departure selected as their leader Col. James Knox, "of Revolutionary memory and fame." As the long line of emigrants strung out on the "serpentine trail around craggy peaks, and through narrow defiles where ten Indians could defeat one hundred men," Knox took special care, appointing an advance guard of ten men to patrol the vicinity of the upcoming trail. A rear guard protected stragglers. Knox placed himself at the head of the main body of emigrants. That night, Colonel Knox "laid out the encampment in expectation of an attack by the Indians; for Indians had been seen all during the crossing of the mountain by spies the entire day, watching carefully." A river protected one side, with horses tied in the camp's center and the packsaddles placed within the upper line from the river with a guard, with sentries posted along other sides as well. "The women who were armed, as most of them were with pistols, took positions with their husbands. The balance of the women and children were placed in a position near the river, supposed to be the safest." In addition to sentries, fires were set up outside the camp lines to illuminate any approaching attackers. The Indians made no attack, but the emigrants trying to sleep could hear their movements beyond the circle of light.[76]

Large contingents on the Ohio adopted similar practices. "The descending boats [numbering 63 vessels] were arranged in order of defense," recalled William Lytle. "Pilot boats headed the advance. The boats manned by the young men sustained each wing, having the family boats in the center and the [live]stock boats immediately in the rear of them, and the rear guard boats floating still behind them." When Rev. Robert W. Finley brought his family down the Ohio, their group followed similar arrangements. "The boat which led the way as pilot was well manned and armed, on which sentinels, relieved by turns, kept watch day and night." The other boats followed close behind. His son James recalled, "While floating down the river we frequently saw Indians on the banks, watching for an opportunity to make an attack." Similarly, the memoirs of James Taylor record that when he descended the Ohio the people selected a commander to coordinate the cumbersome group of twenty-five boats. When he returned to Virginia via the Wilderness Road, Taylor joined a group of about 350 people, again prompting a move toward some organization. "A Colonel, Lieut. Colonel, Major and several Captains were appointed." These leaders coordinated guards and sentries. Few journals or memoirs provide much detail, but casual references to a recognized leadership hierarchy indicate that it was common for simple reasons of practical necessity.[77]

The need for leadership combined with the volume of travelers apparently produced some entrepreneurs. In early 1794, a company of seventy individuals left Crab Orchard. According to one member, some men sought employment as guards at a rate of fifty cents a head. The travelers, however, judged the price too high and declined. When they were attacked a short distance into the trip, some members suspected that the attackers were not Indians at all, but the disgruntled "guards" whose services had been refused.[78] On the Ohio, emigrants sometimes hired local men to pilot the boats down particularly bad rapids.

Many emigrants who escaped attack encountered close reminders of the danger around them. Pioneer Ben Guthrie came to Kentucky in late 1783 and recalled many years later, "Came in Company with 16 horsemen and without any families. A family, on the way, was defeated—and the next day we passed the place, but was not attacked." Another man traveling in 1785 stated, "Scarce a day [went by] but we found the mark of a defeated company." William McClelland, who traveled the Wilderness Road as a boy in 1787, recalled seeing a site where the previous fall an attack had occurred. The dead "had been covered up under a log, but they were torn out by animals, and their bodies lay scattered over the ground." Likewise, "One Walter Carooth was in a defeated camp beyond Raccoon Spring—in about 1786 or 1787," recalled another settler whose party narrowly escaped attack. At night, "we knew that indns. Were all around us, and had repeatedly heard their firing in the woods." In 1790, Daniel Deron recalled having "passed the defeated camp on Yellow Creek." In 1792, James Walker's company came upon the remains of five or six bodies on the Wilderness Road. Similarly, William Boyd recalled, "The Indns., but a day or two before had killed 27 on Big Laurel River." One woman could not forget how "they saw packsaddles, beds, &c., in the wilderness on their way out." The night before reaching Crab Orchard, several travelers stopped to bury thirteen bodies in a mass grave. Lewis Flanagan reported "One McNutt came and 100 got killed the day before I came along." Flanagan's party blew a ram's horn and a number of the McNutt survivors who had scattered into the woods came forward. F.F. Jackson and some neighbors went to rescue a company attacked at Raccoon Spring in 1785. "When we got there they [the Indians] had ripped open the [bed] ticks for 1/4 of a mile, the feathers they had strewn out, made it light like snow."[79]

The danger of attack was also vividly illustrated on the Ohio River. In 1786, James Taylor observed, "On our passage we saw several parties of Indians, our commander fired his swivel [gun] at them, they fired their rifles at us, but we were too far off for their balls to reach half way to us." Emigrating a few years later, in 1789, Benjamin Van Cleve's party met no Indians but worried about reports that some Indians near the mouth of the Scioto River "had taken a number of boats & destroyed families descending the river." William Sudduth descended the river with his own and several other families and remarked, "We saw a great deal of Indian signs . . . but were not interrupted." John Graves recalled that in 1786, "We were often asked by Indians to come ashore for freshment, and in turn asked them to come aboard; but were not interrupted."[80] Probably few travelers, particularly on the Wilderness Road, failed to discover some signs of previous disasters.

The close encounters with Indians undoubtedly helped maintain discipline and vigilance. At times, the lesson learned came in grisly forms. Allen Trimble's memory of the trek includes coming upon the site where the preceding company had been attacked. The site of the "Defeated Camp," recalled Trimble, who was just a boy at the time, "impressed the minds of all with fearful forebodings." Trimble and his fellows "saw the bodies of some fifteen of their countrymen strewed upon the ground, some [toma]hawked and scalped, some stripped naked, and their bodies torn by wild beasts and vultures, exhibiting little of the human frame but bone and sinew." Despite their own danger, the "men stacked their arms and gathered the fragments of their slaughtered brethren and gave them such burial as in their power, sufficient to protect them from the wolf, the panther, the bear and the vulture." This delayed further travel and the group camped near the site of the attack. Young Trimble recalled the aggressiveness of several huge vultures hovering in the vicinity. He also remembered how a large bear lumbered into the camp that evening and was shot down. "[It] would have furnished a delicious morsel for breakfast but for the fact that no one could think of eating the flesh of an animal that had been fattening upon the flesh and blood of human beings."[81]

Most of the attacks are known only by brief references, but a few incidents were more fully described and capture at least a hint of the terror and loss. Margaret Paulee's family took the Wilderness Road in late 1779. The first few days were generally easy travel over undulating ground. The horses were fresh and provisions still plentiful. "It was about 12 o'clock, when I was riding in front of the cattle we were taking with us, with my baby in my arms." Suddenly, "I was alarmed by the report of a gun which seemed to have been fired from behind a log, at which my horse took fright." At the same moment, "I heard my husband's voice calling me repeatedly to ride back." Just as she began to do so, however, one of the Indians "came from behind a tree, pulled me from my horse and struck me senseless with his club." Her baby was wrenched from her arms and killed. She recalled there were six Indians. One other woman was also captured. "My husband when he saw me dragged from my horse, ran up and fought over my body with three of the Indians, using nothing but the but-end of his gun," Paulee recalled. Then one of the Indians pointed his gun and shot her husband in the chest and he fell dead. That night Paulee was compelled to cook with the scalps of her family and friends hanging nearby to dry.[82]

James Taylor's future wife traveled the Wilderness Road in 1784. As her group set up camp one night, another party of about a dozen emigrants came up from behind, but instead of joining together for safety, decided to push on another mile or so. That night the advanced group was attacked. "There was a man & wife who had two children. The woman came back to the camp that they had earlier passed with her infant in her arms. The other child was killed." The husband ran on toward Kentucky, "and each thought the other & children were killed." The next morning the slower group came upon the fresh scene of destruction, "horror-struck" at what they observed. "The dead were buried as well as they could, under the circumstances of the case."[83]

Militia leaders residing near the Crab Orchard, particularly militia leader William Whitley, tried to rescue those who were attacked as they approached Kentucky. In his memoirs Whitley recalled one incident, known as McClure's Defeat, that occurred on Skagg's Creek in 1785. McClure and others fled. Mrs. McClure herded her three small children a short distance away and hid, but one of the children cried and gave away their location The children were killed immediately. When the news reached Whitley, he organized a group of twenty-one men "as true as Steel" and went after the attackers. Whitley's group found the seven Indians on the second day, rescuing Mrs. Whitley, a black woman, and much of the property that had been taken. "They had six scalps stretched in hoops [drying by the fire]," he noted, and "Mrs. McClure had to cook in sight of the scalps." Mr. McClure, however, was not one of the rescuers. According to Whitley's daughter, "Col. Whitley could not prevail upon Mr. McClure to join his party," and after the rescue, "advised Mrs. McClure not to live with such a cowardly man." Whitley led a number of other such rescues, especially where captives were involved or survivors had fled into the woods and become lost. He would take care of them at his home until relatives could be located.[84] Whitley and his "men as true as Steel" aided many victims.

Ohio River emigrants observed less evidence of previous disasters, but the danger of attack was ever present on that route as well. In very early years, it was sometimes possible to camp discreetly on shore but once the volume of traffic increased, the boats became a regular target of attack. Those floating too close to shore made easy prey. One subterfuge was for Indians to hide behind bushes while white captives tried to lure passing boats into coming ashore. The captives claimed to have escaped from the Indians or been stranded while traveling the river.

One of the more notorious incidents occurred in March 1789. A boat conducted by Virginia land speculator John May was hailed from shore near the mouth of the Scioto River by two young men. When May's boat resisted the beseeching entreaties, the two men persisted, following the boat along the shore. Some of the boat's passengers began to waver in their resolve and begged May to rescue the two men. Against his better judgment, May allowed one man to go ashore in a canoe, but once out of the main current the boat moved much more slowly, allowing several Indians enough time to rush from cover. In the midst of gunfire, May sought to get the boat away from shore. Meanwhile, "Their horses, of which they had a great number on board, had broken their halters, and mad with terror were plunging so furiously as to expose them to a danger scarcely less dreadful than that which menaced them from shore." Except for May, none of the others had ever before beheld an Indian and the sight now "struck a terror in their hearts which had almost deprived them of their faculties." Intense gunfire continued from the shore. One of the females received a ball in her mouth and died almost immediately. One of the men received a bullet in his right shoulder that then proceeded under the skin across his back, plus a wound in his other shoulder. When May raised his nightcap to signal surrender, he received a ball in the middle of the forehead and died almost immediately. The attackers then climbed aboard, taking the survivors captive and helping themselves with delight to the boat's ample cargo.[85]

This successful attack was followed in the next days by more, with the two original decoys and two children augmented by the three new captives. The next morning "All of us were compelled to go to the side of the water" and draw approaching boats toward shore. After the attackers killed four men in a canoe, three flatboats came into view, but remained beyond gun range. The Indians used May's boat in an attempt to chase them down, forcing the captives to row. By taking on the passengers from the front and rear boats and leaving those boats behind, the remaining boat escaped. But the Indians were delighted with the two abandoned boats, which were filled with horses and dry goods for resale in Kentucky. "The booty surpassed their most sanguine expectations." Charles Johnson, one of the captives, recognized some of the belongings as those of Thomas Marshall (father of Justice John Marshall). Now amply loaded with plunder, the Indians retired to their village in Ohio.[86] Using white captives as decoys was a common stratagem.

Another notorious river attack occurred in 1791. Captain William Hubbell had gone east on business and was returning home. Descending the Ohio, he shared a boat with a large family and picked up several other emigrants so that the total number of passengers included nine men, three women, and eight children. As they descended the Ohio they noticed "evident traces of Indians" along the banks. At Gallipolis they received warning that a large body of Indians lurked farther down along the river, preying on passing boats. Hubbell, as commander of the boat, assigned sentries for the night, and the guns on board were prepared for use. They passed a slower group of six boats, one of which (that of Captain Greathouse) attempted to join Hubbell but could not keep pace. Expecting an attack at dawn, Hubbell's men were awake and alert, the women and children huddled down in the center of the boat surrounded by baggage for protection. At daylight, a voice called out from shore and "in a plaintive tone repeatedly solicited them to come to shore" and pick up some refugees. Hubbell ignored the cries, which then turned to curses, and soon three Indian canoes were seen through the morning mist advancing toward the boat. "Every man took his position, and was ordered not to fire till the savages had approached so near, that (to use the words of Captain Hubbell,) 'the flash from the guns might singe their eyebrows,' and a special caution was given that the men should shoot successively, so that there might be no intervals." The three canoes were seen to contain twenty-five or thirty Indians, who placed themselves on three sides of the boat, raking it with fire. Almost immediately, a Methodist preacher named Samuel Tucker was mortally wounded but kept up a heroic fire. Another man was hit in the chest. Hubbell was wounded in an arm. The canoes were now so close that some of the Indians could grasp the boat's sides. Hubbell grasped a pair of pistols and killed one Indian as he climbed aboard, then grabbed a kettle and swung it forcefully at the others. Passengers without guns threw firewood at the assailants. Confronted with this determined resistance, the canoes retreated.

At this moment, Greathouse's boat came into view. Instead of mounting a defense like Hubbell, the people huddled in the boat's cabin and were easily captured. Greathouse and an older boy were killed. According to one account, two girls taken from the Greathouse boat "were placed in the bow of the canoes so as to protect the Indians," which now chased after Hubbell's slower flatboat. "But the girls said to Hubbell's men not to mind them, but fire away." Another furious exchange commenced in which another of the boat's defenders was killed. Particularly alarming was that, in the midst of the chaos, the boat had drifted perilously close to shore where the current was slow. Desperate work with the oars brought the boat back to a faster channel and Hubbell's vessel reached Limestone the next night. Three men were dead and Tucker died the next day, but the only other injuries were to a small boy and Hubbell's arm. The boat was densely pocked with bullets and four of the five horses on board were dead. When a detachment of Kentuckians went to the scene of the attack they discovered the bodies of several Indians on shore, as well as the bodies of Greathouse and his passengers. "Most of them had been *whipped to death*, as they were found stripped, tied to trees, and marked with the appearance of lashes; and large rods, which seemed to have been worn with use, were observed lying near them."[87]

Departing emigrants knew about the use of captured whites as decoys and of other Indian stratagems. James Finley's family was alerted that, "Many boats were taken and many lives lost through the deceit and trechery of the Indians and white spies employed by them." Yet sometimes shoreline appeals were genuine. Jacob Van Bibber escaped his Indian captors and made it to the Ohio. He hailed a passing canoe and begged the occupants to come pick him up. "He said he was a prisoner from the Indians. They said they reckoned he was a prisoner from hell and had a hundred Indians to welcome them if they were to go after him." Fortunately Van Bibber was able to convince the canoe's inhabitants, by naming common acquaintances, that he was truly a refugee.[88]

Placing these sorts of individual tragedies in the larger perspective is difficult. "For several years many passing Kentucky boats had been attacked and seized by the enemy; the Indians having provided themselves with boats in order to make their attack," recalled John Heckewelder. "It is said that within two years about 150 people have either lost their lives or been led into captivity from this place." According to one historian, about 100 people taking the Wilderness Road were killed annually, with probably 3,600 civilians killed in the first two decades of Kentucky settlement. Often the casualties suffered en route were pooled with those in the Kentucky settlements. Kentucky judge Harry Innes reported to Secretary of War Henry Knox in 1790 that since his arrival in 1783, "I can venture to say that 1,500 souls have been taken in the [Kentucky] District & migrating to it," as well as 20,000 horses and much valuable personal property. The trans-Appalachian frontier must be ranked as one of the bloodiest in American history.[89]

Some casualties were kept captive rather than killed and

eventually recovered. The Treaty of Fort Greenville, following Gen. Anthony Wayne's victory at Fallen Timbers in 1794, required the release of all white captives. Lexington's *Kentucky Gazette* printed a list of returning captives in hope of reuniting them with their families. Jenny Corder, age twenty-eight, had been captured by Wyandotte Indians in early 1793. Sally Mitchell, age seventeen, had been taken in October 1790 by Mingos. James Hughes Mitchell had been taken by Shawnees on the Ohio in April 1787 or 1788. Polly Ford was captured in 1786 by Wyandottes on the Wilderness Road, aged eight when taken. Some captives were not redeemed until much later. An unknown number of others had died in captivity, could not be found, or refused to leave their new Indian families.[90]

Sublime Natural Scenery and Ancient Curiosities

Despite the danger and hardship, numerous emigrants paused to notice the natural beauties around them. John Smyth, traveling in 1775, gazed westward from a promontory toward the Clinch River and felt moved to write, "Throughout the whole of this amazing and most extensive perspective, there is not the least feature or trace of art or improvement to be discovered." He continued, "It totally absorbs the senses, overwhelmes all the faculties, expands even the grandest ideas beyond all conception, and occasions you almost to forget that you are a human creature." Despite the passage of many years, Felix Walker clearly recalled his first sight of the Bluegrass. "As the cane ceased, we began to discover the pleasing and rapturous appearance of the plains of Kentucky. A new sky and strange earth seemed to be presented to our view. So rich a soil we had never seen before; covered with clover in full bloom, the woods were abounding with wild game," he wrote. "We felt ourselves as passengers through a wilderness just arrived at the fields of Elysium, or at the garden where was no forbidden fruit." Young Daniel Trabue was also touched by what he saw, writing, "I was truly Delighted in seeing the mountains, Rivers, hills, etc., spruce, pine, Laurrill, etc., Everything looked new to me." Jane Stevenson observed, "The pretty springs of waters, & the woods, rendered Powell's Valley so exceedingly beautiful, I could have stopped freely in it." Later in the trek she noted, "But the woods

were more beautiful in Cumberland Valley than any other place."
Although Lewis Condict struggled with muddy terrain as he returned east, he nonetheless appreciated the beauty around him,
remarking, "The mountains on each side of the [Cumberland] river
form a romantic scene, some of which are 700 feet high & are
almost perpendicular."[91]

Visages of natural beauty also struck emigrants who took the
Ohio River. Reported William Brown in 1790, "The Ohio is a
beautiful river, and as you sail along you have some delightful
views—The verdure of the trees—shady level banks, smooth water and great distance you can see before you in some of the reaches
of the river." As the sun set, Brown judged it "the most enchanting
view I ever beheld." Similarly, Baptist preacher John Gregg noted
in his journal, "I am continually seeing a beautiful river, gently
gliding along, a mountain or hill on one side or the other, lined on
either shore with rich soil and the flourishing verdure of the sugar-
tree, sycamore, walnut, etc."[92] Although the eastern settlements
retained much forested land, the dramatic vantage points from river
and mountain, the excitement of a new personal adventure, and
the unfamiliar terrain, apparently sensitized observers of the trans-
Appalachian landscape. At least for some emigrants, discomfort
and fear could not obscure the wilderness's natural beauty.

It was frequently during the migration that people caught their
first sight of another element of western nature. By the eighteenth
century, bison were virtually unknown east of the Alleghenies. Thomas Rogers was only three years old when his family came down
the Ohio River in 1783, but he had a clear memory of his first
sighting. "There was a great bustle in the boat, looking at something in the river. I being a pretty inquisitive little fellow was anxious to see," he recalled decades later. "A man in the boat held me
up above the sides of the boat and told me to look down the river
and I saw the buffaloes, head and shoulders out of the water. And
even to this day it seems as vivid as it was at that day." The first
sight of buffalo was equally vivid for others as well. Recalled Robert Jones, "The first buffalo I ever saw was on the last day of March,
1786, 6 miles above Limestone, feeding on the Cabin Creek bottom." Mrs. McFarland recalled of her first sighting that the buffalo "roared . . . almost as bad as thunder."[93]

Travelers often attempted to describe buffalo for readers who had never encountered one. Englishman Laurence Butler wrote, "the[y] are like your cattle, only larger, and have bones growing up from their withers about nine inches; they have a kind of a mane, and the hair on their forehead is about nine inches long." Englishman Nicholas Cresswell visited Kentucky in 1775 and frequently encountered bison in the course of his western travels. In his journal he recorded unusually detailed observations. "Buffalo are a sort of wild cattle, but have a large hump on the top of their shoulders all black, and their necks and shoulders covered with long shaggy hair with large bunches of hair growing on their forethighs, short horns bending forward, short noses, piercing eyes and beard like a Goat." Cresswell noted that the thickness of the coat changed with the season. "Their tails are short with a bunch of long hair at the end. When they run they carry them erect." Cresswell thought buffalo meat was good eating, "particularly the hump, which I think makes the finest steaks in the world." Cresswell shot several buffalo during his journey, observing "They feed in large herds and are exceedingly fierce when wounded. Their sense of smell is exquisite." A frontier physician who examined a carcass noted that the distinctive hump "is formed by the Spinal Processes of the nine first Vertebrae of the back gradually rising in hight . . . and the process of the third rising sometimes in bulls to the length of Eighten Inches the nineth to 3 or four inches."[94]

Although early Kentuckians encountered buffalo with regularity, the animals became increasingly rare as the western population swelled. One settler as a boy in 1775 "once encountered eleven hundred buffaloes going in single file to the Blue Licks." But the buffalo disappeared quickly. "When we came to this county in 1787, the buffalo were gone," said one woman. "Never saw a wild one." John Hedge, arriving around 1790 reported, "When I first came here, buffalo bones covered the grounds." Too many previous settlers would "kill them for sport, and leave them lie." The survivors retreated to more remote regions.[95]

Buffalo attracted the greatest comment, but among Ohio River travelers, the variety and large size of the fish also drew attention. "The Ohio abounds in fish of different kinds; the most abundant is the cat fish," reported one traveler, some of which he claimed weighed as much as 100 pounds. According to another person, "This river affords a vast quantity of fresh water fish: they have a kind that is called cat, which weighs upwards of 100 weight, and a perch that weighs from eight to twenty pounds, which I think is a finer fish than the salmon or sole you have in England." Another European traveler noted the great quantity of perch. "This fish is the size of a large carp on the Rhine; its flesh is white and well tasted, but it is altogether unlike the perch of Europe." Wrote another Ohio voyager, "We catch a great number of fish in the river, such as the Cat-fish, some of which I saw weigh 60 odd pounds; the Buffalo fish which is very strong; the Bass and Perch which generally weigh from 4 to 10 lbs, also others." One of the Ohio Valley's early historians reported that Ohio River catfish often weighed as much as eighty pounds in the eighteenth century. Other varieties of fish also reached uncommon size. Buffalo fish weighed between five and thirty pounds, pike between four and fifteen, sturgeon between four and ten, and perch reached an amazing twenty-five pounds. Fish in eastern rivers had once been just as large, but by the eighteenth century such sizes were rare.[96]

Many travelers also noted two prominent prehistoric sites, the large Indian mounds on Grave Creek and the prehistoric remains at Big Bone Lick. Both were within easy reach of Ohio travelers having a curious or scientific mind. Numerous smaller mounds and rectangular formations interpreted as ancient fortifications were scattered throughout the Ohio Valley. Most American visitors were satisfied with climbing to the top and speculating about their origin and purpose. A few dug into the smaller mounds and discovered human remains with a variety of primitive relics, concluding that these marked formal burials. From Big Bone Lick, specimens were collected as souvenirs or sent to interested parties such as Benjamin Franklin and Thomas Jefferson.

Big Bone Lick received the greatest notice. Among the earliest American visitors was Robert B. McAfee in 1773, who recalled seeing "a great number of the frames of the mammoth." Some of the men with him used the rib bones for tent poles and the vertebrae for stools. Thomas Hanson, who accompanied a surveying party in 1774, recorded, "There is a number of large teeth to be seen at this Lick which people imagine to be elephants. There is one seven feet and three inches long." On his return to Fort Pitt in 1775, Nicholas Cresswell found an opportunity to visit "Elephant Bone Lick," as he called it. According to Cresswell, "Where the bones are found is a large muddy pond, a little more than knee deep with a Salt spring in it which I suppose preserves the bones sound. Found several bones of a prodigious size, I take them to be Elephants, for we found part of a tusk, about two foot long . . . Ribs 9 inches broad, Thigh bones 10 inches diameter. What sort of animals these were is not clearly known." One of the men with Cresswell had on a previous visit found a tusk six feet long. Cresswell also noted "Several Indian paintings on the trees." Another Englishman, visiting Big Bone Lick in 1784, reported, "I saw a thigh bone which at the big end measured three feet round, and a jaw bone that must have weighed 50 pounds." He continued, "Some say they are elephants' but I think they are larger."[97]

Grave Creek received its name from a prominent Indian mound near its mouth (modern Moundsville, West Virginia). This was the most conspicuous mound along the Virginia shore, being nearly 100 feet in height. A few other ancient sites also attracted pioneer curiosity. One of the most noted was on the edge of Marietta, with the remains of fortifications close by. "When they were discovered, they were full of trees," reported one traveler in 1802. "These trees have been hewn down, and the ground is now almost entirely cultivated with Indian corn." The citizens of Marietta later made the large mound on the edge of town the center of their own cemetery, thereby preserving this ancient edifice. River travelers who visited Marietta often incorporated a visit to the cemetery mound, sometimes also noting the rectangular shapes of ground on which the village was built.

The large mounds at Grave Creek and Marietta, plus dozens of smaller ancient mounds and rectangular edifices baffled eighteenth-century Americans. Traveler Lewis Condict expressed unusual curiosity about several edifices he encountered, but "neither the oldest inhabitants, nor the Indians, can give any account of them, nor does history inform us any thing concerning them." Their regular shape indicated some sort of purposeful design, which "induces some to suppose, that this Country was formerly inhabited by some warlike people who are now entirely extinct." Occasion-

The Great Mound at Marietta was originally forested, but in the nineteenth century the town made it the center of their cemetery. Source: Ephriam G. Squires and Edwin H. Davis, *Ancient Monuments of the Mississippi Valley, Comprising the Results of Extensive Surveys and Explorations* (Washington, D.C.: The Smithsonian Institution, 1847).

ally American curiosity went further. At the mouth of the Miami River, one traveler recorded, "We have by digging discovered a great many human bones covered with large stones which must have been brought from the river as there is none near this grave."[98]

Travelers from the South who chose to reach the Ohio River from the Kanawha River rather than the Monongahela, noted a phenomenon they called Boiling Spring about fifteen miles above the river's mouth on the Ohio. According to an early surveyor, "Put a blaze of fire within 3 or 4 inches of the water and immediately the water will be in a flame, and continue so til it is put out by the force of the wind. The Springs are small and boil continualy like a pot on the fire. The water is black and has a taste of nitre."

Missionary John Heckewelder wrote, "The spring is now visited by many gentlemen travelling down [to] the Ohio, and they tell me, that when it has been set on fire, it usually burns for about three quarters of an hour. It does not however burn down to the ground, but only to the surface of the water."[99]

The Stream of Population Westward

The "rage for Kentucky" drew people from a wide range of the new American republic. A resident of Spottsylvania County in central Virginia commented in 1779, "*People are Running Mad for Kentucky Hereabouts.*" After the upheaval of a long war and the subsequent economic collapse, many white Americans were eager to make a fresh start in a new region. "Everybody coming to Kentucky," recalled a young settler named William Clinkenbeard, "Could hardly get along the road for them." His brother Isaac claimed that the line of packhorses in 1779 "strung fr[om] Cumberland Mn. to Boonesborough." An emigrant on the Wilderness Road in 1784, one of many who believed that the close of the War for Independence would make western settlement safer, found "vast crowds in the wilderness, large droves of cattle, and the trace small." Another traveler that season was likewise struck by the army of westward migrants. "Having arrived at the place where all roads which lead to Kentucky meet, I kept an account of the number of souls I overtook in one day to that country." Although riding at a moderate pace of thirty miles that day, he overtook 221 emigrants. "They seemed absolutely infatuated by something like the old crusading spirit to the holy land." (The major exception, of course, but seldom noted in contemporary accounts, were the several thousand slaves.)[100]

The volume of traffic on the Ohio River was also impressive. The *Pittsburgh Gazette* reported in early 1787, "Since the 10th of October, 1786, to May the 12th, 1787, there has passed down the Ohio river for Kentucky, 177 boats, 2689 people . . . a number passed in the night unobserved." It reported later that year, "Since Sunday evening last upwards of one hundred and twenty boats have passed by this town on their way to Kentucky, which at an average of 15 persons each, will add 1800 inhabitants to that young settlement." Down river at Fort Finney, army paymaster Erkuries Beatty commented in 1786, "Great numbers of Kentucky and keel boats passing every day." While briefly at Fort Pitt in early 1788, John May witnessed four Kentucky boats passing in a single day, calculating about twenty people per boat, and commented, "Tis surprizing the number of these boats that have passd this spring. 200, are taken account of, and many go down in the night." A resident of Marietta noted in April 1789 that "Kentucky boats have passed this place in very large numbers this past week." James Hedge, who came via the Ohio River in 1791, recalled that the "Emigration to Kentucky, for 2 or 3 years, about this time, was very great," perhaps encouraged by Kentucky's admission in 1792 as the fifteenth state. An observer at Pittsburgh in 1795 noted, "An immense crowd of people from all parts are constantly passing through to Kentucky."[101]

The pace of trans-Appalachian migration was not constantly high, but each autumn and spring saw a fresh surge of movement. The first census in 1790 reported a Kentucky population of 74,000, nearly 18 percent of whom were slaves. The ensuing decade witnessed a constant flow of immigrants, especially after 1794, following American military victories against the Shawnees in the North and Chickamaugas in the South. By 1800, more than 220,000 Americans lived in Kentucky, 106,000 in adjacent Tennessee, and 230,000 in Ohio. Roughly 7 percent of the national population lived west of the Alleghenies.[102]

With such high rates of migration, the experience of crossing the Appalachian Mountains could not help but undergo some changes. The most important of these was the end of danger from Indian attack, which persisted on both routes of travel until about 1795. In addition, whereas the trip had originally entailed roughly 200 miles of uninhabited territory, the brave establishment of small settlements had greatly reduced this distance by the end of the eighteenth century. Many of these frontier footholds had endured years of vulnerability to Indian attack. Furthermore, although difficult to measure, by the 1790s westward migrants enjoyed better access to information about routes of travel. Unlike their predecessors, they had benefit of more than two decades of trans-Appalachian travel.

The most important change involved the danger of attack.

Frontier defense usually operated at a neighborhood or local level during the eighteenth century. The Indian raids, from both northern and southern groups, were unpredictable and swift, and any response had to be conducted immediately. By 1781 the problem was frequent enough that western authorities pressed harder on the Confederation government for additional support. Any counter-raid required ammunition, arms, and provisions. The militia needed some sort of compensation for their time, but the government unfortunately had little to give. Col. Arthur Campbell, from Washington County in the remote southwestern corner of Virginia, repeatedly appealed to the governor for a garrison and for regular patrols to warn of trouble. In late January 1781, Campbell reported that already Indians "have killed one of the Settlers in Powell's Valley, and carried off 14 Horses, belonging to a party of men coming from Kentucky." Although he did not know which particular group of Indians was responsible, "this with their former successes near the same place, may encourage them to attempt further depredations, and so render the passage to kentucky exceeding unsafe." He therefore on his own authority as militia commander organized a company of patrollers for the region around Cumberland Gap and began construction of a fort. In March, 150 volunteers residing in the remote settlement of Watauga had attacked three large Cherokee settlements and several small ones, and a second contingent was en route to attack several more south of Cumberland Gap. "If this party is fortunate in their attempts," wrote Campbell to Governor Jefferson, "I trust our South Western Frontier and the Kentucky path will be less infested the remaining part of the year, than they have for some time past."[103]

A year later, little improvement was evident. Lt. Col. John Evans of Monongahela County reported to Gov. Benjamin Harrison, "The murders committed on our Frontiers at such a[n early] time of the year, and the repeated applications of our Suffering Inhabitants, Occations me to trouble your Honour . . . we are few in number and much Exposed. Our fronteers are so Extensive that the few inhabitants there Settled are so scattering that the Enemy murder one part before the others can be alarmed to come to their assistance." Without military assistance, the settlers would begin abandoning their homesteads. By late summer, Col. William

Christian of Montgomery County feared that recent Indian successes would soon bring more. "People are now on the road," he reported, retreating to less exposed places. Furthermore, "If no succor is sent to Kentucky, and the war with the British continues another Year, it is more than Probable the whole of the inhabitants will be killed, taken to [British] Detroit, or driven away." By December, the British threat was past but the Virginia frontier had contracted significantly. In western Pennsylvania and North Carolina, the situation was similar. The British had surrendered at Yorktown, but Britain's native allies remained formidable foes.[104]

Yet, with the peace with Britain, the migration to Kentucky could be expected not only to resume to earlier levels but to swell. Colonel Christian urged the government of Virginia to provide some degree of safety. Christian recommended that Col. Joseph Martin, who had distinguished himself during the Revolution as an official Indian agent for North Carolina at Long Island on the Holston River, be retained by Virginia and move his operation to Cumberland Gap. "The Gap is near half way betixt our settlements on Holston [River] and Kentuckey, and a post there would be a resting Place for our poor citizens going back and forward & would be a great means of saving the Lives of Hundreds of them," wrote Christian. "For it very seldom happens that Indians will kill People near where they Trade: and it is thereabouts the most of the mischief on the Road has been done." This location would be more convenient also for the Cherokees to the south. Moreover, the change would be "of great Importance to the Frontiers of Washington [County, Virginia]; to our Peoples Journeying to and from Kentucky, particularly the poor families moving out; to the Indian Trade and to the Indian Agency in general." Joseph Martin did within a short period of time relocate his agency on the route to Kentucky, about twenty miles east of Cumberland Gap. At the new location, Martin's Station became an extremely important outpost for trade and diplomacy, and a welcome rest stop for travelers. As has been shown, however, the Indian threat would remain substantial for years to come.[105]

The way west to Kentucky also saw important physical improvements in these years. As the only practical overland route through the mountain ridges, public officials realized the importance of repairing and improving the Wilderness Road. Roadwork was customarily a local obligation, which posed a complication for a route that bridged such a wide uninhabited distance. Allocations of labor therefore required special legislation. The importance of a good link between Virginia's eastern and trans-Allegheny counties, however, was undeniable. The legislature made its first allocation in 1779. The goal was limited to making the packhorse trail more passable, but with an eye toward building a future wagon road. Two commissioners were appointed to establish the route, while others were to supervise the workers. The nearest militia officers were to provide a guard due to the risk of attack.[106]

Although the result was recognizably better, the heavy volume of traffic after the close of the Revolution demanded further attention. By 1790, the Virginia legislature again took notice that the "road leading through the Wilderness to the district of Kentuckey, is much out of repair, whereby the intercourse between the inhabitants of the said district and the eastern part of this state is greatly obstructed." Six hundred pounds of public money was allocated for repairs, although it was drawn not from the state treasury but from the taxes to be collected in the five Kentucky counties (still part of Virginia) most proximate to the road and its benefits. Because cash was in short supply, workers would receive a tax credit for their labor.[107]

Shortly after Kentucky became a state in 1792, Virginia decided to widen that part of the road still within the Old Dominion to accommodate wagons. Thus, travelers could go by wagon from the old Block House (in Washington County) to Cumberland Gap (Russell County, modern Lee County). Responsibility for the rest of the route belonged to the new state of Kentucky, which had an equal interest in widening the trail for wagons but could not muster the public resources to match Virginia's plan. In such a recently settled region, sufficient tax revenue was not available. A few of Kentucky's enterprising leaders undertook improvements by private subscription in 1792, hoping to recoup their investment through tolls, but passage beyond Virginia by wagon remained impossible. After several failures, the Kentucky legislature voted to widen the road for wagons in 1795.[108] Lexington's *Kentucky Gazette* proudly announced a year later, "THE WILDERNESS ROAD from

Cumberland Gap to the settlements in Kentucky is now compleated. Waggons loaded with a ton weight, may pass with ease, with four good horses,—Travellers will find no difficulty in procuring such necessaries as they stand in need of on the road; and the abundant crop now growing in Kentucky, will afford the emigrants a certainty of being supplied with every necessary of life on the most convenient terms."[109] The cost of this long-awaited achievement involved the unpopular necessity of levying a toll, although people using the road with an intention of residing in Kentucky were given a special exemption in 1798. Thus, it was not until the closing years of the eighteenth century that Daniel Boone's Kentucky path assumed the character of a true road. Compared with 1775, the transformation was impressive. The actual experience of bringing a wagon across the gaps and rivers remained so difficult, however, that the famous Boone trail was, by the end of the century, a second choice to the Ohio River.

The shear volume of travel in the eighteenth century brought other changes as well. Early travelers had been forced to camp. If a horse became maimed, or food proved inadequate, or any other accident occurred, the consequences were often costly. By the close of the eighteenth century, inns and taverns were still rare, but enough settlers now lived along the road to offer services or provisions. Land speculator Gilbert Imlay exaggerated when he wrote around 1790, "The Wilderness, which was formerly two hundred miles through, without a single habitation, is reduced from the settlement of Powell's Valley, to nearly one half of that distance" But his prediction was correct, "that in a few years more that the remainder of the distance will afford settlements for the accommodation of people travelling that route; when a good road may be made quite to Kentucky."[110] The experience of crossing the mountains remained challenging, but it soon resembled the discomforts encountered in long-distance travel elsewhere in America.

Whereas the governments of Virginia and Kentucky made physical improvements to Boone's wilderness pathway a public undertaking, the low water levels and shifting sandbars of the Ohio remained problematic for decades. Nearly all of the improvements undertaken during the eighteenth century lay within the shadow of army fortifications and would have been impossible without federal support. Because the river did not lie within any state's territory, none would address the Ohio's obstructions. It was not until well into the nineteenth century that the Army Corps of Engineers removed the more substantial obstructions.

As with the Wilderness Road, new settlements along the Ohio's shore made a major difference. Traveling around 1790, Gilbert Imlay claimed that ten or twenty miles below Wheeling "is generally well settled. There are few settlements on the opposite shore until you came to the Muskingum, and the country now wears the face of a wilderness on both sides of the river, there being no habitation worth notice, except at the mouth of the Great Kanhaway, until we arrive at Limestone."[111] Imlay exaggerated, but in the course of the next decade, his inflated description approached reality. Small towns multiplied and nearly every pocket of arable land seemed to hold a cabin or two. The line of settlement along the Ohio River made a tremendous difference. Just as on the Wilderness Road, river travelers could likewise find roofed lodging and prepared meals on a regular basis by the end of the century. Francois Michaux, who traveled down the Ohio in 1793 and again in 1802, saw a dramatic difference. "Till the years 1796 and 1797 the banks of the Ohio were so little populated that they scarcely consisted of thirty families in the space of four hundred miles." By the end of the century, however, the number of settlers had so greatly increased that "they were not farther than two or three miles from each other, and when on the river we always had a view of some of them."[112] Thus, in a single generation, crossing the Appalachians by either land or river had been transformed from a blind incursion through an extensive wilderness into a fairly well charted course.

Conclusion

The Overland Trail to Oregon and California is usually considered the premier migration experience in American history, with the trans-Appalachian migration in the late eighteenth century a much lesser event. The accounts left by the early immigrants to Kentucky indicate that this impression merits reexamination. Although the migration to Kentucky involved a much shorter distance across a much lower mountain divide, it was an event of comparable stature for the people who experienced it. The trans-Appalachian crossing loomed just as large in the eighteenth-century imagination as did that of the Overland Trail several generations later. Both migrations involved arduous labor and expense, as well as isolation from established settlement areas. For nearly two centuries, westward settlement had been essentially contiguous with existing settlements. During times of border unrest, refuge and military aid had been comparatively near at hand. Kentucky settlement involved a frontier of a much greater magnitude. As with the Overland Trail, most emigrants knew they would never see home and kin again.[113] Return journeys, however, were not unknown. Some people had come only to locate vacant land with the intention to settle it later. Some, particularly during the Revolutionary War, could not withstand the constant danger and the human loss and deprivation it wrought. Others returned east on personal or public business. Most eastbound travelers took the Wilderness Road, but the Ohio River was not impossible to ascend using canoes.

Furthermore, earlier as well as later episodes of expansion transpired under the supervision of established governments. The beginning of Kentucky settlement, however, coincided with the eight-year-long Revolutionary War. Although General Cornwallis's surrender at Yorktown secured American independence, the final major engagement, a defeat, occurred at Kentucky's Lower Blue Licks in 1782 where a British-led-and-armed Indian force exacted a devastating toll. Virginia, facing the British army and naval forces, could offer her westernmost citizens only minimum support. The Confederation, even if it could have afforded aid, found itself overwhelmed by more pressing national issues. President Washington's administration was likewise beset with numerous problems. Had there not been the possibility that discontent in Kentucky might lead to secession or an alliance with the Spanish at New Orleans, the federal government probably would have postponed taking military action against the Indians bordering the western settlements. Hoping to avoid the violence that had accompanied Kentucky's settlement, the federal government disallowed American occupation of national territory until Indian claims had been extinguished and the land surveyed. The prospect of secure title, a major problem in Kentucky, discouraged squatting.

Also unlike the better-known experiences recorded on the Overland Trail, trans-Appalachian emigrants suffered greatly from Indian attacks. Although Overland emigrants were forced to appease the Great Plains native people with an occasional "gift" of cattle, they passed on largely unmolested. The immigrants to Kentucky, on the other hand, faced an organized and well-armed adversary. Particularly during the Revolutionary War, the British garrisons around the Great Lakes provided their Indian allies generously. British officers led several major campaigns across the Ohio River. A strong trade relationship continued after the close of the war, enabling countless raids on emigrants and settlers. The main purpose of these postwar hostilities was plunder, particularly horses, but many American lives were lost, too. From the south, Spain followed a similar policy, arming Creeks and Chickamaugas and enabling them to prey upon travelers of the Wilderness Road. Trans-Appalachian travel remained unsafe until nearly the close of the century.

Consequently, whether eighteenth-century immigrants to Kentucky and neighboring regions chose the Ohio River or the Wilderness Road, they joined a group when possible. Contrary to popular impression, many of these groups were quite large, of a size to rival the wagon trains that crossed the Rockies. And like the wagon trains, the trans-Appalachian emigrants organized and chose leaders to coordinate the group.[114] In times of crisis, fellow travelers offered mutual aid, fended off attackers, took in refugees, and buried the dead. The assignment of sentries, the defensive layout of encampments, and the rate of travel were determined by the "captain."

The trans-Appalachian crossing also resembled the Overland Trail in that it often entailed considerable loss and suffering. The terrain through which the Wilderness Road passed was not nearly as high as the Rockies, but was nonetheless challenging. Both the ascents and descents often involved treacherous loose rock. In sections, the narrow trail bordered high precipices where any accident could result in a fatal end. Fording unfamiliar rivers presented danger as well. The innumerable small creeks often had steep and slippery banks to maneuver. Pressured to keep moving by the danger of Indians, the Wilderness Road wore out many a beast. When the Wilderness Road was opened for wagons, simply widening Boone's trail was impossible and certain sections had to be rerouted. Descending the Ohio likewise presented challenges such as buried obstacles, low water levels, rapids, and ice. Boats often had to be pried off a snag and pushed back into a deeper channel. These accidents could easily damage the boat, and stopping for repairs risked attracting hostile Indians.

And, finally, like the experience of the Overland Trail, the passage of time wrought change. Whereas the early trans-Appalachian emigrants were dependent on their own resources, travelers by the closing years of the eighteenth century—at least those with money—could avail themselves of taverns, had ample opportunities to restock provisions, and could find settlements for help in times of need. Most of all, later travelers enjoyed a safe passage.

Reading the firsthand accounts by actual emigrants establishes the trans-Appalachian crossing as a worthy bracket for the nineteenth-century crossing of the continent's other great chain of mountains.

Part One

The Revolutionary Era

The beginning of Kentucky settlement coincided with the outbreak of the American Revolution. Yet even in wartime, the attraction of Kentucky's lush Bluegrass region remained strong. Indian attacks sponsored by British garrisons at Detroit and elsewhere in the Great Lakes region made western travel and settlement dangerous. Many of the people who undertook Kentucky settlement in these years lost their lives or suffered other great losses. Some abandoned Kentucky and returned east. Other people visited Kentucky only to secure land for settlement at some future, safer point in time. Moreover, the way west to Kentucky was not yet well known. Emigrants sometimes became lost or encountered unforeseen problems. Many found themselves underprepared for the rigors of the journey. Travelers were truly entering a wilderness.

1

❦

William Calk, 1775

William Calk was born in 1740 in Prince William County, Virginia, and after his marriage moved to Orange County. Calk left his family behind when he went to inspect prospects in Kentucky on March 13, 1775, with four friends who seem to have been neighbors with equal curiosity (Abraham Hanks, Philip Drake, Enoch Smith, and Robert Whitledge). Several slaves were taken to perform such services as starting the morning fire, preparing the meals, and similar mundane or domestic duties. The source of Calk's interest, inspiring these four comfortably situated men to plunge themselves into a wilderness, is unknown, but is probably similar to the verbal praises that Daniel Boone had heard of, such as a "great meadow" beyond the mountains. Calk took with him surveying instruments, indicating an intention to claim land. Along the way, Calk's party fell in with that of Richard Henderson, who was en route to join Boone and his trailblazers at Boonesborough, so they joined this larger group. The selection presented here begins where Calk's diary opens, a succinct reminder that just reaching the eastern terminus of the Wilderness Road exposed travelers to many difficulties, even, as in Calk's case, when not burdened by a dependent family and essential belongings.

1775 March 13th mond[ay] I set out from prince wm.[County] To travel to Caintuck. on tuesday Night our company all Got together at Mr Prises on Rapadan [River] Which was ABraham hanks philip Drake Eanock Smith Robert Whitledge & my Self. then abrams Dogs leg got broke by Drake's Dog—[1]

wedns 15th we started Early from prises. made a good Days travel & lodge this Night at mr cars on North fork [of the] James River.

thurs 16th we started Early. it Raind [the] Chief part of the Day. Snowd in the Eavening very hard & was very coald. we travld all Day & Got to Mr Blacks at the foot of the Blue Ridge [Mountains].

fryd 17th we Start Early. cross the Ridge. the wind Blows very hard & cold and lodge at James loyls.

Satrd 18th we git this Day to William andersons at Crows ferrey & there we Stay till monday morning.

mond 20th we Start early cross the fery and lodge this night at Wm adamses on the head of catauby [Kanawha River].

tuesd 21st we Start early and git over pepers ferey on new River & lidge at pepers this night.

Wedns 22nd we Start early and git to foart chissel [Chiswell] whear we git some good loaf Bread & good Whiskey.

thurs 23d we Start early & travel till a good while in the Night and git to major Cammels on ho[l]ston River.

fryday ye 24th we Start early & turn out of the wagon Road to go across the mountains to go by Danil Smiths. we lose Drive [a negro slave belonging to Calk]. Come to a turabel mountain that tried us all almost to death to git over it & we lodge this night on the Lawrel fork of holston [River] under a grait mountain & Roast a fine fat turkey for our Suppers & Eat it without aney Bread.

Satrd 25 we Start Early. travel over Some more very Bad mountains one that is caled Clinch mountain & we git this night to Danil Smiths on clinch [River] and there we Staid till thursday morning. on tuesday night & wednesday morning it Snowed Very hard and was very colad & we hunted a good deal there while we Staid in Rough mountains & Kild three Deer & one turkey. Eanock ABram & I got lost Tuesday night & it asnowing & Should a lain in the mountains had not I a pocket Compas By which I Got in a little in the night and fired guns and they heard them and caim in By the Repoart.

thursd 30th we Set out again & went down to Elk gardin and there Suplid our Selves With Seed Corn & irish tators.[2] then we went on alittel way. I turned my hors to drive afore me & he got Scard Ran away threw Down the Saddel Bags & Broke three of our [gun] powder goards & ABrams flask Burst open a walet of corn & lost a good Deal & made aturrabel flustration amongst the Reast of the horses. Drakes mair ran against a sapling & noct it down. we cacht them all agin & went on & lodgd at John Duncans

fryd 31st we suplayd our Selves at Dunkans with a 108 pounds of Bacon & went on again to Brileys mill & suployd our Selves with meal & lodged this night at clinch By a large cainbrake & cuckt our Suppers.

April satd [the] first. this morning there is ice at our camp half inch thick. we Start Early & travel this Day along a verey Bad hilley way cross one creek whear the horses almost got Mired. Some fell in & all wet their loads. we cross Clinch River & travell till late in the Night & camp on cove creek having two men with us that wair pilates.[3]

Sund 2d this morning is avery hard frost. we Start Early. travel over powels mountain and camp on the head of Powels valey whear there is verey good food.[4]

mond 3d Start Early. travel down the valey cross powels River [and] go some throw the woods with out aney track. cross some Bad hils. Git into [Richard] hendersons Road.[5] camp on a creek in powels valey.

tuesday 4th Raney. we Start about 10 oclock and git down to capt [Joseph] martins in the valey where we over take Coln [Richard] henderson & his [Transylvania] companey Bound for Caintuck & there we camp this Night. there they were Broiling & Eating Beef without Bread.

wednesday ye 5th Breaks away fair & we go on down the valey & camp on indian Creek. we had this creek to cross maney times & very Bad Banks. ABrams Saddel turned [over] & the load all fell in. we go out this Eavening & Kill two Deer.[6]

thurd 6th this morning is ahard frost & we wait at camp for Coln. Henderson & companey to come up. they come up about 12 oclock & we Join with them and camp there. Still this night waiting for Some part of the companey that had their horses Ran away with their packs.

fryday ye 7th this morning is avery hard Snowey morning & we Still continue at camp Being in number about 40 men & Some Negroes. this Eavening Comes aletter from Capt [Daniel] Boon at caintuck of the indians doing mischief and Some turns back.

William Calk His Jurnal April ye 8th 1775 Satterday

Satrd 8th We all pact up & Started. Crost Cumberland gap about one oclock this Day. we Met a great maney people turnd Back [from Kentucky] for fear of the indians but our Company goes on Still with good courage. we come to a very ugly Creek With Steep Banks & have it to Cross Several times. on this Creek we camp this night.[7]

Sunday 9th this morning We wait at camp for the cattel to Be drove up to Kill a Beef. tis late Before they come & people makes out alittel snack & agree to go on till till [*sic*] Night. we git to cumberland River & there we camp. meet 2 more men turn Back.

Monday 10th this is alowry morning & very like for Rain & we keep at camp this day and Some goes out ahunting. I & two more goes up avery large mountain. Near the top we Saw the track of two indians & whear they had lain under Some Rocks. Some of the companey went over the River a bofelo hunting But found None. at night Capt. [Nathaniel] Hart comes up with his packs & there they hide Some of their lead to lighten their packs that they may travel faster.[8]

tuesday 11th this is a very loury morning & like for Rain But we all agree to Start Early. we Cross Cumberland River & travel Down it about 10 miles through Some turrabel Cainbrakes. as we went down abrams mair Ran into the River with Her load & Swam over. he followd her & got on her & made her Swim back agin. it is a very Raney Eavening. we take up camp near Richland Creek. they Kill a Beef. Mr Drake Bakes Bread with out Washing his hands. we Keep Sentry this Night for fear of the indians—

Wednesday 12th this is a Raney morning But we pack up & go on. we come to Richland creek it is high. we toat our packs over on a tree & swim our horses over & there We meet another

Company going Back. they tell Such News [of Indian attacks that] ABram & Drake is afraid to go aney further. there we camp this night—

thursday 13th this morning the weather Seems to Brake & Be fair. ABram & Drake turn Back.[9] we go on & git to loral [Laurel] River. we come to a creek before wheare we are obliged to unload & to toate our packs over on a log. this day we meet about 20 more turning Back. we are obliged to toat our packs over loral River & Swim our Horses. one hors Ran in with his pack and lost it in the River & they got it [again].[10]

fryday 14th this is a clear morning with a Smart frost. we go on & have avery mirey Road and camp this Night on a creek of loral River & are Surprisd at camp By a wolf—

Satterday 15th clear with a Small frost. we Start Early we meet Some men that turns & goes With us. we travel this Day through the plais Cald the Bressh & cross Rockcase [Rockcastle] River & camp ther this Night & have fine food for our horses—

Sunday 16th cloudy & warm. we Start Early & go on about 2 mile down the River and then turn up a creek that we crost about 50 times. Some very Bad foards with a great Deal of very good land on it. the Eavening we git over to the waters of Caintuck & go alittel Down the creek & there we camp. keep Sentry the forepart of the night. it Rains very har[d] all night[11]—

monday 17th this is a very Rany morning But Breaks about 11 oclock & we go on and Camp this Night in Several companeys on Some of the creeks of caintuck.

Tuesday 18th fair & cool and we go on. about 11 oclock. we meet 4 men from Boons Camp that Caim to cunduck us on. we camp this night Just on the Beginning of the Good land. near the Blue lick they kill 2 Bofelos this Eavening—

Wednesd 19th Smart frost this morning. they kill 3 Bofelos. about 11 oclock we come to where the indians fired on Boons Companey & Kild 2 men & a dog & wounded one man in the thigh. we campt this night on oter creek[12]—

thursday 20th this morning is Clear & cool. We Start Early & git Down to Caintuck to Boons foart [Boonesborough] about 12 oclock wheare we stop. they Come out to meet us & welcom us in with a voley of guns.

fryday 21st Warm this Day. they Begin laying off lots in the town
   and pre[p]aring for peopel to worek to make corn[13]—
Satterday 22d they finish laying out lots. this Eavening. I went
   afishing and Cacht 3 cats. they meet in the night to Draw for
   choise of lots But Refer it till morning—
William Calk his Jurnal April ye 23d 1775
April Sunday 23d this morning the peopel meets & Draws for Chois
   of loots [lots]. this is avery warm day.
monday 24th We all view our loots & Some Don't like them. about
   12 oclock the Combsses [family] come to town & Next morning they make them a bark canew and Set off down the River
   to meet their Companey—
Tuesday 25th in the Eavening we git us a plaise at the mouth of the
   creek & Begin clearing this day. we Begin to live without Bread.
Wednesday 26th We Begin Building us a house & a plaise of Defence to keep the indians off.
thursday 27th Raney all Day But We Still keep about our house—
Satterday 29th We git our house kivered with Bark & move our
   things into it at Night and Begin houskeeping Eanock Smith
   Robert Whitledge & my Self.

*Calk returned to Virginia, but did not bring his family to Boonesborough
until 1784, after the Revolutionary War. He had made an early land
claim some miles east of Boonesborough, in modern Montgomery
County. In addition to improving his large homestead (with the help
of slaves), Calk's income was augmented by work he did as a deputy
surveyor. He also built a mill and a tannery, becoming one of the
county's most prosperous men. He died at age eighty-two in 1823.*

2

Nicholas Cresswell, 1775

Nicholas Cresswell was a young Englishman who visited Kentucky in early 1775 as part of an extended tour of the American colonies. He was impressed by the quality and affordability of land and even considered moving to Virginia permanently. One of the more unusual aspects of Cresswell's American tour was his determination to visit not only the settled regions but also the Indian country of the Ohio Valley. His account is interesting because it was not written by a western settler making a major life transition but by a tourist, one for whom many aspects of America were novel. It therefore involves a different quality of detail, noting natural curiosities and expressing an interest in Indian culture. In addition, Cresswell's small party joined with that of James Nourse, whose journal is also among the selections in this volume, offering a rare parallel account.

The western expedition required special preparation. Cresswell found it difficult to find a guide, but eventually hired a man named George Rice at the town of Winchester in Frederick County, Virginia, where he also made special purchases for the journey. These included blankets, gunpowder, lead, flints, a camp kettle and frying pan, and a tomahawk. He also obtained "leggings." This type of apparel was novel to Cresswell, who felt compelled to explain, "These are pieces of coarse woollen cloth wrapped round the leg and tied below the knee with a string to prevent snakes biting you."[1] Also at Winchester, Cresswell found two more travel companions who accompanied him as far as their homes in the Fort Pitt area.

This selection from his American journal begins on the Monongahela, where the guide George Rice undertook to make a canoe, which would require about two weeks.² (Cresswell meanwhile took this opportunity to explore the Fort Pitt region and shop for provisions.) It includes his descent of the Ohio with the Nourse group and about ten days spent near Harrodsburg. Because of personal conflict with Rice and his inability to replace him, Cresswell abandoned his hope of continuing on to Illinois. Having little interest in remaining in Kentucky, where Nourse stayed to scout for a land claim, Cresswell joined a group of men who were returning from Kentucky back up the Ohio River to Fort Pitt.

April 14th 1775. This morning, Rice and another man began to cut down a tree to make a Canoe. Have left entirely to his management. Captn. Douglas and Captn. Stephenson to the Steward's Crossings to Major [Valentine] Crawfords. Returned to V. Crawfords in the evening. Agreed to go with Captn. Douglas for Fort Pitt to-morrow.

Saturday, April 15th, 1775. Left Mr. Crawford's in company with Captn. Douglas. Crossed Jacob's Creek and Saweekly Creek. Got to Mr. John De Camp's. Land very rich and level.

Fort Pitt, Virginia, Sunday, April 16th, 1775. Left Mr. De Camp's. Travelled over small hills, woods, and dirty roads to Bush Creek, called at a Mill where by acting the Irishman,³ got a feed of Corn for our horses. Crossed Turtle Creek. Dined at Myer's Ordinary [tavern]. After dinner got a man to conduct us to the place where General Braddock was defeated by the French and Indians the 9th. July 1755.⁴ It was on the Banks of the Mon-in-ga-ha-ly River. Found great numbers of bones, both men and horses. The trees were injured, I suppose by the Artillery. It appears to me the front of our Army never extended more than 300 yards and the greatest slaughter seems to have been made within 400 yards of the River, where it is level and full of underwood. Farther from the River it is hilly and some rock where the enemy would still have the advantage of the ground. We could not find one whole skull, all of them broke in pieces in the upper part, some of them had holes broken in them about

an inch diameter, suppose it to be done with a Pipe Tomahawk.[5]
I am told the wounded were all massacred by the Indians. Got
to Fort Pitt in the evening. Land very good, but thinly inhabited. Our landlord seems to be very uneasy to know where we
come from.[6]

Monday, April 17th, 1775. After breakfast waited on Major John
Connoly, Commandant at the Fort, to whom I had a letter of
introduction.[7] Find him a haughty, imperious man. In the afternoon, viewing the town and Fort. It is pleasantly situated at
the conjuction of Moningahaley and Allegany Rivers, the
Moningahaley on the S.W. and the Allegany on the North side
[of] the town. These two rivers make the Ohio. The town is
small, about 30 houses, the people chiefly in Indian trade.[8] The
Fort is some distance from the town close in the forks of the
Rivers. It was built originally by the French, deserted by them,
and the English took possession of it under the Command of
General Forbes, November 24th, 1758. Beseiged by the Indians but relieved by Colonel Bouquet in August, 1763. Deserted
and demolished by own troops about three years ago, but repaired last summer by the Virginians and has now a small garrison in it.[9] It is a pentagonal form. Three of the Bastions and
two of the curtains faced with brick, the rest picketed. Bar-
racks for a considerable number of men, and there is the remains of a genteel house for the Governor, but now in ruins, as
well as the Gardens which are beautifully situated on the Banks
of the Allegany well planted with Apple and Peach trees. It is a
strong place for Musketry, but was cannon to be brought against
it, very defenceless, several eminences within Cannon Shot.
Spent the evening at Mr. Gambel's, an Indian Trader in town.

West Augusta County, Virginia, Tuesday, April 18th, 1775. This
morning Mr. Gambel informed me that Adam Grant lived about
12 Miles from town. Left Fort Pitt. Dined at Turtle Creek. Escaped drowning very narrowly in crossing Turtle Creek. Got
to Adam Grant's late in the evening. Great scarcity of every
necessary of life in this house, but the man is glad to see us and
gives us the best he has got with a hearty welcome. He has got
a small tub mill and land enough, but it is of little value in this
part of the world. Very heavy rain all day.

Wednesday, April 19th, 1775. Left Adam Grant's. Got to Saweekly Creek, but it is too high to Ford. Returned to Mr. De Camps. We have been lost several times to-day. The by-roads are only small narrow paths through the woods and in some places not the least appearance of a road.

Thursday, April 20th, 1775. Left Mr. De Camp's. Crossed Jacob Creek and Saweekly Creek. George Rice has joined some other people that are going down the Ohio in assisting them to Build canoe. They go about 600 Miles down the River and will be ready to set out in eight or ten days.

Friday, April 21st 1775. This day made a full agreement with George Rice to go with me to the Illinois Country, on condition that I will wait for him at the Kentucky River Ten days.[10] I have agreed to do this and give him 500 acres of Land for his trouble. This Contract was made before Captn. William Douglas, who wants to take one half of my purchase, paying half my expenses in going to the Illinois and coming back. Am to give him a positive answer in two days. Wrote to Mr. Kirk.

Saturday, April 22nd, 1775. Employed in getting provisions for the voyage.

Sunday, April 23rd, 1775. Went to Major Crawford's, who gave me an account of the different Rivers on the Ohio and the distances between them.

Monday, April 24th, 1775. Employed in getting provisions. Find them very scarce and dear.[11]

Tuesday, April 25th, 1775. Agreed to let Captn. Douglas have one half of any land I may purchase of Mr. Kirk or Mr. Sydebottom at the Illinois. He is to pay half my expenses there. Have nothing to do with the Land that Messrs. Kirk & Sydebottom give me, or anything to do as a Surveyor. Wrote to Mr. Kirk that will take his share if the times are settled as formerly. Captn. Douglas is to advance all the money and I am to pay no interest for Five years after the money is paid. I have now a prospect of making money without advancing any. This suits my circumstances very well.

Thursday, April 27th 1775. Got our Canoes finished and our provisions collected together. Intend to set out to-morrow.

Yaughagany River, Virginia—Friday, April 28th, 1775. Left part of my clothes with Mr. Crawford till my return. Parted with Captn. Douglas by whom I returned the Horse. Launched our Canoes. One of them we call the *Charming Sally*, and the other *Charming Polly*. They are 30 foot long and about 20 inches wide, made of Walnut trees, dug out something like a manger. Proceeded down the Yaughagany River. Obliged to get Pilots to carry the Canoes down the Falls, very bad navigation. Full of dangerous rapids. Camped at Washington's Bottom, expect the rest of the company to join us in the morning. I may now bid adieu to sleeping in beds or houses for some months.

Saturday, April 29th, 1775. This morning we were joined by Mr. James Nourse, an English gentleman going down to the Kentucky River to take up land in right of his Brother who is an Officer in the Navy, Mr. Benjamin Johnston and Capt. Edmund Taylor, who are going to take up land on the Kentucky River. Got all our provisions on board. Mr. Nourse, Captn. Taylor, Mr. Nourse's servant, and me in the *Charming Sally*, Mr. Johnston, his servant, George Rice, Captn. Taylor's brother and a servant of his in the *Charming Polly*, proceeded down the River to the mouth of Saweekly Creek. The navigation very bad. Obliged to push the Canoes over the shoals for two miles together. A great number of rapids, is a very dangerous navigation. Mr. Nourse insists on me taking one half of his tent; this is very agreeable.

Sunday, April 30th, 1775. This day we have been detained by the rain. Settled our accounts concerning Vessels and provisions. The Land from the foot of the Laurel Mountain to Fort Pitt is rich beyond conception. Walnut and Cherry Trees grow to an amazing size. I have seen several three foot diameter and 40 foot before they come to a limb. Great plenty of Wild Plum Trees and a Species of the Pimento, these are small Bushes. The soil in general is Black and of a Fat Loamy nature. Coal and Limestone in the same quarry. I have seen stratums of Coal 14 foot thick equal in quality to the English Coal. Land is at a very low rate, 1000 acres might be purchased for £100 Pennsylvany Currency. Very thinly inhabited. The few there is, are in general great rascals.

Yaughagany River, Virginia—Monday, May 1st, 1775. After breakfast left Saweekly and stood down the River. Crossed several Fish pots. These fish pots are made by throwing up the small stones and gravel something like a mill weir, beginning at the side of the River and proceeding in a diagonal line, till they meet in the middle of the stream, where they fix a thing like the body of a cart, contracted where the water flows in just to admit the fish, but so contrived as to prevent their return or escape. Got over the shoals by hauling our canoes. Fell into the Mon-in-ga-ha-ley about noon. Eat our dinner at Mcgee's [McKee's] Fort. This is a stockade fort, built the last summer.[12]

Mon-in-ga-ha-ley River — Monday, May 1st, 1775. This River is about 100 yards broad and it confluxes with the Yaughagany, and has continued its breadth. Upon the banks of this river, where they are high and broken, I observed stratums of leaves about a foot thick twenty foot below the surface of the earth. They appeared to be sound and not concreted together, much like those that are driven together by winds in autumn. Fell down a little below Braddock's Field, where we camped in a heavy shower of rain. One of our company shot a wild Turkey, which made us an excellent supper.

Ohio River — Tuesday, May 2nd, 1775. Proceeded down the River. Our Canoes are so heavily loaded that we are in great danger of oversetting, the water is within three inches of the gunnel which adds to the general crankness of our vessel and makes me uneasy. Called at Fort Pitt and bought some necessaries such as lead, flints and some silver trinkets to barter with the Indians. Dined at Mr. John Campbell's. After dinner proceeded down the Ohio River. Passed McKey's Island, it is about a mile long, and belongs to Captn. Alexander McKey, Superintendent of Indian Affairs. Camped at the lower end of Monture's Islands, three fine Islands belonging to John Monture, a half Indian. The Land exceedingly rich.[13]

Wednesday, May 3rd, 1775. This morning Mr. Robert Bell and one Harrison left us to go to their plantations in this neighbourhood. They had come with us from Yaughagany River and have been very serviceable in instructing us how to navigate our little barks. Proceeded down the River, passed Logg's Town (an old Indian town but now deserted). It is on the W.

side, then Big Beaver Creek on the W., then little Beaver Creek on the W., neither of them so large, but they may be foul in dry weather. A little before dark stopped at a farmer's house to bake bread. Agreed to lash our vessels together and float all night. The River is very high and rapid, suppose we can float two miles in an hour.

Thursday, May 4th, 1775. In the morning found ourselves opposite Yellow Creek on the W. Very heavy rain for several hours. Very few inhabitants, not a house to be seen in 40 miles, tho' the land is exceedingly rich, in general. The River is exceedingly crooked, full of small Islands and rapid. If there is high land on one side there is always a rich level bottom on the opposite shore. Got to Wheeling Creek, Fort Fincastle on the East side of the River. This is a quadrangular picketed Fort on a little hill beside the River, built last summer by Lord Dunmore, a small garrison in it. Here we took into our company Captn. George [Rogers] Clark.[14] Lashed our canoes together and drifted all night. Stopped at Grave Creek about 2 in the morning.

Friday, May 5th, 1775. Got up very early and went to view the [ancient] Grave. It bears East of the River, about a mile from it and above the mouth of the Creek. The great Grave is a round hill something like a sugar loaf about 300 feet in circumference at bottom, 100 feet high and about 60 feet diameter at top where it forms a sort of irregular basin. It has several large trees upon it, but I could not find any signs of brick or stone on it, seems to have a trench about it. There are two other hills about 50 yards from this, but not much larger than a Charcoal pit and much in that shape, with other antique vestiges. Some appear to have been works of defence but very irregular.

Friday, May 5th, 1775. All these Hills appear to have been made by human art, but by whom, in what age, or for what use I leave it for more able antiquarians to determine. The Indians' tradition is that there was a great Battle fought here and many great Warriors killed. These mounds were raised to perpetuate their memory. The truth of this I will not pretend to assert. Proceeded down the River, entertained with a number of delightful prospects in their nature, wild yet truly beautiful. Passed several Creeks and small Islands, few inhabitants but rich land.

Got to the head of the long reach where we have a view of the River for 15 miles. Drifted all night.

Saturday, May 6th, 1775. Found ourselves opposite Muddy Creek. The heavy rain obliged us to take shelter in a lone house and stay all night.

Sunday, May 7th, 1775. This morning Captn. Clark (who I find is an intelligent man) showed me a root the Indians call pocoon, good for the bite of a Rattle Snake. The root is to be mashed and applied to the wound, and a decoction made of the leaves which the patients drink. The roots are exceedingly red, the Indians use it to paint themselves with sometimes. Left Muddy Creek, passed two small Islands to the Big tree Island, so called from the number of large trees upon it. Went ashore on the Big tree Island and measured a large Sycamore tree. It was 51 feet 4 inches in circumference one foot from the ground, and 46 foot circumference five feet from the ground, and I suppose it would have measured that twenty feet high. There are several large trees, but I believe these exceed the rest. One of the company caught a large Catfish which made a most delicious pot of Soup. Past the Muskingum River on the W. Fine land between that and the little Muskingum. Passed the Little Kanhawa River on the East. Barren land about the mouth of it. Stopped to cook our supper at Fort Gower, a little picketed Fort built last summer, but now deserted at the mouth of Hokkskin [Hocking River] on the W. Drifted all night.

Monday, May 8th, 1775. Heavy rain this morning which obliged us to make a sort of awning with our tent cloths and blankets. Got round the Horseshoe, a large curve of about 4 Miles made by the River in the form of a horseshoe from whence it takes its name. Here is excellent land. Passed a number of small Islands. River continues rapid. Camped about 4 Miles below the Horseshoe, where we met with some people who gave us very bad encouragement, say that the Indians are broke out again and killed four men on the Kentucky River. My courageous companions' spirits begin to droop.

Tuesday, May 9th, 1775. Proceeded down the River. Passed four Islands. About noon got to the mouth of the Great Kanhaway or Conhanway River. Here is a large picketed fort called Fort

Blair, built last summer by Colnl. Andrew Lewis, who entirely defeated the Shawannee Indians about a mile from it, in August 1774.[15] It is now garrisoned with 100 Men, under Captn. Russell, who invited us to dine with him, and treated us as well as his situation would admit. Confirms the account we heard yesterday. My companions exceedingly fearful and I am far from being easy, but am determined to proceed as far as anyone will keep me company. Drifted all night.

Wednesday, May 10th, 1775. Found ourselves opposite Guiandot Creek on the east side of the River. Rowed hard and got to Sandy Creek to breakfast, where we found Captn. Charles Smith encamped with 22 men. He was taking up land as we are now out of the inhabitants. I intend to stay here for Captn. Lee.

Thursday, May 11th, 1775. Employed in washing our linen and mending our clothes.

Friday, May 12th, 1775. This day held a Council whether we should proceed or turn back. After much altercation our company determined to proceed, tho' I believe they are a set of Damned cowards. With much persuasion prevailed upon them to let me endeavour to make our Vessels more safe and commodious. This has been an arduous task to effect, so difficult it is to beat these people out of their own course when it is for their safety.

Saturday, May 13th, 1775. Camped at the mouth of Sandy Creek. Employed in fixing our Canoes together by two beams, one athwart the heads, the other at the stern, setting the Canoes about one foot apart. In the middle of the aftermost piece, I fixed a strong pin, on that hung the rudder, made something like an oar, but bent down towards the water and projected about two feet astern of the Vessel, rigged her out with four oars and called her the *Union*. Some of our company laughs at it and declare she will not answer the helm. But it pleases me well and hope it will deceive them.

Sunday, May 14th, 1775. Camped at the mouth of Sandy Creek. This morning very wet. After breakfast Mr. Edmund Taylor and I entered into discourse on politics which ended in high words. Taylor threatened to tar and feather me. Obliged to pocket the affront. Find I shall be toryfied if I hold any further confab with these red-hot liberty men. (Mem. Taylor's usage to be remembered.)

Monday, May 15th, 1775. Left Sandy Creek. Captn. Lee not arrived. Find our Vessel answers very well and gives universal
satisfaction to the company. One of the company shot a turtle
which made us an excellent supper. Land good and level in
general. All of us strangers to the River. Drifted all night, but
keep watch, spell and spell about.

Tuesday, May 16th, 1775. Passed the mouth of the Sioto [Scioto]
River in the night. This river is on the N.W. side. Stopped to
cook our breakfast on a small gravelly Island where we found
plenty of Turtle eggs, with which we made pancakes equal in
goodness to those made with hen's eggs. It must be people of a
nicer taste than me that can distinguish the difference. These
animals come out of the water and lay their eggs in the sand to
be hatched by the Sun. They are white, but smaller than those
of a hen and perfectly round with a tough skin instead of a
shell. The inside has all the appearance of a fowl's egg. Generally find about twenty together, about two inches below the
surface.

Tuesday, May 16th, 1775. After breakfast attempted to fix a sail
in our Vessel but the wind soon blew up the River which rendered it useless. Passed several Creeks and Islands, but unknown
to us. This evening Mr. Rice and I went ashore and each of us
killed a wild Turkey, which made us an excellent supper. Drifted
all night.

Wednesday, May 17th, 1775. This morning did not know where
we were, or whether we had passed the mouth of any River in
the night. I believe our watch had slept most of the night. Fell
down to a Creek. By the description Mr. Johnston had from
his Brother we take it to be Bracken Creek.

Wednesday, May 17th, 1775. Stopped at Bracken Creek and went
a hunting as they call it here. Mr. Rice, Johnston and I went
together. In a short time Mr. Rice fired at a Buffalo. Johnston
and I went to him and found him standing behind a tree loading his Gun and the beast laid down about 100 yds. from him.
As soon as he was ready we fired at him again, upon which he
got up and run about a quarter of a mile, where our dogs bayed
him till we came up and shot him. It was a large Bull, from his
breast to the top of his shoulder measuring 3 feet, from his

nose to his tail 9 feet 6 inches, black and short horns, all before his shoulders long hair, from that to the tail as short as a mouse. I am certain he would have weighed a thousand. Camped a little below the Creek.

Thursday, May 18th, 1775. All hands employed in curing our Buffalo meat, which is done in a peculiar manner. The meat is first cut from the bones in thin slices like beefsteaks, then four forked sticks are stuck in the ground in a square form, and small sticks laid on these forks of a gridiron about three feet from the ground. The meat is laid on this and a slow fire put under it, and turned until it is done. This is called jerking the meat. I believe it is an Indian method of preserving meat. It answers very well, where salt is not to be had, and will keep a long time if it be secured from the wet. The lean parts eat very dry. The Buffalo flesh differs little from beef, only ranker taste. Hot weather.

Friday, May 19th, 1775. Proceeded down the River. Passed the mouth of the little Miamme River on the N.W. and Salt River or Licking Creek on the S.E. Saw an Elk and a Bear cross the River, but could not get a shot at them. Got to the mouth of the Great Miamme River on the N.W. It is about 100 Yds. wide at the mouth and appears to be a pretty gentle current. Stopped to cook and take a view of the land on the S.E. side of the Ohio River. It is a little hilly but rich beyond conception. Wild Clover, what they here call wild Oats and Wild Rye, in such plenty it might be mown and would turn out a good crop. The great quantity of grass makes it disagreeable walking. The land is thin of timber and little underwood. Drifted all night.

Saturday, May 20th, 1775. In the morning in doubt whether we had passed Elephant Bonelick or not.[16] Went ashore at a small Creek on the S.W. side in quest of it, but in vain. Believe we are too low down the River according to our Charts. Begun to rain about noon. Floated down the River till night where we moored to a stump in the middle of the stream. Some of our company are in a panic about the Indians again. Shot at a Panther this afternoon, but missed him. Hot weather with Thunder.

Kentucky River — Sunday, May 21st, 1775. Proceeded down the River. About noon, got to the mouth of the Kentucky River on the S.E. side. The Ohio is about three quarters of a mile here, the Kentucky is about 130 yards wide at the mouth and continued its width about two miles when we camped in a Beechy bottom. Our company is in great fear of the Indians. Some of them insisted on sleeping without a fire. After a long contest it was agreed to put the fire out when we went to sleep, but I believe it was not done. Whatever my companions might be, I am not uneasy. I suppose it is because I do not know the danger of our situation. Rainy weather.

Monday, May 22nd, 1775. Notwithstanding the danger of our situation last night I slept sound and undisturbed, tho' some of the company were kept in perpetual alarm by the barking of the dogs and their own fears. This morning held a council to consult our present safety, when after many pros and cons it was determined to keep two men on each side [of] the River as scouts, the rest to work up the Vessel and relieve each other by turns. It happened to be my turn to walk as a scout, but found it disagreeable clambering over gullies and wading amongst the weeds as high as my head in some places and raining all the forenoon. Saw several Buffalo tracks and a flock of Paroquets. At noon went aboard and rowed all night. Find the current here pretty strong. Camped on a hill in a Beech thicket, all hands well tired and D——d cross. One of the scouts killed a deer.

Tuesday, May 23rd, 1775. Proceeded up the River, found several rapids which obliged us to get out and haul our vessel up with ropes. The current stronger than yesterday. Saw several roads that cross the River which they tell me are made by the Buffaloes going from one lick to another. (These licks are brackish salt springs which the Buffaloes are fond of.) With hard labour suppose we have come twenty miles to-day. No signs of Indians. Camped on a stony hill near a Buffalo Lick. Saw several of them and killed two Calves and a Bull. [Found] Limestone impregnated with shells.[17] Large Beech bottoms but our scouts inform me the Land is better a distance from the River. Believe G. Rice does not intend to go down the Ohio which will be a great disappointment to me.

Wednesday, May 24th, 1775. Proceeded up the River, find the navigation worse, more rapids and strong current. Surrounded 30 Buffaloes as they were crossing the River, shot two young Heifers and caught two calves alive whose ears we marked and turned them out again.[18] About noon Captn. Michael Cresop met us, informed us it is 100 miles to Harwood's [Harrod's] Landing the place our company intends to take up land. No danger of the Indians. Captn. Clark left us and went with Captn. [Thomas] Cresop.[19] Clark always behaved well while he stayed with us.

Wednesday, May 24th, 1775. Land in general covered with Beech. Limestone in large flags. Few rivulets empty into the River, which makes me suppose the country is badly watered. Camped at a place where the Buffaloes cross the River. In the night were alarmed with a plunging in the river. In a little time Mr. Johnston (who slept on board) called out for help. We ran to his assistance with our arms and to our great mortification and surprise found one of our Canoes that had all our flour on board sunk, and would have been inevitably lost, had it not been fixed to the other. We immediately hauled our shattered vessel to the shore and landed our things, tho' greatly damaged. It was done by the Buffaloes crossing the River from that side where the vessel was moored. Fortunately for Mr. Johnson he slept in the Canoe next the shore. The Buffaloes jumped over him into the other, split it about fourteen foot. Mr. Nourse and Mr. Taylor's servants usually slept on board, but by mistake brought their blankets on shore this evening and were too lazy to go on board again or probably they would have been killed.

Thursday, May 25th, 1775. Repairing our Vessel by putting in knees and calking her with the bark of the white Elm pounded to a paste, which is tough and glutinous, something like Bird-lime and answers the purpose very well. Some of the company shot a Buffalo Bull, saw several cross the River while we were at work. Two canoes full of men passed us down the River going to Fort Pitt. Am convinced Rice will not go with me, find he is a great coward. On inspection find our Flour is much damaged, obliged to come to an allowance of a Pint a man per day. Had we come to this resolution sooner it would have been better. Great quarrelling among the company.

Friday, May 26th, 1775. Proceeded up the River. Met 2 Canoes bound to Redstone. Shot an old Buffalo Bull that had his ears marked. Passed a bad rapid which took all our force to tow our Vessel up. Much tormented with Ticks, a small animal like a Sheeplouse, but very tough skin. They get on you by walking in the Woods in great numbers, and if you don't take care to pick them off in time they work their heads through the skin and then you may pull the body away but the head will remain in the skin, which is very disagreeable. If they are not removed in a short time they grow like the Ticks on a Dog. Beechy bottoms. Camped at the mouth of Elk Horn Creek. Our company still continues to be crabbed with one another and I believe will be worse as Bread grows scarce.

Saturday, May 27th, 1775. This day got up several smart rapids. Thunder, Lightning and rain. Some high rocks and Cedar hills. Find Rice does everything in his power to quarrel with me, am determined not to give the first affront.

Sunday, May 28th, 1775. Proceeded up the River. Saw a great many Buffaloes cross the River above us, all hands went ashore to surround them. I kept on the outside of them and shot a fine young Heifer, some of the rest shot a Cow and Calf. Our stupid company will not stay to jerk any, tho' we are in want of provisions. Camped on a gravelly Island. Beech bottoms and cedar hills with few rivulets.

Monday, May 29th, 1775. This morning George Rice (without any provocation) began to abuse me in a most scurrilous manner, threatened to scalp and tomahawk me. I was for bestowing a little manual labour upon him, but he flew to his Gun and began to load, swearing he would shoot me. I did the same, and had it not been for the timely intervention of my worthy Friend, Mr. Nourse, I believe one of us would have been killed. A great deal of abusive language was given on both sides, but nothing more. I have expected this for some time. He did it on purpose to get off his engagement to go down the Ohio, which it has effectually done. Proceeded a little way up the River to a great Buffalo crossing, where we intend to kill some meat. Our provision is almost out.

Tuesday, May 30th, 1775. This day Mr. Nourse, Mr. Taylor and Rice went to take a view of the Country. Mr. Johnston and I took a walk about 3 miles from the River, find the land pretty level, a blackish sandy soil. Timber chiefly Beech. In our absence those at the Camp caught a large Catfish which measured six inches between the eyes. We supposed it would weight 40 pounds. Don't expect our company back tonight.

Wednesday, May 31st, 1775. At the Camp washing and mending my clothes. In the evening Mr. Nourse and company returned and say the land a distance from the River, is the levelest, richest and finest they ever saw, but badly watered.

Thursday, June 1st, 1775. Proceeded up the River, bad navigation, many rapids and strong currents. Saw a Gang of Buffaloes cross the River. Shot a Bull. Saw some Deer but killed none. Camped at a place where we found some Corn in a Crib, a Gun and some clothes, supposed to be left there by some people coming to take up land. Rocks, Cedar Hills, and Beech Bottoms.

Friday, June 2nd, 1775. This day met eight Canoes bound to Redstone and Fort Pitt. Went about 9 miles and camped, to hunt, shot at some Buffaloes, but killed none. Land good, weeds as high as a man. Pleasant weather. Our company continually quarelling, but I have the good luck to please them all but Rice, whom I treat with contempt.

Saturday, June 3rd, 1775. Proceeded up the River, till noon, when after being wet to the skin we camped about 10 miles below below Harwood's [Harrod's] Landing. Another Canoe passed us this day bound to Wheeling. Rocks, Cedar hills and Beech bottoms.

Harwood's Landing, Sunday, June 4th, 1775. Arrived at Harwood's Landing in the evening. Saw a Rattle Snake about 4 feet long. A bark Canoe at the landing. We have been Fourteen days in coming [only] about 120 miles. My right foot much swelled, owing to a hurt I got by bathing in the River. Rocky and Cedar hills, along the banks of the River. My foot very painful.

Monday, June 5th, 1775. This is called Harwood's Landing as it is nearest to a new Town, that was laid out last summer by Captn. Harwood [James Harrod], who gave it the name of Harwoodsburg about 15 miles from the Landing for which place Mr. Nourse, Mr. Johnston, Taylor and Rice set out this morning.[20] I would have gone with them, but my foot is so bad I am scarcely able to walk. Applied a fomentation of Herbs to assuage the swelling. Very little to eat and no possibility of getting any flour here. Must be without Bread very soon.

Tuesday, June 6th, 1775. Mr. Nourse and company returned this evening. He gives good account of the richness of the land, but says it appears to be badly watered and light timbered. They lodged in the town. Mr. Nourse informs me there is about 30 houses in it, all built of logs and covered with Clapboards, but not a nail in the whole Town. Informs us the Indians have killed four men about nine miles from the town. This has struck such a panic that I cannot get anyone to go down the Ohio [to the Illinois Country] on any account. Determined to return by the first opportunity. My foot much better. Much provoked by my disappointment.

Nicholas Cresswell's foot continued to heal, and a few days later he joined a group of wayfarers returning by canoe to Fort Pitt (modern Pittsburgh). Poling up the Ohio presented less of a struggle than had the ascent of the Kentucky River, but the group still encountered numerous difficulties. The canoe became leaky and required a stop for repairs. At one point Cresswell's group found themselves surrounded by several canoes of Indians, who caused quite a fright but turned out to be friendly. The biggest problem, however, was hunger. For several days not even game could be found, and Cresswell struggled to keep working the canoe upstream. On a more positive note, Cresswell did get to spend a couple of days of the return voyage at the famous Big Bone Lick, which he had missed earlier, and collect some prehistoric souvenirs. But even before reaching Fort Pitt, rumors were circulating of an armed clash with the British army near Boston. At Pittsburgh, the rumors were confirmed, with the added information that Governor Dunmore of Virginia had abdicated and gone aboard a British Man of War. Despite his tory principles, Cresswell prolonged his travels in the upper Ohio frontier for some months more and visited other parts of the seaboard states before returning to Britain in 1777.

3

❦

James Nourse, 1775

James Nourse began productive life as a London woolen draper. He sailed with his family for America in 1769, arriving at the port of Hampton, Virginia. After a year there he settled with his family at Piedmont, a plantation he purchased near Charlestown, Virginia, now Berkeley County, West Virginia. Located fairly close to Fort Pitt, Nourse's region was among the first to hear about the land in Kentucky. In 1775, Nourse led a small group of neighbors to Kentucky to claim land. He kept a journal on this trip down the Ohio River, the opening page or two of which is missing. The surviving section begins while he was still in Berkeley County, in midsentence.

[April 21, 1775] . . . the timber lofty, yet the country not so desirable, being more hilly; very disagreeable riding, especialy in wett weather, the side of the hills being dangerously slippy, and ride which way you will you are continualy mounting or descending—got my linen washed and Miss Gist altered my hunting shirt.[1] The inhabitants so distressed this spring that they are going [east] over the mountain continualy with pack horses for flour. Mr. Taylor gave 20 p[er] hundred P:C for flour at Gregg's ordinary and 9 p lb for bacon—

Saturday 22d Tom not being at Gist's, when I got back from Crawford's.[2] Taylor's and Johnstons Servants neglected to drive up my horses with theirs and this morning they were not to be

91

Replica of a late eighteenth-century hunting shirt, worn by western riflemen as an overgarment. The cape and fringed edges were typical of the style. Courtesy of the Colonial Williamsburg Foundation.

found—persuaded on Lyons and Clifton to hunt them to no purpose, neither this day nor Sunday the 23rd.

Monday 24th rode to the great madows 12 miles. Lynch's [?]could hear nothing of them—went over the large meadows behind Fossett's beautifull, but the high land bad—offered 4 dollars reward—returned to Gist's in the evening, Johnston came back from Rice's.

Tuesday 25—did little else but mend my tent.

Wednesday 26th went to the Yongheany [Youghiogheny River], workt a little at the Canoes, paid 4 dollars on account of them and returned at night with Johnston and A. Taylor, missed our way, being very dark—

Thursday 27th, prepared for moving our things tomorrow in a waggon. Tom Ruby acquainted me he was afraid to go. Some acquaintance he had in that neighborhood had told him it was dangerous; however after a little talking to him resolved to proceed—

Friday 28th, Sett off with the waggon. Tom under pretense of killing a turkey joined us not till night. A very disagreeable day I had of it, walkt all the way and what was worse Johnston's horses not drawing [the wagon] well was obliged at every bad place which was very often to put my shoulders to the wheel, however by dark we arrived at Simpson's, overseer for Geo. Washington at Washington's bottom where he is building a large grist mill,[3] tis a valuable bottom and said to contain 1800 acres, but the expence he [is] at there, seems not to be proportioned to profit that can possibly arrive in that part of the country for some years—

Saturday 29th April—embarqued on board our Canoes about 2 miles from Simson's; joined there Mr. Creswell an Englishman— George Rice—Taylor's with Beal and Harrison two that were only going a few miles below Fort Pitt—the River so low and shallow at places, that a dozen times a day all hands were obliged to jump overboard and lead the canoes. once our Canoe Struck upon a Rock in the Midst of the River, and Edm. Taylor was in much danger. about an hour before sunset, encamped at the mouth of Sweetly's [Sawicky] creek having gained about 15 Mile—of 2 old fowls that were in the Canoe one died, the other made soup of, very hungry, eat fat bacon and bread very heartily, pitched my tent, lodged with me Mr. Creswell and Tom— Slept well—

Sunday Apr. 30th—breakfasted upon Bacon Soup thickened with Crumbs of Bread. Rained hard. Shaved &c—kept my tent up not being likely to move forward, read and walked and lay at the same camp—

May the 1st Monday—embarked again, again obliged to wade several times [due to low water], dined at little Sweetly creek— past on to the mouth where it loses its name by joining the Mohongahala constituting a fine river, nor obliged to wade any more—had we taken water at Redstone Fort upon this river we should have entirely avoided it and the land carriage much the same—put in on acct of a storm—Rice shot a turkey, past a man that had just caught a Sturgeon, judged to weigh 30 lb—

encamped 7 mile short of fort Pitt, tryed our fish lines but without success, one of my larger hooks snaped off, supposed by a Catfish, Tom having fixt the line to a Stump instead of bending bow—Rained very hard before we pitched our tents. Supped and Tuesday May the 2nd breakfasted upon turkey and soup. The trees began to look green—shaved and changed entirely—coming down the river had put my flannell waist coat under my shirt on acct. of being so often wett [illegible] the wind blowing right ahead made the water very rough, at Fort Pitt by 12 oclock. Lord Dunmore had the assurance to attempt the Changing its name to Fort Dunmore—He in some measure repaired it, rebuild'g the points of the Angles, which with a handsome brick house &c. had been destroyed by orders from Lord Hillsborough tis said whilst secretary of state for America—about 2 oClock embarqued again and as soon as we past the junction of the river got into smooth water—the river here is about ¼ mile wide, passed by McGee's [McKee's] (the Indian agents) plantation, came also to another where tis said he keeps a squaw and has Children by her, past several beautifull bottoms some on one side some on the other—came to Montcure Islands on the bottom opposite on the east shore encamped, where we parted with Rob't Beale and Benj. Harrison who had lands a few miles back from this, here Tom went a fishing at some distance from us and a Canoe coming down seeing his fire halloed to him, on which he run for it, supposing them Indians, however before he got to us the people had joined us, being fellow travellers bound for Kentuke.

Wednesday May 3, the men that joined us last night set off before us, we having some leaks to stop but we passed them and 3 More canoes bound also for Kentuke, at Gibson's which is opposite to Logstown 18 mile below Pitsburg,[4] a little below it on the west side is the appearance of a French settlement, came to Beaver Creek below, went on shore on the Indian [west] side, fine sands past little Beaver Creek, eat our diner on board and let the Canoes float—came to a plantation on east bank, went on shore, ground our axes, baked bread and by an hour after sunset went on board, lashed our Canoes together, 2 & 2 keeping watch found in the morning we had floated about 20 miles.

Tuesday [Thursday] May 4th soon after day rained very hard at
the two creeks, cleared up, rowed to Wheeling, a tolerable good
Stockade on a high situation called Fort Fincastle met there a
Capt.[George Rogers] Clarke from Caroline county [Virginia]
who joined us, went on board a little before sunset and floated
to Grave Creek, lay there till day light.

Friday May 5. The gentlemen went to the Indian grave. It appears
to them to be an artificial mount about 100 feet high and ¼
mile round. Came to a plantation that Capt Clark claims but is
disputed.[5] Tom and I cooked, G. Rice helping me, a small fish
the two the liquor being made into soup, dined 9 of us the
most delicate meal I had made, sauce melted butter with walnut pickle, past Capitaine Creek and 4 mile below Fish creek,
being obliged by the weather to stop, we came not to the Strait
Reach till dusk or we should there have had a view 17 or 18
miles down the river floated all night—

Saturday 6th May. In the morning a violent storm of rain and not
being dressed got thoro wett, Blankets cloaths &c, rowed about
8 miles and just below Muddy Creek was an empty house of
Capt. Cressop's, here we made a large fire dryed ourselves and
the weather continuing uncertain, resolved to pass the night
here, being also joined by the other Canoes, it holding up some
went a hunting, others a fishing but to no purpose except one
lad that catched one cat [fish], which with two he had taken in
the morning and some bacon made a good supper but had no
sauce—

Sunday May the 7th I alone shaved and shirted,[6] embarqued in
good time past 2 Islands and on the 3rd went on shore where
on the right hand side of the island is a large tree which a foot
from the ground measured 51 foot circumference about breast
high 8 ft less it forks about 20 foot high and its forks larger
than most trees—from thence we came to little Muskingum
then great Muskingum Creeks an handsome river—came to
some Rocks on the east side where we dined upon the cold
fryed fish and bacon. Johnston near an hour taking the lattitude
[with instruments], in the mean time the dogs eat his dinner. I
believe an accident undesigned by any tho' when happened on
account of the man's Selfish behavior nobody seemed to feel

for him—the young fellow that had been before successfull a fishing at the mouth of a small creek catched a cat about 12 lbs.—found Dr. Briscoe's servants fishing on the bank side, delivered the 2 letters [to home], the sons gone for Berkley [County]. Stopped at little Kanaway, while Johnston viewed a piece of land on the south side, very ordinary, overtook a man in a canoe solus bound for the Nachez. from little Kanaway past several Islands the bottom opposite little hocking [River]. Col. Washington's, by dusk arrived at Fort Gower on the west side of Ohio at the mouth of Hock hocking [River] a ruined stockade a well covered log house where we cooked and supped . . . and floated 16 miles

Monday 8th May. At sunrise unlashed [the canoes and] rowed about 8 miles, stoped by thunder and rain, went on shore, held up, proceeded to some rocks, dined, but obliged to put in before night by bad weather, about 12 mile above the great Kanaway [River].

Tuesday May 9th arrived early at Fort Blair on the point at the mouth of the big Kanaway—breakfasted and dined with Capt [William] Russell,[7] Lieut. Shelby, ensigns Robert and Sharp, all very obliging. Capt. Russell much of the gentleman, here we learnt from Capt. Russell who had been up Sandy Creek to Clinch [Valley] Settlement, for corn for the fort, that he had certain intelligence that the Indians had killed 4 and wounded 2 men upon [the] Kentuke [River], the company all resolve to continue there rout, myself undetermined, but having come so far [am] loath to return without my errand—

Wednesday morning May 10th arrived at the mouth of Sandy creek as it is commonly called, though it may be rated amongst rivers, it being navigable for canoes nearly to the settlements upon Clinch river from whence as I observed before Capt. Russell had fecht corn—the Governor's large bateau full which must be at least 200 mile—at a cabin on the lower point of Sandy river we found Charles Smith and 10 others surveying and dividing soldier's rights to lands by lot.[8] breakfasted upon Capt. Smith upon lean venison. Tom catched two cats on which and the Soup we made an excellent diner.

Thursday 11th May breakfasted upon coffee and bread and but-

ter, went a fishing, catched none but exchanged a piece of bacon for 2 cats, stewed under Capt. Smith's direction in an iron
pot with half a pint water and between each layer butter, pep-
per and salt putting sticks to keep the fish from the bottom and
then put fire over and under the pot, a good dish for those that
love seasoned meat. Our hunters went out but killed nothing,
brought home some turkey eggs.

Fryday, May 12th—Bacon frays with the turkey eggs for breakfast. Capt. [Michael] Cressop with 6 men arrived, wrote [to
Mrs. Nourse] by Capt. Smith.[9] the men that bound in the other
canoes for Kentuke set off—as did soon after Cressop.

Saturday 13th May. Tom finished washing my linen and dying my
Hunting Shirt, the company being tired of waiting for Le[illegible]
it was resolved to set off tomorrow morning—

Sunday 14th May a very rainy day.

Monday 15th May having loaded our canoes once more embarqued
rowed till 2 o'clock, eat bacon on board, in the afternoon Rice
shot a Soft Shelled turtle, it is flatt and in the water, looks like
a turbot, went on shore at night to dress it, found in it 21 full
grown eggs and as many lesser ones, made nice soup, meat and
soup both very good, floated all night, moonshine, very cool
and in the morning,

Tuesday 16 May, a great fog and violent dew about 2 oClock this
day came two a gravelly island supposed to be that markt in
my list, 14 ½ below Scioto which we past in the night, went on
Shore on the island, a fine bank of Vines running upon the
sand, dined upon bacon frays made of the turtle's eggs, the
Wind being fair for us, we cut a Mast and hoisted sail—but the
wind shifting we were soon obliged to take it down—tis remarked by every body that the wind scarce ever (not one day
in seven) blows down the river, the canoes being lashed together at about a foot apart, with a high Mast and large sail
bore the strongest gust without being affected, towards the
evening Creswell and Rice each shot a turkey, a fine moonshine. Creswell [night] watched for me—

May 17th shot at a turkey standing on the shore, out of the canoe—
two others also shott at it but it walked away very composedly—
went on Shore on a Stony beach, cooked our turkeys. Tom

catched a small Catt, the hunters went out but no success, came to Bracken's creek, said to be 10 miles above little Miamme [River], the hunters went out, Rice and Taylor killed a very large bull buffaloe, Clark a Buck—the buffalo tho' not very fatt was supposed to have weighed 1000, the buck not fat but fleshy, here we resolved to stay the next day to barbecue and jerk our meat and have had no fresh meat lately and all along upon allowance as to bread, we eat all day long from turkey to beef, from Beef to Venison, fish &c, &c.—

Thursday 18th, Fryday the 19th, got under way by 5 oClock— came to little Miamme—a pretty river, then 8 mile farther to Salt lick Creek or rather river—Catched a Cat, saw a bear crossing the Ohio—rowed hard but was to late to kill it, rowed to the Miamme, went on shore opposite to it, fine land but very hilly—dressed our Victuals—were rather imprudent in having a fire so late on shore [for fear of attracting Indians], it being quite dark before we quitted it—

Saturday May 20th passed 3 Creeks, but are very uncertain which was the [Big] Bone lick Creek—passed without knowing which—Moored to a stump all night for fear of passing [the] Kentuke [River].

Sunday May 21 half past nine P.M. (having shaved and striped from head to foot) arrived at the mouth of Kentucke river—expected a larger river, [but it is] not larger than the little Kanawah or but little difference. Set in to raining, rowed up about one mile and encamped, spent the rest of the day in my tent, it continuing raining, staid there all night, had no fire on account of the Indians, but the dogs barked so incessantly (being a bundance of wolves in all these parts) that had any Indians been near, they might have found us by the Dogs.

Monday May 22nd Set off about 5 oClock, rowed thro' the rain past a pretty creek about 7 miles upon the north side—another about 2 miles farther on the lower or south side—another about 2 miles farther on the lower or south side—(believe Greening Creek) that comes from Greening (famous buffaloe lick) then 2 mile farther up a considerable creek that looks like a fork of the river (Eagle Creek I since learned) about 20 mile up the river, landed on a high Shore, a young Venison killed, made a fire but it got dark before the cooking was over, the company promising to put out the fire [so as not to attract Indians]. When twas over I went to sleep in my tent, but was waked by the blaze between 3 and 4 in the Morning and [be]rated them for breach of promise and they engage that the next night they will Cook time enough to have it all out before dark.

Tuesday May 23d—came to a rapid about 3 Mile up the river— the first (afterwards there were several of them, at least 12 or 13).

Fryday 26th of May, 1775. Loaded our canoes; came to a bad ripling—at which place are very large slabs of very fine stone.

Sat. May 27th passed two riplings—dined at a good spring—proceeded to a place that is an Island when the river is high getting around it, a Considerable ripling, above a Creek on the upper side, supposed to be Elkhorn creek—where we encamped, pitched my tent [but] the others did not. About midnight, violent thunder and lightning, E. Taylor and Johnston creeped into my camp, the others lay'd out.—

Sunday, May 28th. Fine morning—breakfast, shave and dress all clean. Half past 2 before we sett off—very hot—in two hours and a half, saw a great quantity of Buffaloes, all sizes, went on to a small Island that the lowness of the water had made a bed of stones—cut down a kind of Pea Vine, blue Blossoms, no smell—I made a bed under my tent. Mr. Creswell thought it so bad he went and lay in the canoe. Slept well, got on board

Monday, May 29th, by six o'clock—rowed till ten, Rice and Creswell quarreled, Rice Vulgar & ill behaved in the morning—this last I did not hear the beginning of, but from Tom's acct, Rice first to blame; when I came to them neither would have discredited a Billingsgate education. Rice on my declaring my opinion of his manner before, drew in and it became a Calm—we went ashore—breakfasted—proceeded and got to the buffalo Crossing, about 3 o'clock pitched our tents; purposing going tomorrow a day's journey by land back to see the Country, being come opposite where E. Taylor supposes he has a tract of land. Fine Stone all up the river, a kind of gray marble and Shell stone of all sizes—Slabs of any Breadth & thickness, even to tile stone and fine pavement.

Tuesday 30th of May, 1775, set off on foot with E.T. & G.R. (having first breakfasted) with my great Coat tied to my Back;[10] walked 3 miles and came to the River—Struck off again by the paved landing along a buffalo path, which soon led to good Buffaloes, all sizes (Tom here) [illegible] except Johnston, self and George E. Taylor, bring wood, they have killed three, a Cow, a Yearling and a Calf, Mr. Creswell killing [the] Yearling to his great satisfaction—a ripling a head or we should follow them with the Canoes, they brot the heart, suet, marrow bones and some beef of the Cow. Went on to a small island [illegible] land a good bottom and high land tolerable—came to the foot of a steep hill or mountain over which the path led—steep and rocky but not so bad but a horse might now go up and is capable of being made a waggon road—it is about 2 miles from the river on the top of the Hill, the land is level and well timbered with oak, afterwards it is light with timber—little oak—mostly sugar tree, Walnut, Ash and Buckeye (horse chestnut) but the tops of the trees mostly scraggy, the surface of the ground covered with grass along the path which was as well trod as a Market-town path. about Twelve mile the farther we went the richer the land, better though of the same sort of timber, the ash very large and high, and large locusts of both sorts—some Cherry—the growth of grass under amazing—blue grass, white clover, buffalo grass and seed knee & waist high: what would be called a fine swarth of Grass in cultivated Meadows, and such was its appearance without end—in little dells in this. We passed several dry branches but no running water our course S.E. At about twelve mile came to a Small run and soon after I discovered a pretty spring that joined its waters—here we resolved to dine, being both hungry and thirsty. We had seen in our walk about 5 herd of Buffaloes. At this place was the last, but they smelled us and away they ran (you may go close to them if you chance to be to the leeward, but their smell is quick off to the windward). By the blessing of that God that feedeth the ravens, they left one calf asleep, and whilst we were kindling a fire he started up and Rice soon fetched him down and in a trice his heart, liver, kidneys, Sweetbread and about 10 lbs of the best part of the meat was soon broiled upon forks and a

most excellent dinner we made, left the meat we eat not at the
fire and proceeded about 3 mile farther; the path decreased but
the growth of the land bespoke its being still richer. We returned to our spring—a thunder gust threatened us, but we
had no great quantity of rain—put on my great coat—lay down
under a tree, but got no sleep till after 12 o'clock, lay too slant-
ing and missed my [illegible] for a pillow.

Wednesday, May 31—Returned to our Camp, eat heartily of a
large Cat they had catched—about twenty pounds weight. Lay
down and slept most soundly—by the time eating and baking
was over they thought it too late to proceed—gave my Gun a
thoro cleaning, supped upon rice Broth and went to bed. Slept
well.

Thursday, June 1st—Called them all up by daybreak and got in
the canoe before 5 oClock. Passed two Riplings in the course
of two hours and one more at the end of the 2d two hours—
went on shore to a spring—examined the Virginia Spider Wort—
3 foot high—beautiful stem and leaf and fragrant smell. Still
the banks every now and then walled with regular stone in
beds Horizontal with the river, which in some places appear to
be paved all across. Saw several Buffaloes—went on shore—
shot at one, but when after other shots, he having stood at bay
the dogs, found him Old and poor—so took none of him—
rowed till one—dined upon jerk beef and soup made of [illeg-
ible] All quiet—no disputes. N.B. [P.S.]—Last night very
cool—cold though wrapped up in my blanket—took my great
coat from under me to keep me warm and the air all day fresh
and cool—except in the sun. Rowed till one—eat cold jerk and
a cup of broth for diner—rowed again—Stopped soon on acct.
of getting some meat. The hunters went out on both sides but
no success—went to bed—cool again before morning.

Fryday, June 2nd—Morning cloudy—set off about 6 oclock met 5
Canoes [descending the Kentucky River, presumably headed
for the Fort Pitt area]—one gave us the best half of a Buck,
rowed to where they Camped, found good part of a doe and a
fire still burning—cutt some of it, put it on the coals, dressed
our venison and went a hunting—high acct. of the lands on
Elkhorn creek, but fear it is most of it surveyed—other [de-

scending] canoes passed—in all the day eight—no success, one deer saw on one side and one buffalo on the other, but neither killed, fitted my camp with a bark floor and matt at the door, walk with Creswell thro' the woods about 3 miles, saw nothing, returned and eat venison steaks.

Saturday, June 3d. Set off at 6 oClock—rowed till twelve. Hard rain before we got on shore—the others out about an hour in worst of the rain making a bark tent, whilst mine was up in five minutes—Supposed ourselves within about fifteen mile of Harwood's [Harrod's] landing—afternoon cleared, but being hazardous, resolved to stay here all night—for had they moved another tent would have been to have made which consideration more than once lost us half a day.

Sunday, June 4th, Cloudy set off about 6 ock, rowed about 3 hours, rained again, went under a cave in the rocks stayed about 2 hours (having passed 6 bad ripples this day) about 2 oclock arrived at Harwood's landing—

Monday, June 5th, breakfasted upon thickened broth. E.T., G.R., B.J. and I.[J.]N. set off with a Cane and my Great Coat slung to my back, walked along 15 Miles to Hardwoodstown which Consist of about 8 or 10 log cabbins without doors nor stopped [illegible] about 70 Acres in Corn—the land most part of the way rich—weeds as high as your head—the path but badly trod and continual logs and sticks across that I fell twice—very tired I was—B.J. though he walked much better there than I no sooner was arrived but he was taken with a violent pain in his thighs, which never left him till he had borrowed a horse to carry him back and fetch his goods [from the canoe at Harrod's Landing].—When we got there an acquaintance of Johnston's treated us with bear fat and hot bread for diner (their meat being just out) and hominy for supper, hominy also for breakfast.

Tuesday, June 6th. B.J. on horse back and the rest on foot, returned to our landing.—

Wednesday, June 7th, B.J. drew out his 2 shares which left us only about 20 pounds of flour a hand and about 1 gall[on] of Corn, and no prospect yet when I can attend to my business the Surveyor being out a Surveying and not knowing where to meet with him or when he will return.

Thursday 8th Mr. Creswell resolved to return with some Men going by water to Wheeling; divided flour and corn—in the night,
George Noland, servant to E. Taylor, and a servant of G. Jones
ran off, had taken Mr. Creswell's share of flour, but being
alarmed, they fled to the woods and left it in the canoe.

Fryday June 9th Creswell left me the others being out seeking the
run-aways, they return without success, engage Welch to go
after them—a Man that Johnston sent down for his things and
a horse that brot Creswell's company's things, when loaded
with mine &c. Tom and I set off once more for Harrodstown,
very hott, mett about half way 3 young Men, who told us of
the Boston engagement [at Bunker Hill] and of 39 Negroes
being hanged near Williamsburg, said to be 900 of the English
troops killed. About 6 arrived in town, eat some beef and
hominy at Mr. Slaughter's, pitcht my tent about 10 yds from
them and slept well.

*James Nourse remained in Kentucky the rest of June, determined to
find good land not already claimed, working with James Harrod and
John Floyd (the deputy surveyor for Fincastle County). Previous visitors to Kentucky had already engrossed many of the region's prime
locations. His journal entries record his exploration of Kentucky and
assess the land's potential. Nourse returned to his family by way of
the Wilderness Road. He later settled permanently in Kentucky.*

4

❦

James Smith, 1783

James Smith was born in 1757 in Powhatan County, Virginia, and came from a family of means. At the time of his first trip to Kentucky in 1783, he owned a large plantation and a number of slaves. At an early date Smith joined the Methodist Church and later the dissident Republican Methodists organized by James O'Kelly and became a preacher. It is perhaps as a Republican Methodist that he eventually came to deplore slavery, a major factor in his eventual decision to relocate in 1798—not to Kentucky, but to Ohio.[1]

This selection is drawn from his first trip to Kentucky. Smith explained, "Having long had the desire to see that famed western country, to wit Kentucky, and conscious to myself that I should never rest well satisfied till I did see it, occasioned me to fix a determination if God should spare me to travel to that far distant territory, fully to satisfy my restless curiosity and also to enable me the more effectually to determine concerning my future proceedings."[2]

Smith began his 1783 journal as he departed from home with his half-brother George Rapin Smith and his slave Manuel and traveled for nearly two weeks across Virginia. The portion of Smith's journal presented here begins with his approach to the Block House at the head of the Wilderness Road. Another half-brother, George Stovall Smith, had settled near the Crab Orchard in Kentucky several years earlier, and this is where he headed first.[3] Disappointed in the quality of Kentucky land, he soon returned home by way of the Wilderness Road, departing the Crab Orchard on December 1 in the company of

his brother, but was shortly forced to turn back due to snow, illness,
and the loss of a horse. A second, more successful attempt was under-
taken about a week later. This selection omits his time in Kentucky,
much of which was spent ill in bed, and picks up with his winter
journey home as far as the Block House.

Mon. [October] 13th. Mr. Fendley [who had hosted Smith the pre-
    vious night] having just returned from Kentucky, gave us the
    following information. That some Indian traders at the
    Chickeymogey [Chickamauga][4] nation had sent express to Col.
    [Joseph] Martin, superintendent of Indian affairs, residing at
    the long islands on Holstein [Holston River] informing him
    that a body of Indians in number about 150 had started from
    the nation, and it was conjectured that their destination was
    either for the Kentucky road or the Cumberland settlement [fu-
    ture Tennessee]. That the like information had been despatched
    to Col. Ben Logan at Kentucky. In consequence of which Col.
    Logan had ordered a body of 150 men to guard the road as far
    as Cumberland mountain. Mr. Fendley informed us further that
    a considerable number of horses had been stolen on the Ken-
    tucky road and that one company just before the one he came
    with had lost [illegible] and several other companies had lost
    horses likewise.
        On receiving the above information we judged it advisable to
    collect as large a company as we could and accordingly appointed
    the Thursday following to rendezvous at the Block-house; by which
    time we judged a considerable body would be collected together.
    We then started from Mr. Fendley's and took up at Tho. Caldwell's
    about a mile beyond Washington [County, Virginia] Court-House.
Tues. 14th. We started late, traveling slow and took up the night
    with Messrs. Fowler and Bray where they had lay encamped
    about 3 weeks waiting for the rest of their company.
Wed. 15th. We lay by all day in order to rest our horses and pro-
    vide ourselves with necessaries to carry us thro the wilderness
    and accordingly got about 30 lb. Of flour, 1–2 bushel corn-
    meal, 3 bushels of oats, and having provided ourselves thus
    determined to start early in the morning for the Block-house.

Thurs. 16th. We started pretty early and arrived at the Block-house about 1 or 2 o'clock, but we found ourselves altogether disappointed as to finding company for not a man was there traveling to Kentucky, neither could we hear of any that were before. However we pushed forward and in the evening overtook Mr. S. Taylor with whom we encamped about 4 miles above Mockerson [Moccasin] Gap.

Fri. 17th. Thro neglect having omitted stretching our tent and having made our fire in an open place, when we arose in the morning our bed covering was as wet with the dew as if a small shower of rain had fallen on it. My head seemed much clogged up but as yet I felt no other bad effect. We fixed off towards Clinch and rode up the same about 2 miles. The water of this river is the clearest that I ever saw; in riding along up the river we could with perfect plainness see fish which I suppose were several feet under water, and the bottom, which I suppose was 8 or 10 feet deep, was plain to be seen. We traveled on in an exceeding bad road and about 1 o'clock we made a stop to let our horses feed. I then turned out a hunting and ascended a very high mountain which fatigued me very much. On my return I was immediately taken unwell with a fever which increased all the afternoon. Nevertheless I pursued my journey and about the middle of the afternoon crossed Powell's mountain which is the worst both for length and steepness that we have hitherto passed. After passing this 6 or 7 miles we were again obstructed in our passage by another lesser mountain. Tho exceeding steep and rocky we without much difficulty ascended. But the descent being much steeper than the ascent and likewise much rockier, night having overtaken us and it being very dark, we were in the utmost danger of being dashed to pieces. But at length [we made] a very dangerous and disagreeable passage in safety. We arrived at the foot of the mountain where we encamped. We had not been long lay down before it began to rain and continued raining the greater part of the night.

Sat. 18th. was a close, foggy, drizzley morning: however we started and in a little time arrived at the Valley [Martin's] Station; we there made a halt hoping the weather would break; here we also refreshed ourselves and horses, but seeing no likelyhood of the weather breaking we again set forward in order to over-take the company before [and join together for mutual protec-tion]. We had not been long set out before it set in raining very hard which continued the greater part of the day. Nevertheless we pushed on and overtook the company about an hour by sun at night. But riding thro the rain threw me again into a fever with which I was very sick all night.

Sun. 19th. was still cloudy and raw, and I was also still very unwell after one of the most disagreeable night's lodging that I ever had in my life, for the ground being wet, all our bedding wet, the wind all night blowing exceeding hard and either rain or snow frequently beating in upon us was the cause of my being seized with a shivering ague, which continued till the middle of the day. I then laid down on the ground and covered myself thick with clothes (the company having stopped to feed their horses). But a severe fever coming on caused me to throw off the clothes, but the fever still rising soon rendered it difficult for me either to go or stand upon my feet. The time was now come when I was to see trouble, for being taken so violent I had little expectation of ever surviving it, even were I at home where I might lie at ease upon my bed with proper attendance. But here I was in a wild uninhabited part of the world having nearly 150 miles to travel without any proper nourishment, under an absolute necessity of traveling without so much as an acquaintance except my brother and 2 or 3 others (whom I but barely knew by sight) from whom I could reasonably expect anything of consequence in my situation. Under these circum-stances I was at an entire loss what to do, whether it would be best either to go back or forward; my brother's advice was that I should return to the valley with [slave] Manuel and stay there till an alteration either for the better or worse, which notwith-standing the distressing thought of being in a distant country from home among a people of bad character and entirely des-titute of friend or acquaintance, I agreed to and was preparing to return when I was persuaded by several of the company to try to go forward, they promising me their friendly assistance on the way. On these conditions I again determined to go forward as far as I could; one of the company having sent me his beast which went very well, we again set forward with a determination if possible to reach Parker's Spring it being 12 miles; but of all the rides that I ever had this was the worst. I seemed to be in a kind of insensibility and blindness. By which means the way seemed to be exceeding long and tedious, but at length we arrived at the place appointed and took up camp.

Mon. 20th. Soon after we left our encampment we came in sight of Cumberland Gap and about an hour after passed thro the same. This is a very noted place on account of the great number of people who have here unfortunately fallen prey to savage cruelty or barbarity. The mountain in the gap is neither very steep nor high, but the almost inaccessible cliffs on either side the road render it a place peculiar for doing mischief. However we passed it without molestation, or seeing any sign of Indians, except one mockerson [moccasin] track. We had not passed the gap far before I was again taken with an exceeding hard ague, which on its going off was succeeded by as hard a fever, nevertheless I was obliged to travel, and with extreme weakness and fatigue reached the appointed encampment about 66 miles beyond Cumberland [River] Ford.

Tues. 21st. We rode thro a barren and exceeding badly watered country; about 10 o'clock my ague again came on and it was with great difficulty that I sat upon my beast. But I still was able to keep on with the company tho many times thinking I should not be able to proceed. This day we pushed hard, traveled late and took up camp near Racoon Spring.

Wed. 22nd. The weather having changed from fine, fair and warm to cloudy, rainy and raw, rendered it disageeable traveling and my ague at the usual time of day coming on weakened me very fast, but I still made out to travel. We took up in the evening at Rock Castle [River].

Thurs. 23rd. We fixed off, traveled hard and in the evening after a fatiguing journey accompanied with distress and disappointment we arrived at Englishe's Station, the first in the Kentucky settlement.[5]

Fri. 24th. After getting breakfast at Englishe's we started for Bro. George's[6] but before we arrived there I was seized with my ague again. We then called at Capt. Kincaid's where we tarried till toward the evening. We then set forward again and arrived at Bro. George's about sunset or a little after. We had the satisfaction of finding him and all his family in health and enjoying the happiness of being in a safe part of the country and having plenty of what is necessary for the support of nature.

Smith remained extremely ill until November 21; most of his journal entries during this period report on his health. A week later he and his brother prepared for their journey home via the Wilderness Road.

Sun. [November] 30th. We were somewhat surprised when we arose in the morning to find it snowing very fast, the evening before having been very warm, fair and pleasant. It continued snowing till about 12 or 1 o'clock by which time it was an ankle deep or more, which prevented our going to the Crab Orchard. It ceased snowing about 1 o'clock but continued cloudy and raw all the remainder of the day.

Mon. Dec. 1st. After having fixed up our luggage and taken breakfast we started from Capt. Owsley's, but being detained longer than we expected made it near 12 o'clock before we arrived at the Crab Orchard. When we arrived we were informed the company had been gone from there about an hour. We were then obliged to push hard to overtake them, but being much plagued with our packs, and being also obliged to call at English's [Station, apparently a social call in return for the earlier kindness] prevented our overtaking them till they encamped. I was enabled this day to ride thro the snow and frequently obliged to get down to alter our pack without feeling any perceivable damage; we traveled about 22 miles and took with the rest of the company on Scagg's creek.

Tues. 2nd. We left our encampment just as it was well light and traveled pretty fast. About 12 o'clock it clouded up and began to rain and continued to rain all day; we traveled till near dark and then took up on Racoon creek. But riding thro the rain with the fatigue of traveling about 30 miles threw me into a smart fever. Bro. George also having took a great cold was likewise very unwell. As soon as we arrived at the encamping ground we immediately turned our horses loose into the cane, thinking before we lay down to confine them, but we were both so unwell that we were scarcely able to move from camp so they remained loose all night. After a very wet night and bad lodging we were blessed with the light of

Wed. 3rd. but to our no small disappointment our horses were not to be found. Bro. George made what search he could till towards 8 or 9 o'clock without success and then offered a reward of 10 dollars to any person who would bring them. But in vain, for after searching till sometime in the afternoon we were under the disagreeable necessity of returning to Kentucky. This was truly a wretched shift but nevertheless it was the best we could make and notwithstanding our case was bad yet we had great reason to be thankful that it was no worse. For first, we had one horse left, which I had luckily tied up over night; secondly a company of our old acquaintance coming by mere accident to our camp about 10 at night, who (happy for us) were detained in the morning as well as we; and when we were driven to the necessity of returning assisted us on our way back; and thirdly when we arrived at Kentucky we had the good fortune to find our horses, who had got there about 2 hours before us, so that we came off much better than we could reasonably have expected.

Thurs. 4th. The weather was still cloudy, cold and raw, but we pursued our journey. But I think I suffered the most cold that I almost ever did in one day in my life; for I was so weak that I was unable to walk which was the only expedient we could have recourse to to warm ourselves when cold. Having made it rather late in starting from our encampment (which was on Rock Castle) we did not arrive at Kentucky till about 9 o'clock at night.

Fri. 5th. was cold and blustering which brought on a heavy shower of snow which was soon over and then it cleared away. Bro. George and myself having taken a walk down to the river to wash ourselves saw the greatest curiosity I ever saw in Kentucky. Which is as follows; On the river bank lie several large rocks the gritt of which as well as I recollect is much like grindstone gritt; within these rocks there are innumerable appearances of some kind of shells which are turned into solid stone, the greater part of which a good deal resemble buck's horns. What was the cause of this strange phenomenon of nature I am at a loss to determine, nevertheless I must think that these stones were once covered with water, and that these appearances were once perfect shells. Otherwise I can form no idea how they should come there. But of this enough.—Having parted with our provisions both for ourselves and horses we were obliged to provide more, having determined to start with the company that were coming from Crab Orchard. We accordingly got enough to carry us thro the wilderness and with it once more started for home. But the company having got the start of us thro our being unavoidably detained in providing our provisions, we were again obliged to travel by ourselves till late in the night, when we at last overtook them at their encampment near the mouth of Scraggs [Skaggs] creek.

Sat. 6th. We started pretty early, travelled slowly and encamped in the evening on Fraser's creek. We were in number about 35 men and there being a good deal of danger of Indians, caused us to be much on our guard. Wherefore it was thought proper to place out 4 centinels one on each corner of the encampment, which after a list was obtained for the purpose were accordingly ordered to their several posts.

Sun. 7th. We fixed up and started from our encampment as soon as it was well light. Soon after our setting out we were struck with horror at the sight of the fresh grave of the unfortunate Fielding, who had fallen a prey to the savage barbarity of a merciless, cruel and bloodthirsty enemy; who after it was his fatal misfortune to have his thigh bone shattered to pieces was inhumanely butchered and bruised and at length scalped to complete the horror of that mournful scene. Soon after we had passed this monument of cruelty, our front were alarmed at the fresh signs of horses that had come up to the road on a high hill, which was doubtless a party of savages, who had come hither to learn if there had any company just passed. Nevertheless we pursued our journey without any interruption. We travelled on till night when we came to the place where poor Fielding and his companions received their mortal wounds; the company who survived the shocking massacre had built for their preservation a kind of fort, into which they repaired but unhappily their cautious proceedings came too late for their unfortunate friends. We proceeded a few miles farther and took up camp.

Mon. 8th. Having determined if possible this day to get into Powell's valley we started about 2 hours before day. When the daylight came on the front were again alarmed by a mockerson track, which appeared not to have been gone an hour. On seeing this repeated sign of Indians, a council was held wherein it was decreed that the gun men should divide, some in front and some in the rear in case the rear should be attacked. In this position we marched until we passed Cumberland river. When we arrived at the foot of Cumberland mountain we were again halted and the whole of the guns (being about 12 or 15 in number excepting pistols) were put up in front; thus we marched uninterrupted thro the gap. But 2 men, one of whom had a foundered and the other a tired horse, being quite out of sight of the rest of the company behind, when they had a little passed the top of the mountain one of them chancing to cast his eye some distance to the left hand was suddenly startled by the sight of 6 Indians running with their guns in their hands as tho they meant to head the body of the company by taking advantage of a crooked part of the road. They immediately set up a continued cry for assistance, which being heard and answered by those before, made the very mountain seem to be alive with people. But when the company collected again on the top of the mountain no Indian was to be seen. A council was then again held, when Col. Martin gave it as his opinion that we should certainly be attacked some time in the night by those Indians. Whereupon the guns were again divided, some in the front and some in the rear. We then marched on in close and good order in a single Indian file; we marched thus about 5 miles and then stopped, fed our horses and determined to travel the greater part of the night. As soon as our horses were done eating we set forward again it being at this time about 2 hours in the night; after traveling about 6 miles farther we came to the encampment of a company bound for Kentucky with whom we encamped all night.

Tues. 9th. Hoping we were now out of danger, several of the company talked of not starting till towards 8 or 9 o'clock, but my brother and me with a few others pushed on with an intention to get to the Valley Station. We travelled on till towards the middle of the day, when all except my brother and me stopped to let their horses eat cane. We pushed along, thinking to go somewhat farther and wait for them while our horses should feed, but seeing no convenient place we kept on, when our pack horses were going along before and coming to the brow of an hill suddenly started back and came meeting us; my brother immediately dismounted and bore off to the left hand and I bore off to the right. We could make no discoveries of anything, but this so alarmed us that we were not at ease all the day after; we also saw several mockerson tracks along the road which still tended to increase our fears. But safely and undisturbed we arrived at the Valley Station about 10 o'clock at night.

Wed. 10th. Being now quite beyond danger we did not start so soon as usual so that all our company came up again and we all set off together about 11 o'clock from the Valley Station and took up camp at night on Clinch river.

Thurs. 11th. We started pretty early and arrived at the Blockhouse about 1 o'clock, so that we have been but 6 days since we started from Englishe's. We fed our horses at the Blockhouse and then rode on to Campbell's.

Smith arrived home on the twenty-first. As he neared the end of his journey, the pace of travel quickened. His eagerness is apparent in his journal entries, which omit observations about nearly everything except the distance covered and the weather. He relocated his family to Ohio in 1798.

5

❧

Peter Muhlenberg, 1784

Peter Muhlenberg, the son of a minister, began his adult life as a minister himself in a German-language community in western Virginia's Shenandoah County. During the course of the American Revolution, he achieved the rank of general and for his services received a grant of 13,000 acres of western land in Ohio.[1] When peace finally returned, the Virginia Assembly appointed Muhlenburg, as an officer of high rank and a man of unimpeachable moral character, to help locate the western land allocated to war veterans who had served as state troops. Muhlenberg commenced his journey down the Ohio River in early 1784, setting out not from his own home in western Virginia but from his father's house in Philadelphia County, Pennsylvania. He traveled with a man known only as Captain Paske.

By the time Muhlenberg had traversed the length of Pennsylvania to Pittsburgh, his physical appearance had been altered in ways that gave little indication of his status. "I have at present the perfect resemblance of Robinson Crusoe: four belts around me, two braces of pistols, a sword and rifle slung, besides my pouch and tobacco pipe, which is not a small one," Muhlenberg observed with some amazement. "Add to this the blackness of my face, which occasions the inhabitants to take me for a travelling Spaniard."[2] Muhlenberg was bemused by this mistake rather than resentful. His comment is very telling, however, for it illustrates the rigors of early American travel even in well-settled regions.

The portion of Muhlenberg's journal presented here begins with *his approach to Pittsburgh and follows his route down the Ohio River as far as Louisville. Muhlenberg's first language was German, although his journal indicates an equal comfort in English. No way exists of knowing whether or to what extent his editor and son, Henry A. Muhlenberg, anglicized the original journal for publication in 1849. Some alteration must be assumed. The journal in its published form suggests little ethnic distinctiveness. His birth in America and advancement to the rank of general in the Revolution indicate an advanced degree of acculturation. His journal, at least in the form published by his son, records no encounter with language barriers or similar problems.³ As an ethnic German raised in Pennsylvania and living in western Virginia, Muhlenberg may have encountered little that was culturally alien. Furthermore, the rigors of long-distance travel in early America may have ironed out most ethnic differences. Everyone, regardless of background, had to deal with flea-infested accommodations, harsh weather, and inflated prices for essential commodities.*

March 10th [1784]—We rode ten miles to Turtle Creek, which was very high; and the ice breaking, we cut down trees, and with their assistance got over. We crossed first, and then drew our horses over by a long rope. We got over in about two hours, and arrived at Fort Pitt in the afternoon, where I found Colonel Anderson, the principal surveyor, Dr. Skinner, and some other of my friends, waiting the clearing of the river [of ice], in order to proceed to the Falls [of the Ohio River, modern Louisville]. Colonel Anderson was kind enough to offer me a passage in his boat, which is nearly ready, and to carry one horse for me. I shall consequently keep but one, and have given away my baggage horse.

March 11th.—The ice is driving very fast on the Monongahela, and I expect that stream will be clear in a day or two. The Allegheny [River] seems not yet broken up, so that in all probability it will be eight or ten days before we can set out. This will give us time to settle matters properly. This day I have delivered my [land] warrants, and those entrusted to my care, to Colonel Anderson for the Continental [veterans], and Major [George] Croghan for the [Virginia] state line, and have now fixed everything for the voyage, except a few necessaries which are yet to provide.[4] The remaining part of my leisure I employ in preparing my lines, and trying to catch some Ohio fish, which, according to report, are very large; but hitherto I have been unsuccessful, as the river is still too full of ice.

Sunday, March 14th.—Rains hard; keep within doors. The ice has now broken up, and both Allegheny and the Monogahela have risen upwards of twenty feet. This week we are preparing our horses, &c., but do not expect our boat to be ready in less than ten days.

Sunday, 21st.—Doctor Skinner, Captain Fitzhugh and others, left for Kentucky, the river being still full of ice.

Sunday, 28th.—This day our boat arrived, with 22,000 weight of flour, 1500 weight of bacon, &c., on board.

March 29th.—Still engaged in getting our horses aboard.

March 30th.—This morning prevented from sailing by a severe snow-storm from the northwest. A boat belonging to Mr. Lewis, of Virginia, having himself and brother on board, and one belonging to Captain Ellis, from the Eastern Shore [of Chesapeake Bay], go with us in company.

March 31st.—The weather is more moderate. At half past ten we set out from Fort Pitt, passed Logstown and Fort M'Intosh,[5] but about thirteen miles below the fort, near sunset, we were carried by the force of the current on the point of an island, where we ran the greatest risk of losing both vessel and cargo. In this situation we continued all night; and as I was requested to take command of the company, we formed four watches, each taking the guard in turn. What added to our uneasiness was, that we were near the Indian shore, and, in our situation, would have become an easy prey to the Indians, who, however desirous they might be of obtaining a peace, would not have been able to withstand the great temptation of plundering a boat so richly laden as ours. I likewise observed how misfortunes depress the spirits, and raise gloomy ideas from causes which at other times would have no effect; for I must confess that I did not hear the noise of the wild fowl, the screaming of loons, the whooping of owls, and the howling of wolves, which continued around us all night, with total indifference.

April 1st.—At break of day our difficulties seemed to increase, but by one lucky effort we at last extricated ourselves, and got the boat into the river clear of the trees. We found our consort about three miles below waiting our arrival. We continued our course without accidents to Decker's Fort [a small fortified settlement], where we stopped a few hours, and then went on to Fort Wheeling [officially Fort Fincastle]. This fort was built by the Governor of Virginia in 1774, and was during the late war several times attacked by the Indians, and once by the Indians and a detachment of British from Detroit, who beseiged it several days, and at last endeavoured to compel the garrison to surrender, by making a cannon of wood, and firing it upon the fort. The cannon, however, did not stand proof, and the Indians, who made a close attack, were beaten off and the garrison relieved. The fort is now totally decayed, and Captain [Ebenezer] Zane, the only inhabitant at or near the place, makes use of it for firewood.[6] This place lies about one hundred miles below Fort Pitt, and as it is the last settlement we shall come to until we reach the Falls, we have agreed to stay all night, especially as it rains and snows hard, and we have the promise of some mush and milk for supper.

April 2d.—This morning we were joined by two boats more, with families going to the Falls. To avoid any danger from Indians, they wish to keep us company, so that we have now five sail: the Muhlenberg, the Lewis, the Ellis, the Dowdon, and Carpenter's Mistake. As the weather was moderate and fine, we continued under way all night, and at 4 p.m. passed Fish Creek, at 8 o'clock passing Fishing Creek, and at 4 in the morning passed Muskingham [River], one hundred and eighty-nine miles below Fort Pitt.

April 3d.—A fine day; but as we are without wood and fresh meat, the whole company have agreed to land. Finding it impracticable, however, to bring our boat to shore, we were obliged to continue our course all night. Captain Harrison in the small boat ran ashore, and brought a large turkey-cock. About midnight we passed the mouth of Sciota [River].

April 4th.—Cloudy and raining; in the morning we went in the barge to the Indian shore and killed two turkeys, some ducks and pigeons. At 12 o'clock we passed the Little Cannauway

[River], and afterwards passed the Hockcockin [River], and continued our course all night without accident.

April 5th.—Continued on our course until 9 o'clock, when a heavy storm came on, and we were compelled to come to shore on the Indian [Ohio] side. After we had taken every precaution to keep our boat from harm, a hunting party turned out and killed one buffalo and one deer, but both were very poor. This is part of the land allotted to the Virginia line [of state Revolutionary veterans]. The storm continued very severely, and obliged us to lay by all night.

April 6th.—As the morning promised a fair day, we set out, but the storm coming up again, we were obliged to come to on the Indian shore. Here we landed our horses to recruit them a little, and rode five or six miles into the country to view the lands, which are exceedingly fine, especially the bottoms. We killed three buffaloes, but found them too poor to eat, so that we determined to kill no more. The winter must have been very severe here, and hard for the game, as we have this day found several deer, one bear, and four buffaloes dead in the woods, which seem to have perished through want. Two boats passed us in the night for Kentucky, and one went up the river with a sail.

April 7th.—The weather is something more moderate. We set out about sunrise, not caring to remain too long in our position on the Indian shore. We kept a guard out all last night for fear of a surprise [attack]. In the afternoon, we went on shore with the barge, and killed eight turkeys. At sunset, the wind rising and the prospect of a squally night, determined us to land, where we continued until dawn of day.

April 8th.—This morning at 7 o'clock we passed the Little Miami [River], and at 9 o'clock, Licking Creek. The lands on both sides of the river still continue to evince the appearance of being of the best quality. At 10 o'clock went on shore with the barge and killed two turkeys and some ducks; in the afternoon went on shore again and killed two turkeys. At 3 o'clock we passed the mouth of the Great Miami, a beautiful river, having from appearances excellent bottoms on both sides. From what I have hitherto seen of the River Ohio, and the lands on both sides, I make no doubt that in time this will be the first and most valuable settlement in North America. At present, it is inhabited by wild beasts only, whose music in the night sounds rather harsh to the ear, and puts me in mind of heavy iron doors grating on their hinges. At sunset we came to, in order to wait the rising of the moon.

April 9th.—At 4 o'clock we started, and about 10 came opposite the Big Bone Lick, on the east side, about three miles from the river. Here the company consulted whether we should make a halt in order to view the Big Bone Lick, but on examining the map, we find that we have already passed it. The ravages among the game, made by the severity of the winter, are still visible, as we see numbers of buffaloes and other game lying dead along the shore. At 11 o'clock, a heavy squall came on, which compelled us to come to on the Indian shore. At 3 P.M. the wind lulled, and we put off, but coming opposite to Mr. Lewis's boat, we were informed that Mr. Lewis and Mr. Towles had gone hunting immediately on our landing, and had not yet returned. On receiving this information, we put to shore again, and kept firing signal guns until some time in the night, but could hear nothing of our lost companions. Various are the conjectures with regard to their fate. Some are of opinion that they have lost themselves, and are unable to find their way back to the boat; others again are as positive in believing that they have been intercepted by a party of Indians and carried off; for my part, I hardly know what to think. It rained and blew very hard all night.

April 10th.—This morning the rain still continues, and we have no account of our lost companions. We have, however, agreed to wait for them until 10 o'clock, and perhaps longer, as their situation must be sufficiently distressing already, but will become much more so if we go off and leave them in the wilderness, and on the opposite side of the river, where there are no white inhabitants. At 4 o'clock, P.M., we gave up all hopes of finding the two gentlemen who are lost, and therefore concluded it would be both needless and dangerous to continue in our present position. We, however, left three men with the barge, directed them to cross the river to the opposite side, and wait there until to-morrow evening, and then if the gentlemen should not come, to bring off the boat. Shortly after 4 o'clock we got under way, much distressed at being compelled to leave two of our companions behind, without knowing what may be their fate. If they have been taken by the Indians, it must have been by a small party who were afraid to attack the boats, as they must have heard from the firing of the signal guns that we were not badly provided with fire-arms. It is a sharp lesson to young hunters and poor woodsmen.—At 6 o'clock, after coming about ten miles, we had the pleasure of being hailed from the shore, where we found Mr. Lewis and Mr. Towles, who had been travelling at random the whole night, and had got to the river about 11 o'clock this forenoon; so that we now still three men behind us, who will follow us to-morrow. At sunset we passed the mouth of the Kentucky [River], where I caught a catfish of about eight pounds weight, which came very seasonably, as we were almost tired of turkeys. We kept under way all night, and at break of day found that we were about twenty-five miles from the Falls.

April 11th.—Passed several islands, and now begin to see canebreaks along the shore. About 11 o'clock we arrived at the Falls, and came to in Bear Grass Creek, opposite Louisville; here we found Colonel [George Rogers] Clarke and a number of gentlemen waiting for us. We were saluted from Fort Nelson, where Major Wales has command, with three guns.

Peter Muhlenberg made Louisville his main base of operations, noting that the town "consists of a court-house, a jail, and seven huts, besides the fort."[7] His initial choice to begin surveying was in modern Ohio, where a tract had been set aside for Virginia veterans. This, however, required the protection of a substantial guard because the Indian occupants still regarded the territory as theirs. The Cumberland region south of Kentucky was likewise dangerous. Furthermore, the arrival of summer made surveying among the weeds and underbrush a near impossibility. Finding it impossible to conduct the work he had set out to perform, Muhlenberg took the opportunity to investigate the interior of Kentucky and admitted, "I was surprised to find it so fine a country."[8] Unfortunately, further exploration was hindered by illness. Not until late May was Muhlenberg strong enough to begin his return via the Wilderness Road. His journal entries for this stage of his travels equal his earlier voyage down the Ohio in terms of vivid and revealing detail. In late June he reached Philadelphia and submitted his reports to the national government.

Part Two

Postwar Expansion

Peace with the British and the economic recession that followed released a pent-up surge of westward migration. Initially, prospects appeared promising. Although the British had been defeated, their Indian allies had not. The Cherokees and Chickasaws to the south preyed upon travelers of the Wilderness Road. From the north, the Shawnees, still bitter from their defeat in Dunmore's War, and their Delaware, Wyandotte, and other allies haunted the Ohio River. Native leadership was often divided in this period, but the militants were numerous, and for years they found the Spanish and British reliable sources of support. As the number of western American settlers increased, however, the prospects for halting their expansion dwindled. This realization was often hardly perceptible, because if the intruders could not be expelled, at least they could be exploited. Horses, liquor, axes, and any other useful booty became the primary focus. Any resistance that stood in the way was dealt with aggressively. Indian attacks therefore continued to effectively keep the border settlements in a defensive position. Migrants were especially vulnerable.

6

Samuel Shepard, 1787

Samuel Shepard left Weston, Massachusetts, in early April 1787. It was a momentous departure for the young man, traveling alone, for he had never before left his native state. He carried only a gun and a pack of personal belongings. Shepard's journal is of special interest because his New England origins made him unusual as a Kentucky settler. Shepard traveled by boat from Connecticut to New York, then proceeded by land to Philadelphia. He spent the summer working for a farmer in nearby Chester County. After an initial period getting oriented in Kentucky, Shepard settled near modern Georgetown in Scott County.

Although Shepard began his journal upon his departure from Weston on April 10, 1787, this selection begins with Shepard's departure from his employer's house in October and includes some preliminary detours in which this young New Englander first encountered unfamiliar conditions. He appears to have kept the journal with the intention of later sharing it with someone left behind in Massachusetts, but the identity of this person is not given.

October 4 moved on for Kentucky. I started in company with two other men going to Kentucky one Hadrian Moss [?] & I hired him to take about 13th [lbs.] weight of my load mostly clothing. I had still about 23 wt to carry beside my gun. I have lived the past summer with a good farmer & lived well.

5 arrived at Lancaster.

6 crossed the Susquehannah [River, Pennsylvania].

10 crossed into the state of Maryland as Mr Froman [who] I was with had business there.

11 Froman having many places to go to I took all my property on my back about 30th beside my gun. with this load crossed a steep mountain called the south mountain. on this mountain I tarried all night at what they called a house where I believe all their furniture & provision would not be as heavy as my pack.

12 got off the mountain & came to what was called a Tavern a small house with out a chimney. they said they had rum & I believe it for there was a case bottle lying on the bed which was all the vessel in the house that could have held spirits.[1] at 2 OClk came to Fan's Town where we were to stay for Forman who did not arrive untill the

18 I stayed at the house of a Duchman or German who treated me exceeding well without any expense. we set forward this day & passed through Hagers Town [Maryland].

19 midling rough traveling but could not stop to keep my birth day.

21 being near the aligana [Allegheny] mountain we crossed the Potomac River to buy some provisions. this brought us into Virginia but we only entered one house. got what provision we wanted & returned into Maryland. we begin to assend the mountain about 3 miles and put up for the night.

22 traveled 30 miles on the mountain up hill & down. began to fall in with many people going to Kentucky.

23 we crosed the line [back] into Pensylvania.

24 got to the foot of the Alegana mountain having traveled upwards of 70 miles since we first came to it.

25 came to the house of the widow Spears on the Monongahela River. here I expected to take boting for Kentucky but the water is at present to low. I have been unwell for some days but have got much better.

29 removed about 4 miles down the River to the house of Nicholas Crist [Gist] and went to work at farming. here I fell in with a young man from Attleborough by the name of False. he was teaching School. he knew some of my relations being from Massachusetts last summer.

Nov'r 5 I ground some corn on the hand Mill for the first time.[2]

6 the first time I ever eat sower croud.

9 eat venison for the first time.

14 eat some Buckwheat cakes for the first time.

15 assisted to release a boat that had struck a rock and sprang a leak by attempting to get down the River while the water was to low.

18 I saw a famely encamped in a hollow Sicamore tree on the bank of the Monongahala River. the tree was standing one side open which served for a door the out side of which they built their fire the hollow was so large that it contained two beds one Chest and some other firniture beside several persons.

19 the River having raised I went on bord a boat belonging to Joseph Stephens and bound for Kentucky. there was five boats in company.[3]

20 landed at Fort Pitt.

21 a storm of wind arose and blew up the River very hard and we were obliged to land a little below Fort McIntosh about 30 miles below Fort Pitt. we landed on the Indian shore and discovered a boat in distress near the other shore which was fast on a tree. I went with two other men to assist in giting off the boat. the waves ran high the water swift. I was in the forend of the Conoe and as she struck the boat I seized hold of the latter and indevoured to hold the Conoe with my feet but it fell from under me like lightning. I sunk in the water to my waste but kept hold of the boat and got into it without much hurt a number of men came to assist & the boat was released. 2 Negro men were drowned the same day a little below us. one of them got on shore on an Island but died with wet cold and drowning added together.

22 went about 53 miles landed about midnight three miles below the Mingo bottom [modern Steubenville, Ohio].

23 we took nine horses on bord the boat that had been sent to this place by land. we set forward and landed at Wheeling Creek 18 miles. here we were in formed that between 30 and 40 Boats have passed this day. the weather cleared off this morning & the moon being near the full we concluded to move on and either row or float all night.

24 fine weather. we this day passed the Muskinggum River. here
we were informed that upwards of 800 people had passed this
place to day. the River was now strong with Boats. I saw one to
day that had on board 50 souls 21 horses & 45 sheep. we
again moved on the whole night by leting our Boat float on the
water without rowing.

25 we passed the great Kanhawa [River].

26 another man and myself landed on the Indian shore [Ohio] in a
Conoe to take in [fire]wood. this night we passed the Scioto
River.

27 this morning was fogy. just as the fog went off we came to
difficult Island where had it been on we should have been in
much danger. at 11 Oclock we came to the three Islands [a
noted landmark and Indian crossing] and at ¼ past three P.M.
we landed at Limestone Creek in Kentucky in perfect health
and safety.

28 we put the Waggon together that belonged to the Boat. the famelies
packed up their things and prepared to start. I concluded to go
with Mr Stephens about 40 miles into the country.

29 we had a steep and difficult hill to assend and traveled only
between three and four miles. passed through the town of
Washington and encamped in the woods.

Novem'r 30 We traveled 10 miles and encamped in the woods at
Johnsons fork of Licking River not having seen a house since
we started this morning. a number of famelies encamped at the
same place here for the first time. I stood as a Centinel there
being danger of Indians.

Dec'r 1 passed the Lower blue licks. here several famelies live and
are making salt a spring of Salt water and one of fresh break
out of the ground about 16 feet apart. here I eat some Buffaloe
beef for the first time which was very sweet and good. we encamped this night in the woods.[4]

2nd we arrived at the place our destination between sunset & dark
(viz) at Capt Isaac Ruddells, Bourbon County. since we landed
at Limestone the weather has been very pleasant & no accident
happened.[5]

Shepard maintained his diary intermittently for several years after arriving in Kentucky. He lived initially in Bourbon County, where he found work as a schoolmaster. Particularly interesting is his account of establishing an independent household in Scott County about a year later and the small affairs of daily life at a time when conditions for settlers were still dangerous.

Mary Coburn Dewees, 1788

The family of Samuel and Mary Coburn Dewees departed for Kentucky from Philadelphia in late 1788. They, with several close relatives, traveled the length of Pennsylvania by wagon, then descended the Ohio River. In Kentucky, they reunited with family members who had preceded them west. Mary Dewees kept a detailed journal of the trip, apparently to share with friends back home.[1] It is unusual for a journal to have been written by a woman, one responsible for several young children, and is therefore presented in its entirety. Despite her refined background, Dewees's adventurous spirit and good humor carried her over a number of unpleasant experiences. One of the distinctive qualities of her account is the frequent appreciation for wild beauty.

September 27th 1788. Left Philadel. about 5 oclock in the afternoon and tore ourselves from a number of dear friends that assembled to take a last farewell before we set off for Kentucky, made our first stay 6 miles from the City, being very sick the greatest part of the way.

28th We left the sign of the Lamb [a tavern] at half past six A.M. and proceeded to Col. Websters 7 Miles. Where we breakfasted, and then set off for [a tavern known as] the United States which we reached at 5 oclock P.M. and put up for the night on account of my sickness which was excessive, being obliged to go to Bed immediately.

29th Left the United States and arrived at the waggon 40 Miles from Philad. That place which contains so many valued friends. Sister and the Children are very hearty, the Children very diverting to all but poor Maria who was as sick as it was possible to be. we took up our lodging at [a tavern known as] the Compass.

30th. Left the Compass and reached [a tavern known as] the Hat at 10 oclock A.M. much better than I was. Lost all the fine prospects the first days owning to my sickness, which was excessive, being obliged to be led from the waggon to the bed, and from the bed to the waggon.

October 1st. Crost the Conestogo, a good deal uneasiness for fear my sickness should return, the Conostogo is a beautiful creek with fine prospects around it. After refreshing ourselves we took a walk up the creek and I think I never saw a more beautiful prospect, you cant imagine how I long'd for you my friend to join our little party and to be partakers of the Beauties of nature that now surround us, we are seated beneath the shade of intermingling trees, that grew reaching oer the creek and entirely shades us from the noon day sun. Several since I sat here has crossed some on horse back others in boats, while at a fall of water at a little distance adds a dignity to the scene and renders it quite romantic. As the sun was setting we rode through Lancaster. A Beautifull inland town, with some elegant Houses in it. I was quite delighted with the view we have from the corner of the street where the prison stands of the upper part of the town which at once presents to your sight a sudden rise with houses, trees, and gardens, on either side that has a very pleasing effect.

2d 'Tho but a few days since my friends concluded I could not reach Kentucky, will you believe me when I tell you I am sitting on the Bank of the Susquehanah, and can take my bit of ham and Biscuit with any of them.

Returning health has made the
face of nature gay
Given beauty to the sun
and pleasure to the day

Just crosd the river in company with Mrs. Parr and her daughter, not the least sick, what gratitude is owing from me to the great author of nature who in so short a time has restored me from a state of Languishment and misery to the most enviable health.

3d Past through York Town, a pretty little town, and lodged about a mile from that place.

4th This day we rode through Abbots town a trifling place, find the roads much better from Lancaster upwards than from Philad. To Lancaster, reached Hunterstown 113 miles. expect tomorrow to cross the South Mountain. weather exceedingly pleasant.

Octo 5 Left Hunters Town and proceeded to the Mountain, which we began to climb about 10 o'clock sometimes riding sometimes walking; find the roads much better in places than we expected, 'tho in others excessive stony. the length which is ten miles renders it very tedious, Oblidgenly favoured with good weather. We have halted on the top of the Mountain to refresh ourselves and horses. this afternoon decended the west side find it much worse than the east side the road in places for a mile in length so very stony that you can scarce see the earth between. 'Tho at other places beautifully watered by fine springs, took up our lodging at the foot of the Mountain, the people very civil the house right Kentucky.

6 Left the foot of the Mountain, crost the falling spring and proceeded to Chambersburgh a handsome little Town with some pretty stone and brick Buildings in it. After passing the Town we crost the falling spring again, one of the finest springs in this part of the world by which several Mills in this neighborhood are turned. Obliged to stop sooner than usual one of our horses being Lame, find the people a good deal shy, at first, but after a little while very sociable and obliging, treated with some very fine apples which begin to grow very scarce with us, I am much afraid we have be like the Children of Isreal. long for the Garlick and Onions that your city abounds with.

7th Set off for the north mountain which we find so bad we are obliged to foot it up, and could compare ourselves to nothing but a parcel of goats climbing up some of the Welch Mountains that I have read of. [Daughter] Sally very desirous to know whether this mountain is not the one that in Mr. Adgates [a Philadelphia singing master] song. find this the most fatiguing days journey we have had, the roads so very bad and so very steep that the horses seem ready to fall backwards. In many places, you would be surprised to see the Children, Jumping and Skipping. Sometimes quite out of sight sometimes on horseback sometimes in the waggon, so you see we have variety, 'tho sometimes would very willingly dispense with some of it. Believe me my dear friends, the sight of a log house on these mountains after a fatiguing day's Journey affords more real pleasure that all the magnificent buildings your city contains. took up our lodging at the foot of the Mountain and met with very good entertainment.

Oct 8th Left the foot of the mountain and crost scrub hill which is very bad indeed. I had like to forgot to tell you, I have lost my children, dont be concerned for the loss for they are still in the family, the Inhabitants of this Country are [not] so cruel as to deprive me of them, but they were kind enough to give them to Sister Rees, and I am [like] a Miss from Philada you may rest assured I don't take the trouble to undeceive them, unless Sally (as she often does) Crys out where's my Mar, the children are very hearty and bear fatigue much better than we do, 'tho I think we all do wonderfull, you would be astonished to see the roads we have come some of which seems impassible. Rachel mostly passes half the day in Spelling and Sally in Singing. every house we stop at she enquires if it not a Kenty [Kentucky] house and seldom leaves it 'till she informs them she is an Kenty Lady.

9th Crost sidling hill and were the greatest part of they day in performing the journey. the roads being so excessive steep sidling and stony that it seemed impossible to get along. We were obliged to walk the greatest part of the way up 'tho not without company. there was five waggons with us all morning to different parts, this night our difficulties began. we were obliged to put up at a cabin at the foot of the hill perhaps a dozen logs upon one another, with a few slabs for a roof and the earth for a floor & a Wooden Chimney constituted this extrodinary ordinary.[2] the people very kind but amazing dirty, Except Mr. Rees the Children and your maria, who by our dress or address or perhaps both were favoured with a bed and assure you we that thought ourselves to escape being fleaed alive.[3]

10th After Breakfasting at this clean house, set off for Bedford. in our way crosed Juniata [River], past through Bedford a small county town, some parts of the road very bad and some of it very pleasant, for a considerable distance, we travelled along the Juniata, we put up at a house where we were not made very welcome but like travellers we learn'd to put up a few sour looks instead.

11th Set off for the Allagany Mountain which we began to assend in the afternoon, found it as good as any part of our journey. we assen[d]ed in the waggon not without fear and trembling, I assure you. we got about six miles and fell in with a french gentleman and his family going to Pittsburgh. we all put up at a little hut on the mountain which was so small that we prefered lodging in our own waggon [than] to be crowded with frenchmen & negroes on an earthen floor.

12th At the top of the Cloud capt Allagany. It was really awfully pleasing to behold the clouds arising between the mountains at a distance, the day being drisly & the air very heavy rendered the clouds so low that we could scarce se[e] fifty yards before us. this Evening got of[f] the Mountain, It being twenty miles across we passed through Burlain a small town, as the Election was held at this place we could not be accommodated proceeded to a dutch house in the glades where we were kindly entertained.

Oct 13th Proceeded to larel Creek and ascended the hill. I think this and many more of the scenes we have passed through, we have seen Nature display'd in her greatest undress, at other times we have seen her dress'd Beautifull beyond expression. The road excessive bad, some of the land fine, The Timber Excellent and grow to an amazing height the generality of it from 50 to 60 foot high. The day by reason of the Badness of the roads could not reach a stage the hill being 20 miles across and our horses a good deal tired, we in Company with a nother waggon were obliged to Encamp in the woods, after a Suitable place at a Convenient distance from a run of water was found and a Level piece of ground was pitched upon for our encampment. our men went to give refreshment to the Horses. we Females having had a good fire made up a set about preparing Supper which consisted of an Excellent dish of Coffe having milk with us, those who chose had a dish of cold ham and pickled beets with the addition of Bread, Butter, Biscuit, & Cheese made up our repast. after supper Sister, the Children, and myself took up our lodging in the waggon the men with the Blankets laid down at the fireside, the wind being high with some rain, disturbed our repose untill near day light, when we could have enjoyed a comfortable nap had we not been obliged to rise and prepare breakfast which we did on the

14th Set out for Chestnut ridge, horrid roads and the Stony's land in the world I believe, every few hundred yards, rocks big enough to build a small house upon. We arrived at Chenys Mill towards the middle of the day and parted with our Company. Chenys Mill is a beautifull situation, or else the scarcity of such places make us think it more so than it really is. We were overtaken by a family who was going our way, which renders it more Agreeable travelling than by ourselvs. I think by this time we may call ourselves Mountain proof. at the close of the day we arrived at a house and thought it prudent to put up for the night, the people are Scotch Irish, exceedingly Kind but Surprizingly dirty, we concluded (as the Company that was with us Made up 18 besides the family) to lodge in our [covered] waggon which we did. It rained very hard in the night but we laid pretty Comfortably.

15th After Breakfast we set off for Miller Town, you would be surprized to see the number of pack horses which travel these roads ten or twelve in a drove, in going up the north mountain. Betsy took it in her head to ride a horseback, and Daddy, undertook to escort her. on there in a narrow path at the edge of a very steep place they meet with a company of these packers, when her horse took it in his Nodle not to sti[r] one foot, but stood and received a thump from behind from every pack that pass'd and whilst Betsy was in a state of greatest tripedation expecting every Moment to be thrown from her horse, her

Gallant [escort] instead of flying to her Assistance, stood laughing ready to Kill himself at the fun, but the poor girl really look[ed] pitiable. We put up at a poor little Cabbin the people very kind which Conpensates for every Inconveniency.

16th Mr. Dewees and my brother rode about 13 miles to McKees ferry to see how the waters are as we are apprehensive they are too low to go down the river [from about 12 miles above Pittsburgh]. The weather still fine.

17th Left our little Cabbin and proceeded to Mckees ferry where we staid two days in a little hut not half so good as the little building at the upper end of your garden, and thought ourselves happy to meet with so comfortable a dwelling.

18th Our boat being ready we set off for the river and arrived their at 12 O'Clock and went on board immediately. She lay just below the mouth [of the] Youghiogeny [River] which empties into the Monongahela. at 2 o'Clock we push down the river very slowly, [and] intend stopping at Fort Pitt, where we expect to meet the Waggon with the rest of our Goods. our Boat resembling Noahs Ark not a little. at Sun set got fast on Braddock's upper ford where we staid all that night and 'till 10 O Clock the next day.

19th With the Assistance of some people that was coming up in a flat [boat] we got off. The water very low. I am much afraid we shall have a tedious passage. our boat 40 foot long our room 16 by 12 with a Comfortable fireplace. our Bed room partioned off with blankets, and far preferable to the Cabbins we met with after we crossed the Mountains. we are clear of fleas which I assure you is a great relief for we were almost devoured when on shore. The Monongahela with the many coulored woods on each side is Beautifull, and in the Spring must be delightfull. We are now longing for rain as much as we dreaded it on the Land and for it is impossible to get down untill the water raises. We live entirely Independant, and with that there is a pleasure which Dependants can never be partakers of. we are all very hearty, nor have I had the least signs of Sickness Since I came on board. May I ever retain a great full sense of the Obligation due to the great creater for his amazing goodness to me especially, who have every reason from the first of the Journey fear quite the reverse. About 3 O'Clock we passed the field (Just above Turtle Creek) where Braddock's fought his famous battle with the French & Indians, and soon after got [stuck] fast on the lower ford but by the agility of our men soon got off, the river about a Quarter of a mile across. Sammy and Johny gone ashore for Milk.

20th Rose as soon as our men had prepared a good fire, got Breakfast, & Mr. Dewees set off for McKees [ferry] where we left the horses on account of the waters being low, expect to reach Pittsburgh tonight, Just opposite the hill where General Grant fought his battle on with the French and Indians who were in possession of fort Pitt. at that time [1757] As the sun was setting [we] hove in sight [of] the Coal Hill and ferry house opposite Pittsburgh, this hill is amazing high and affords a vast deal more coal than can be Consumed In that place, what a valuable acquisition would it be near your City.

21st We are now laying about a mile from Pittsburgh, and have received several invitations to come on shore. we have declined all, as the trunks with our cloaths is not come up, and we [are] in our travelling dress, not fit to make our appearance in that Gay place. Just received an Invitation from the french Lady we travelled part of the way with to come up. Mr. Tilton call'd on us with Mrs. Tilton's Compliments would be happy to have us to tea, he gone and three french Gentlemen & an Englishman came on board & expressed a great deal of pleasure to see us so comfortable Situated. In the afternoon Mr. and Mrs. Oharra waited on us at the boat and insisted on our going to their house, which in Compliance to their several invitations we were obliged to accept, and find them very polite and agreeable.[4] we staid and Supp'd with them, nor would they suffer us to go on board while we continued at this place.

22nd Mrs. Oharra waited on us to Mrs. Tiltons to Mrs. Nancarrows & Mrs. Odderongs & engaged to tea with mrs. Tilton, Col Butler and his lady waited on us to the Boat, was much delighted with our Cabbin took a bit of Biscuit & Cheese with a glass of wine & then returned to dine at Capt Oharras. Spent the afternoon at Mrs. Tiltons with a room full of Company, and received several invitations to spend our time with the Ladys

A view of Pittsburgh in the late eighteenth century. Source: Georges-Henri-Victor Collot, *A Journey in North America* (Paris: Printed for Arthus Bertrand, Bookseller, 1826).

at Pitts. Called on Mrs. Butler and saw a very handsome parlour, Elegantly papered and well furnished. It appeared more like Philad[elphia] than any I have seen since I left that place.

23rd Drank tea at the French ladys with several Ladys & Gentlemen of this place.

24th The town all in arms, a report prevailed that a party of Indians within twenty miles coming to attact the Town. The drums beating to arms with the Militia collecting from every part of the Town has I assure a very disagreeable Appearance.

25th Left our hospitable friends Capt. Oharra & Lady not without regret as their polite and friendly Entertainment demands our utmost Gratitude, they waited on us to the boat where we parted for ever. Was much disappointed in sending our letters as the man that was to Carry them set off before the Messenger got back from the Boat. About 11 o'Clock A.M. drop'd down the Ohio, & at the distance of a mile & a half had a full view of Capt. Oharras Summerhouse which Stands on the Banks of the Allgahany river which runs about a hundred yards from the Bottom of their Garden. It is the finest Situation that I ever Saw, they live at the upper end, or rather out of the Town, their house in the midst of an Orchard of 60 Acres, the only one in that place. from the front of the garden you can at one view behold the Allegany, the Monongahala, & the Ohio rivers, it is impossible for the most lively Imagination to pai[n]t a Situation and prospects more delightful. Att the close of the day [we] got to the lower point of McKees Island where we came to a Anchor under a large rock near 60 feet high and the appearance of just falling in the water. on one side in a large smooth place arc engraved a number of names which are your Eliza's & Maria's.

26th & 27th Staid at Mckees island waiting for water, which is too low to go down. took a walk up the hill from which we have a fine prospect of boath sides of the Island and saw an Indian grave with three others, on the top of the hill, likewise the remains of an old intrenchment that was throw[n] up ye last Indian war. Saw three boats full of troops going up to Pittsburgh. We suppose they are going up for Provision for the Garison below.

28th Mr. Dewees & Mr. Shelby went up to Pitt. [I] am in hopes they will bring some Intelligence of the warriors that went out against the Indians.

29th Still continue at the Island waiting for water, had the pleasure of two ladys Company from the Island, who gave us an Invitation to visit them. had a very stormy night and a Snow of two or three Inches.

30th The weather much in our favour it rained all day. sewing & reading and when the weather is fine walking are the amusements we enjoy. The Gentlemen pass their time in hunting of deer, Turkeys, ducks, and every other kind of wild fowl with which this Country abounds. A Beautifull doe had the Assurance the other day to come half way down the hill and give a peep at us, but our hunters being out escaped being taken. fishing make up part of their amusement.

31st Still in hopes of the waters raising as we had snow again this

Morning and aprospect of rain, this the most tedious part of our Journey as we still continue in one place.

Nov. 1 The weather Clear and cold & no prospect of the water raising. [I] am little apprehensive we shall have to winter among the rocks. You cant imagine how I want to see you all, often do I indulge myself in fancys eye at looking at my dear friends, in their several families and wish to be a partaker of their happiness. Eliza too, I long to know how she behaves in her new department. I suppose she often Briddles when She looks at My Hariot to this she has got the whip hand of her.

2nd Went over to the Island to see our new Acquaintance and they insisted on our repeating our visits. While we staid a man came in that was wounded by the Indians a few days ago. About 20 Miles from Pitt a party of Traders were surprized by them in the night but got off without any but a little Blood by one who had been wounded in the head by a Taumhawke.

3rd Receiv'd a visit from three french Gentlemen who come to dine with us on board the boat.

4th Today the two Mrs. Williams came to invite us to their house a mile from this place promising to furnish us with horses and sadles, but we declined accepting their invitation Chusing rather to continue where we are 'till we go down the river.

5th Mrs. Hamilton and Miss Conrad from the Island called on us to take a walk up the hill to gether grapes which we got a great Abundance off.

6th Brother and Mr. Shelby (one of our passengers) went up to Pitt[sburgh] to procure some necessarys for us.

7th Dines on an Excellent pike. had the Company of the 3 french Gentlemen before mentioned to dine with us who came to invite us to a Ball held at Col Butlers where 30 Ladys & Gentlemen were to assemble for that purpose. it is hardly worthwhile to say we declined going as it was out of our power to dress fit at this time, to attend such and Entertainment or else (you know) [we] should be happy to do ourselves the honour.

8th Had several Gentlemen to dine on board the Ark expecting a fire hunt [with torches] of some deer who keep about 200 yards from our boat, on a very high hill but a Shower of rain in the night disappointed them, rendering the Brush and leaves to wet for that purpose, they passed the day in Squirrel hunting, and fishing for pike, this being the season for them, I saw one to day weighing 30 weight, the Beatifulist fish I ever saw.

9th Paid a second visit to the Island which keeps us in hopes of rain.

10th From the 10th to the 18 of November we passed our time in visiting, and receiving visit on board our boat, when we bid Adieu to the Island friends and pushed down the Ohio. [We] saw a small Kentucky Boat go down yesterday which induced us to set off as the water has risen but very little But still continues to rise slowly. [We] past Fort McIntosh [in the] P.M. and got fast for a minute on one of the ripples.

19th Passed Backers fort about 10 O'Clock A.M. and proceeded down the Ohio, a very Beatifull river, passed yellow [Creek] which runs near the Indian shore. The Country is very hilly on boath sides of the river, in places a half mile wide in other places much narrower. so near we are to the Indian Country and yet think ourselves pretty safe. The wind blowing very hard and being Contrary Obliged us to put on shore 65 Miles below Pittsburgh, the Boat tossing about a good deal occaisioned one to feel a little quamish [squeamish]. Betsy Rees was so sick she was obliged to go to bed, What strange reverses there are in life. The Children are very hearty & one now is playing with Daddy on the shore. we passed fort Stubane [Steuben] and the Minggo bottom in the night.[5] we should have got up to see the fort But the watch told us we could see nothing as it was Cloudy. The barking of the dogs at the fort, the howling of wolves, & the yelling of the hunters on the opposite shore was a little alarming at first but we soon got reconciled to it.

20th Just as the day broke, got aground on a Sandbar, at the beach Bottom. Just at that time a small Kentucky Boat, that was ashore endeavoured to alarm us by firing of a gun and Accosting us in the Indian tongue But our people could just discern the boat which quieted our fears. at sun rise we passed through Norris Town on the Indian Shore a Clever little Situation with ten Cabbins pleasantly situated. [We] saw another kentucky Boat and passed by Wheeling a place where a Fort was kept and attacked last war, many people waiting [for higher water] to go down the River. An excessive hard gale of wind Obliged us to put to shore. After the wind Abated, we again put out in the Channal and were Obliged again by a fresh gale to put To Shore on the Indian Coast which caused some disagreeable Sensations, as it is not long since the Indians have done some mischief here abouts. after the wind lulled they thought proper to put out again 'tho it still continued to rain very hard which made it very dark & disagreeable, as it is impossible to discern where the rocks and ripples lay; but not withstanding all the Obstructions we have met with, have gone at the rate of fifty miles in the twenty four hours. nor have I felt the least Sickness since the first gale 'tho we have been tossed about at an Amazing rate. my Brother has just come off the watch and tells us we are again anchored 'tho on the opposite shore. the weather being too bad to proceed, we laid all night ashore, it still continued very Stormy: many large trees blew down on the Bank; we expect'd every moment the boat would leave her Anchor.

21st The wind still blowing very hard we staid 'till one O'Clock when we again put out but made little progress. the wind still ahead, some of our people went ashore and brought a fine wild Turkey. Just passed Grave Creek 12 Miles below Wheeling. At dark passed Cappatana Creek, and in the night passed Fishing Creek.

22nd About 10 O'Clock A.M. passed Fish Creek, being the largest one we have passed, there is a beautifull level Bottom on each side, which, with the hills on hills, which seem to surround it, must render it truly delightfull in the summer season, when the woods are cloathed in their freshest verder. About 12 O'Clock got into the long reach it being 15 miles Long ten out of which you may see streght forward, without the interruption of those bends which are very frequently in this river, the diversity of Mountains & Vallys; and the Creeks that empty into the Ohio on both sides with a variety of Beatifull Islands in the river renders it one of the most Beautifull rivers in the World.

23rd The weather hazy but calm. Call'd up by the watch about 5 O'Clock A.M. to look at fort Muskingum. it being hazy could discover nothing but the lights at the fort and a vast body of cleared Land. at day break was agreeable Serenaded by the

drums and fifes at the fort beating and playing the revele. It
sounded very pleasing tho at a Considerable distance. at 10
O'Clock we got to the little Kanawha [River]. half past one got
to little Hocking river, at 4 we passed the big Hockhocking, a
little before dark got opposite Flyns old Station a Clever little
place on the Banks of the river with a large corn field on each
side. At dark came to Billwell a place founded by Mr. Tilton
late of Philad. Tis the most delightfull situation I have seen on
the Ohio, there are about a dozen very little Cabbins built on
the Banks in which families reside, with each a field of corn
and a garden, with a small fort to defend them from the Savages; this Settlement began about [2] years ago, distant from
fort Pitt 220 Miles on the Virginia shore.

24th Rose about 6 O'Clock to look at Latach falls which are very
rapid. in the last 24 hours have come seventy miles; had the
pleasure of seeing a doe and a Beutifull little fawn on the Indian shore at too great a distance to shoot at. The variety of
deer, ducks, Turkeys and geese with which this Country abounds
Keeps us allways on the look out, and adds, Much to the Beauty
of the scenes around us; between the hours of 6 & Eleven we
have seen 12 deer some feeding in the green patches that are on
the Bottoms, some drinking at the river side, while others at
the sight of us Bound through the woods with Amazing swift-
ness. As we rose from dinner we got to Campain [Captain]
Creek the place that General [Andrew] Lewis cross'd when he
went against the Indians, this last war. Just after dark came to
point pleasant, the moon shining very Bright gave us an imper-
fect view of the Beaties of this place. 'Tis Built on the Banks of
the Ohio, and at the point of the Kanawa River, at the point
stands the fort which, in the time of the American war was
Attacked by the Indians, but was defended, & they driven off
across the river by Gen'l Lewis, who owns a vast tract of Land
at this place, there are 12 or 15 houses, besides the fort and a
good deal of Cleared Land about it.[6] The last 24 Hours brought
us 85 Miles further on our voyage.

25th At 6 O'Clock A.M. got to the Guyandot river, but not being
called up lost the sight of it. you can't imagine how much I
regret the time lost in sleep. it deprives me of seeing so many of

the Beaties of nature. Just as we were going to Breakfast we came to a small river call'd the Indian Quindot; at 9 O'Clock came to Tweel pool river & soon after to Big sandy Creek on the other side of which the Kentucky lands begin. At 3 O'Clock passed little Sandy river 30 Miles Below big Sandy. Came to the Sciotto [River] in the Evening: Came 100 Miles this day.

26th At 4 O'Clock A.M. woke up by a hard gale of wind which continued untill Breakfast time, when we had both wind & tide in our favour: at ½ past 9 we came to the 3 Islands 12 Miles from Limestone; at ½ past one Hove in sight of Limestone; at 3 O'Clock Landed safe at that place, where we found Six boats, the place very Indifferent, the Landing the Best on the river; there are at this time about a 100 people on the Bank looking at us and enquiring for thier friends, we have been 9 days coming from McKees Island, three miles below Pittsburgh.

27th As soon as it was light my Brother set off for Lexington without company which is far from being safe, so great was his anxiety to see his Family [already in Kentucky].

28th Left Limestone at 9 O'Clock their being 30 odd boats at the landing the chief of which arrived since yesterday. 3 O'Clock, we got to a little town call'd Washington in the Evening where we stayed, and lodged at Mr. Woods from Philad.[7]

29th We left Washington before light, and got to May's Lick at 12 O'Clock.[8] left there and reached the north fork Where we encamped being 15 or 20 in Company, we had our bed at the fire, the night being very cold and the Howling of the wolves together with its being the most dangerous part of the road, Kept us from enjoying much repose that night.

29th Set at day light for the [Lower] Blue Licks [on the Licking River] which we reached at 12 O'Clock, took a walk to look at the salt works which were a great Curiosity to us. we travelled about seven miles further, and took took [*sic*] up our lodging for that night.

30th Was agreeably surprised by the Company of mr. Rees and mr. merril who came out to Meet us, but having taking a wrong road mis'd us the Evening before. We reached Grants Station that night, where we lodged, and on the first of Decemb'r arrived at Lexington, being escorted there by Mr. Gordon and

[his] Lady, who came out to Bryan's Station to meet us. we were politely receiv'd and welcomed by [sister-in-law] Mrs. Coburn.[9] We all staid at my Brothers 'till the 11th Dec when Betsy Rees left us to begin house Keeping, her house not being ready before.

Jany 1788 We Still continue at my Brothers and have altered our determination to go to Byckeye [?] farm, and mean to go down to south elk horn [creek] as soon as the place is ready.[10] Since I have been here I have been visited by the genteel people in the place and receiv'd several Invitations both in town & Country. the Society in this place is very agreeable and I flatter myself I shall see many happy days in this Country. Lexington is a clever little Town with a court house and Jail and some pretty good buildings in it Chief[ly] Log. my abode I have not seen yet, a description of which you shall have by and by.

29th I have this day reached south Elk horn, and am much pleased with it. tis a snug little Cabbin about 9 Mile from Lexington on a pretty Asscent surrounded by [maple] Sugar trees, a Beatifull pond a little distance from the house, with an excellent Spring not far from the door. I can assure you I have enjoyed more happiness the few days I have been here than I have experienced these four or five years past. I have my little family together. And [I] am in full expectations of seeing better days.

8

⽈

John May, 1788

John May was an affluent and ambitious Boston merchant who had in-vested in western lands through the Ohio Company of Associates, a group of New England investors who had obtained a large land grant from the U. S. Congress. He was about forty years old when he descended the Ohio River in 1788, bound for the company's huge land grant in the Northwest Territory. Believing that the surging western population offered good com-mercial prospects, May brought along a substantial quantity of merchan-dise and several employees. He made the new town of Marietta his headquarters, building a dwelling and a store, and planting crops.

May apparently kept the journal primarily to share with his wife, to whom he also wrote several letters during his western travels.[1] It begins with May's departure from his home in Boston and describes a "tedious and fatiguing journey of twenty-two days," to reach the vi-cinity of Pittsburgh.[2] The original journal also documents May's ac-tivities at Marietta and his return to Boston. The portion selected for the present volume includes only his voyage down the Ohio from Pittsburgh to Marietta. May was delayed near Pittsburgh for several days waiting for his wagon of merchandise to arrive and for a chance to meet with other officers of the Ohio Company who were also en route to the company lands. May took up lodgings opposite the Monongahela River from Pittsburgh late on May 7, 1788.[3]

Thursday, May 8: nothing extraordinary—my people catching fish and cooking and eating our chief business. I took a ramble this

Portrait by Christian Gullager of John May in his military uniform. Courtesy of the American Antiquarian Society.

afternoon, up a very high mountain from whence I could look up and down the rivers a long distance, and see every house in Pittsburgh, distinctly so as to count them. one Fredrick Bossman unfortunately fell out of a scow in plain sight of my window this afternoon, and was drowned—

Friday, May 9: large numbers of people raking and grappling after Poor Fredrick. all kinds of supersticious incantations and old traditions are recalld and used to find him—(he being Dutch). among others the following was much believed in by the

Waglopers [?]—they took a shirt which the drowned man last pulld off, put a loaf of good new bread wt 4 lbs into the shirt and tied it up at both ends—then carried it in a boat to near the place where he fell in, and put it afloat on the water—having previously put a line and togle to it—this they said would swim till it came over him and then sink—the bundle swam some time and then disappeared, but unfortunately for the concerned the line was not long enough, and when the loaf had fill'd with water and sunk the togle disappeard—by this means they lost their experiment not having another shirt charg'd with the same extraordinary virtues—this day I deliverd our horses to a Mr. Kirkendall (a miller near Elizabeths town) to keep, at the rate of 6 s[hillings] pr month. there we left our saddles bridles and mule straps—taking with me only portmants and holsters and pistols—we have had fish for dinner every day since our arrival—and tho there are seven stout hearty men of us—we have never been able to eat more than one fish at a meal[4]—

there are a number of Indians on the other side of the river—many of them are often over at Pittsburgh. I can not say that I am fond of them for, they are frightfully ugly, and a pack of thieves and beggars. one of their chiefs died day before yesterday. these Indians are pretty cross and some almost infernals. they killed a white man 3 days ago—I can obtain no news of General [Rufus] Putnam—only that he went down the river the 3d of April, and some say he arrived safe at Muskingum.[5] just now I receivd undoubted information that 3 large Kentucky boats, were captured by the Indians near the great Miamies, about 2th of March. In one of these was a Mr Pervience of Baltimore, to whom I have letters of recommendation from Gentlemen in Bal[timor]e.[6] this misfortune makes some of my men put on a serious face. however the first opportunity I mean to embark, and not come so far for nothing.

Saturday, May 10th. last night and this day very rainy, from the eastward nothing remarkable, only the rivers rising rapidly.

Sunday, May 11th. the river continues rising—some of the people gone crost the river to [a religious] meeting—4 Kentucky Boats gone past today—tis surprizing the number of these boats which have passd this spring. 200 are taken account of, and many go down in the night. we allow at the least computation 20 souls to a boat—and many bodies without souls.

Monday, May 12th. the river still rising. our men gone after wild turkies—have since returnd without any tho they saw near 20—

Tuesday, 13th. spent the greater part of the day in seeking for a boat to carry me and my effects down the river Ohio—dined at Captn Oharro's. had a very elegant dinner. drank tea at Colonel Butlers,[7] and then cross'd the river to my lodgings—some of my people crossd the Allagahana and brought home a quantity of wild asparagus.

Wednesday, 14th. I will here insert the route, with the different stages, from Baltimore to Pittsburgh by way of Simmerill's ferry[8]—

From Baltimore to Winchester [Md.]	30 miles
over the blue mountain	44
sideling Ridge	42
Foot of the Alleghana [Mountain]	31
Foot of laurel mountain	40
Ellerys	40
Monongahela	20
	___
	247

this day Major [Withrop] sargeant and myself busied ourselves in forming a plan for a house, to be built in the Muskingum settlement [Marietta]—our plan is 24 feet square Block house fashion—I think will at once answer the purpose of convenience Elegance and defence—Majr Sargeant and a Mr. Metcalf, dined with me to-day on gammon, etc. I had some wild asparagus, which we calld excellent—about 4 o'clock this afternoon General's [Josiah] Harmar and [Samuel Holden] Parson's and many other gentlemen crossd the river in the congress barge, row'd by 12 men in white uniform and caps.[9] this barge is 52 feet long. The Genl invited me to take a *row* with him up the Allagahana river which I gladly accepted—this is a rapid but beautiful river. the soil on each side very good. the General has been up [the Allegheny River] to Venango to visit the garrison there under the command of Captn Hart[10]— this post is one hundred and 60 miles from fort Pitt yet he came thence to this place in fifteen hours. we visited a farm of Colonel Butlers on the north side of the river. it is a very beautiful spot. We went to see some Indian Graves, at the head of which are poles fixed, daub'd with red. they are left out of the ground the height of the deceased. we visited the grave of old Rumtony—this is the name of the Chief who died a few days since. Rumtony in Indian is Warpole in english. he had this name on account of his exploits in war. we then returned to my quarters and refres'd ourselves with some good grog, which was the best I had to offer.

Thursday, May 15th Mrs. Hulin has been telling of a sovereign cure for worms in children. Take a half-pint of live angle-worms, put them in a thin linen bag, and sew them up. Then put them, while yet alive, on the child's stomach. There let them remain six hours; then remove them to the navel; there let them remain for the same time; then take them away, and the child will never be troubled with worms again. To cure the rheumatism, take the bark of upland or red willow; boil it in a quart of water; bathe the place affected with this decoction an hour, then put the bark, while warm to the place. This applied three times will work a cure for that kind of rheumatism which swells.[11]

at half past eleven General Harmar and others called in the barge, and invited me to go up the Monongahela river about 12 miles to view Braddocks field the place where that general was defeated in 1756.[12] This was a terrible engagement for the British, but a glorious one for the French and Indians which last creature composed great part of the army—the bone's of the slain are plenty on the ground at this day. I pickd up many of them which, were not much decayed altho tis more than 30 years since the battle. General Braddock gave them platoon firing sometimes advancing in solid columns. the Indians played quite a different game [shooting from cover] and tore him all to pieces—the savages were unmercifully cruel not sparing Man Woman or Child except one woman—A man who was with us was in the action. he says they left 800 dead on the field—we found a delightful spring of water here where we refreshed ourselves with Venison Ham and Crackers and Cool Grog—we went up the river at the rate of 4 Miles an hour, came back 8— some of my people gone to night to try to get me a wild turkey. hope they will speed well—mean time I go to rest—

Friday, May 16th. I am still waiting for a conveyance but my patience almost exhausted—Henry returnd this morning with a fine turkey which weighed 18 ½ lb. Frederick B. just now floated but left the shirt and provision behind him at 2 o clock AM. I crossd the river and dined at General [John] Gibson's in company with many other gentlemen. drank tea at Captn [John] Ervings and returnd home at 8 o clock.[13]

Saturday, May 17th. this morning went on foot 4 ½ miles into the country to view a grind stone quarry—found them difficult to get out therefore bought one ready made—and returnd home— had fine roast turkey and Asparagus for dinner. Several gentlemen dined with me—this afternoon I proved my [new] rifle gun—fir'd her 4 times and made excellent shot. 3 times out of 4 I put the ball within 2 inches of the spot which was the bigness of a dollar—the river has fallen as much as six feet in six days—the Yohogany [River] so low tis difficult coming down [it]—my hope is we shall start in a day or two.[14]

Sunday, May18th. this morning, about 8 o clock 2 lads brought to my quarters, a couple of fine perch weighing 40 lb. there have been some caught here weighing 24 lb. they are very handsome good fish something resembling a hadduck and much better eating. we kept Sunday at home—generally some of us reading—about 5 in the afternoon the Congress barge came over. brought Generals Harmar, Parsons, and a Mr. [James] White, member of Congress from N Carolina, and paid me an agreeable visit of an hour then returned [back to Fort Pitt].

Monday, May 19th. this day employed in making axe-helves, hough handles and sundry other matters in the tool way—purchased one bushel of salt at 20 s[hillings] and 2 bushel potatoes at 2 s, P.C. [Pennsylvania currency]. the river falling at the rate of 12 inches a day, and our boat not come yet—I must confess I feel very uneasy. this delay in the midst of sowing time makes me quite unhappy—notwithstanding I strive to act the Philosopher and my people dont know that I am in the least anxious.

I hope by doubling my dilligence to make up for this delay. this day a Mr. Metcalf, of Dedham [Massachusetts], came here wishing to get a passage down the river, and being destitute of provisions and money I took him into my family. at 6 o clock I accompanied a number of gentlemen up the hill opposite Pittsburgh. this mountain is 300 feet high and almost perpendicular and look's directly into fort Pitt—it abounds with good sea coal which they call here stone coal—

Tuesday, May 20th. our boat not arriv'd therefore we employ ourselves as well as we can—I have just taken a receipt for making bread—from Mrs Hulen—she makes ours and it is as good as any that ever I tasted. The method she takes is this—the evening before she takes a piece of leaven about as large as her hand—and if hard pounds it fine until it is pretty fine and mixes it in about 3 quarts of cold water. if it is not dry mix it without pounding. when thoroughly mixed let it stand and settle till morning. then turn off the water gently, and use the sediment the same as you would yeast. mix your dough with pretty warm water, and let it stand while your oven heats in which time it will rise sufficiently—then make up your loaves, and put them in baskets made purposely. let them stand a little while then set them in the oven. and if your heat is good you are sure of good bread.

Wednesday, May 21st. At 2 o clock PM. our boat hove in sight coming round the point, and in half an hour, was made fast at Pittsburgh. She is 42 feet long and twelve wide with a cover. She will carry a burthen of 45 tons, and draw only 2 ½ feet of water. it has raind steadily and fast for 24 hours which occasions the rivers rising as fast as it has fallen of late.

Thursday, May 22. dined to day on turtle, fish of various kinds soup etc.—a boy brought to my quarters this evening a sturgeon that was 4 ½ feet long. tis a very handsome and well made fish except the head which resembles a horse—he has no kind of bone in any part of his body—but calld a good eating fish—tho I have no mind to try him.

Friday, May 23. still continues to rain and the river to rise. the roads intolerable bad. almost impossible to move in them—this is most certainly is a different climate or a different world. the storms in N. England come from the N. East—these from the S. West, and these last as long as those notwithstanding the rain. I have put our baggage and stores on board the boat in expectation of going down the river tomorrow—at 5 o clock this afternoon Governor St. Clair arrivd at Pittsburg, he is not going down the river now but to returns to his family again[15] —we shall be under the necessity of paying him a formal visit to-morrow. all these things seem against me but no doubt are all for the best. I confess I am mov'd to this visit by two motives one the respect due to the Governor of the Western territory the other (a little selfish—) as we wish him to make the [town of] Muskingum the sea[t] of Government, and his place of his residence. if proper attention is paid to little matters as well as those of greater magnitude I have no doubt this important object may be obtain'd—supd to night on perch that were alive 5 minutes before they were in the pan.

Saturday, May 24 and Sunday, May 25. the rain increasing the river rising. I am tir'd of this world of clouds. tis not forty day's since I left Boston and only 8 I call Fair weather—I have had but little sleep since I have been here chiefly owing to the barking of dogs. I believe here are two dogs to one man—and at my quarters there are no less than seventeen of these wide throated son's of B——,—Pittsburg dogs begin the yell and our on this side echo back with great vehemence. at 11 o clock paid the visit to our Governor wrapped in my Khan sloper [?]. was most graciously received. tarried an hour—then embarked for Hulens. staid a quarter of an hour and took leave of this good family— and went down the river one mile in his Yawl our big boat having gone that distance some time before to get some boards and make a covering—at half past 12 o clock cast off our fast's and committed ourselves to the current of the Ohio—the scene was delightful—without wind or waves we invariably went more than 5 miles an hour. in 8 hours we arrived at little Beaver [Creek], a distance of 42 miles—this is the place General Parsons mentions in his journal, where he says a Mr. [illegible] raisd 600 bushels of corn from seven acres of land. I saw the man who says it is true but that the squirrels robd him of near 60 bushels—so that he did not receive but 540—here we tarried and hour and a half for the moon to rise—and set out again—in six hours arrivd at Cox's Fort, 33 miles.[16] here we tarried several hours and refreshed ourselves—here I bought 303 lb of beautiful Gammon, at 5 d pr lb. [pence per pound] also some red corn and potatoes—our passage thus far down the Ohio is too delightful to be described by me here where I have just room to swing my pen. we are pretty close crowded having 27 men on board—2 cows—2 Calfs—7 hogs—and 9 dogs besides 8 tons of baggage. at Cox's Fort are a number of settlers on very pretty farms, thou quite new it not having been settled more than 5 years. the soil is excellent the best I have seen. this territory is calld West Liberty—and belongs to Virginia.[17] dollars [exchange] at 6s[hillings]. we bought some butter here at 5 d. our seed-corn at 2 s. 6 d [two shillings and six pence], and barrel of pickeled Perch at 3 d per pound—took on board a quantity of excellent sallad—some plants etc. and embarke'd on board our ship again. Cox's fort is 111 miles from Muskingum. we went rapidly down the river and at halfpast 3, arriv'd at Wheeling a distance of 16 miles, and were kindly received by Mrs. Zane,—her Husband being gone to convention.[18] here we purchased some Cows and Calves and other necessaries. stay'd and drank tea and eat excellent bread butter and radish's and about 8 o clock committed ourselves to the waters of this beautiful river—it is true prospect before us was gloomy, a heavy cloud right ahead from whence darted flashes of lightning and the grumbling of thunder roar'd at a distance. it was so dark we could but just discern the black mountains on each side of us, except when the flashes came. then we star'd with all our eyes—it was my turn to stand at the helm this hour, and was relievd in time, but the scene was so grand, so many different noises, that I staid up 6 hours and kept the helm chief of the time, with one to look out and four to rowe. the rest slept sound and we mov'd on still as night—in the thick forests on either hand was the howling of wild beasts— the Owl hoop'd his dismal sound, and the screech Owl scream'd the other and a burst of thunder, all these things and many more kept my imagination awake—I must confess it was the grandest night I ever beheld—about two o clock the sky was serene and clear, the moon about 2 hours high—I then turned in and got some sleep—I have blended Satturday and Saturday night, Sunday and Sunday night, all together, as the whole seems but one long day. however, I will adopt the old plan—and make up my days work in the future.

Monday, May 26. I mean in some future page to give a description of the river Ohio, as I have made several observations which can not conveniently be inserted here—the Sun rose beautifully upon us this morning—and the prospect as pleasing as tis possible to conceive, it would require the pen of a Hervy to describe its beauties—every moment the scene changing Landscape rising beyond landscape constantly attracting the eye.[19] we passing by one beautiful Island after another, floating majestically down at the rate of 4 ½ [miles] an hour, thus moving on spying fresh wonders till 3 o clock, when we arrivd saftly on the banks of the delightful Muskingum [River].

Tuesday, May 27. slept on board last night and rose early this morning. spent the day in viewing and reconnoitering the spot where the City [Marietta] is to be built. find it answers the best descriptions I have ever heard of it. the situation delightfully agreeable, well calculated for an elegant City—the old [Indian] ruins are a masterly piece of work of great extent. how many ages since inhabited none can tell—the trees appear as ancient as the rest of the wilderness. I find many traces of [Indian] art in different places.[20]—our surveying buildings etc. in a very backward state. there appears to have but little done and much time and money spent—there are about 30 Indians now here—who appear very friendly but they are a set of creatures not to be trusted. General Putnam tells me there have been several parties here since his arrival—for my part I am not fond of them neither do I fear them. I dined to day with General Harmer, by invitation, had an elegant dinner. amongst the variety was allamode and boild fish Bear steak roast venison etc. excellent sacketosh [succotash] sallads and cramberry sauce. grog and wine after dinner. viewd Majr Doughty's gardens.[21] found them as well filled with necessaries and curiosities as most of the gardens in Boston—here I saw cotton growing in perfection also a fine nursery of apple and peach trees. purchas'd this eve a quarter of Bear @ 1 ½ d. and one side of venison at 1 d. a pound.

John May returned east to Baltimore in the spring of 1789, probably to establish business relations for his western enterprise. From there, he found an opportunity to sail to his home in Boston. He then made a second trip to Marietta. His industry at Marietta indicates a plan to relocate his family there, but he never did so. His grandson, Richard S. Edes, attributed this to the family's reluctance to leave Boston. Yet May also encountered the same problem that plagued all western merchants—a general lack of cash. When May returned to Marietta in 1789 with a fresh load of goods, he reported that the people "come plentily" and "want to se[e] everything." Although May's prices were judged "Cheep Verry cheap," May sold little, explaining that customers "go away without buying, because they have no money." Taking country produce instead of cash was undesirable, although May indicated he would have done so had there been a cash market for the produce farther downriver. The only item May thought fundable was ginseng. Had commercial prospects been more encouraging, the May family might have been induced to overcome their reluctance to move west. John May retained his Marietta property to the end of his life, but never returned.

9

Joel Watkins, 1789

Joel Watkins was born in 1758 in Prince Edward County, Virginia, to parents who had emigrated from England. A Revolutionary War veteran, he set out from Virginia for Kentucky in late April 1789. He escorted his brother-in-law John Walker, Walker's wife, and their small children. The group began their journey to the Ohio River by a secondary route, overland to the Kanawha River following what was known as the Lewis Trail or Old Indian Road. From a navigable point on the Kanawha River, Watkins's party descended to the Ohio River. After spending the summer in Kentucky while the Walkers got settled in their new home, Watkins returned home by the Wilderness Road.

The portion of Joel Watkins's journal presented here begins as the journal opens because Watkins included a rare declaration of his purpose. In Kentucky, most of his time was spent sick in bed. Watkins returned home via the Wilderness Road, and his account of that return journey provides a good comparison of what it was like to travel the two routes at this time. As Watkins discovered, the journey home involved many of the same sorts of dangers and hardships.

There is nothing perhaps that renders any Persons Travels in a New Country more entertaining than taking a Just memorandum of what ever appears new or curious, Curiosity which is the great Promoter of man kind both to Action and speculation—For several years Past, I have had the greatest Curiosity of seeing the much famed Country Kentucky but could never make Conveniency Comply with my Curiosity untill the much wish'd for Opportunity from which time I began my Journey and Jurnal being Tuesday the 28th of April in year 1789— After taking Leave of my old Cottage and parting with my Friends and Acquaintance I set from my mothers at Ten Oclock in the morning in Company of—David Walker and his family—fed our Horses and eat Diner at Ratclifs old place (being cool & cloudy) from thence we Continued on our way till we came within eight miles of New London Town where we incampt all night—

Wednesday the 29th April we Proceeded on our way and pass'd through the above Mentioned Town at or near Twelve Oclock (being the first time I saw the said Town and never was so far to the Westward before) fed our horses eat at Colo. Calloway's. From thence we moved onwards and pas'd through Liberty Town in Bedford County about sun set—set to a School house a mile from the said Town incampt. (being cool & cloudy)

April 30th Proceeded on our way from the said School House— (being clear and cool) to a place calld McClelins Gap in the Blue ridge where we fed horses and eat (near a Saw & Grist Mill at which place we concluded to go to Kentucky by Water being informed that it was much the best safest way—we had set out with an intention of going through the Wilderness) and and cross'd the Blue Ridge—directing our cours[e] after passing by Howards to the Great Kenhaway [Kanawha River] incampt at one West's within eleven miles of Botetourt Town.[1]—

May 1st Continued onwards & pass'd through the town Last mentioned at Twelve oclock and fed our Horses and eat ourselves at a Mill in sight of Botetourt Town—from thence we directed our course to the sweet springs Cross'd Catawber [Catawba] river and a Mountain Call'd Craigs Creek Mountain cross'd Craigs Creek nine miles west of the said and incampt in a [vacant] Cabbin on the Bank of the said Creek (Cloudy & like for rain).[2]

May 2d Continued our way to the sweet springs. pas'd a very rich Bottom on the said Creek. Crossed the said creek twice. we proseed up a fork of the said Creek to the foot of a Mountain (by some call'd Peters Mountain, by others Potts Creek Mountain) whereafter we prepared the pack horses for passing the said Mountains. We Cross'd the said [mountain] which took near three Hours—Being remarkable High—it commands a great Prospect for the Curious Traveller to the East & West which appears from the top of the said Mountain to be one Continued pile of Mountains—we stopt on the Bank of a small Creek that has its sourse in the said Mountain and fed the horses & eat Breakfast being much fateaged—From thence we Continued down the s[ai]d. run between two breaks of the said to Potts Creek which we Cross'd and encontered the sweet spring Mountain of Equal Hight to the former but not altogether so bad a way as waggons pass'd over the sd. Mountain with [loads of] Eight Hundred pounds—as was inform'd. NB [P.S.] after passing the Rich Bottom mentioned in page the 2d. our travels chief of the day were through a Prodigious Broken barren Country 'till we arrived at the sweet spring which is at the foot of the last mentioned Mountain—after viewing and tasting the said spring & water continued our way and incampt one mile below at the Red Spring—very sightly land below the sweet spring & about the Red spring—there being some as large Buckeye [trees] as I have ever seen growing—we had very Cool fine weather all day.

May 3d Sunday. being fine clear weather—we directed our course for Green Brier County Court house [modern Lewisburg, West Virginia] after travelling down a Creek (the name of which I forget) to a Certain Taggards [Tygerts] we left the said Creek and proceeded up Taggards Valley & Cross'd what they call in that part of the Country a Dr[a]ught (and in our parts a large Branch or Creek) Twenty Eight times which runs down the said Valley before we came to the head or Sourse which is in the Allegany Mountain. We cross'd the said Mountain about twelve oClock and Proceeded down another draught some distance. fed our Horses and Eat (Shaved and shifted myself [changed underclothes]) being the first Western Water I ever drank).[3] from thence we Continued our way down the said Draught and arrived at one Dicksons on Howards Creek (and came to a waggon road from Bottetourt Town to this place chiefly no more than a pathway and perhaps as rough and as bad [as] any in America)—From thence we proceeded down the said Creek to Green Brier River (I went to view the Sulphur spring [modern White Sulphur Springs, West Virginia] which is not far below Dicksons. their is Joining the sulphur spring a Very Rich Bottom on the sd. Creek equal in appearance to any I ever saw but Produces Corn but indifferent).[4] There appears Quantity of Sulphur emited from the said spring and may be smelt at One Hundred Yards distance—We forded Green Brier River at the Mouth of Howards Creek after sunset being from appearance between two and three Hundred yards wide and inCampt not far from the said river and could purchase no kind of Grain for our Horses—

May 4th, Monday being Cloudly & like for rain we proceeded for green Brier Court House where we arrived soon afterwards—it being three miles from our incampment—fed our Horses and Proseded for Kenhaway [River] being Eighty six measured Miles from the Court House to the Boat Yard on the Sd. River—for Ten or Twelve Miles West of the Court House there is some very rich Highland but very much spoilt with lime sinks[5] (Rained and Continued Cloudy). fed our Horses and Eat (We could purchase only Two Bushels of Corn in the Settlement, after Leaving the Court House to feed Our horses the above mentioned distance). we continued our way and incampt at a place cal'd the Meadows about seven Miles out of the inhabitants—(there is no settlements on the road more than twelve miles on the road west of the Court House) the land began to get Very Broken and poor after the above mentioned Distance from the Court House.

May 5th Tuesday Cloudy and began to rain—soon after we set out, which continued till near Twelve Oclock. Cross'd the Meadow river several times. very muddy way up the Meadow River. we left the said River and Pass'd through Very Poor Broken Highland and fed our Horses on a Branch and Eat. From thence we Proseeded onwards. pass'd through remarkable poor & Broken Land but very Heavy Timbored, with chestnut, Chestnut Oak,—Spanish Oak Poplar,—Maple etc. clear'd up very

Cool in the evening—we incampt on a Creek call[ed] 20 mile Creek

May 6th Wednesday clear with Frost. Lost nine of our horses 'till near eleven Oclock which was a very distressing Circumstance as our Provisions began to get very short and the way very bad. Everything that retarded Our Journey was feelingly distressing. after we had got our Horses again we prepared and set out on our way. pass'd Big Laurel Creek & Little Laurel Creek. from thence we cross'd several creeks that I did not know their names, cross'd Sowel Creek & a mountain by the same name. the Trees from near Liberty Town in Bedford County untill we came to the foot of Gauley Mountain had not put forth their Leaves but in particular places, when we arrived at the foot of the said Mountain which is Fifty seven miles West of Green Brier Court House the Trees began to exhibit another appearance as the woods began to appear green which continued to the Kenhaway. we pass'd over Gawley Mountain (which is as high and as Defiant of Access as any We had pass'd) and proseeded down rich land Creek between remarkable High narrows that makes from the said Mountain and incampt On the side of the sd. Creek—very bad way and much fateauged—Kept Centery [sentry] as there might very Probable be some danger of the Indians.

May 7th—Thursday Cloudy and Cool—We prepared and set out on our way down the Creek last above mentioned and cross'd it Forty Eight times and Came to Gawley River at the Mouth of the said Creek and Cross'd Gawley River three times which appeard to be One Hundred and fifty yards wide—from thence we cross'd another Creek by the name of Twenty Mile creek and came to Bell Creek which we Proseeded up to the head spring after Crossing it near as often as rich Land Creek we came to time mountain cal'd the Dividing Ridge and pass'd over the sd. Ridge—and struck the head of Morrises Creek and Proceed down the sd. Creek and arrived at the Kenhaway [River] at one hour besun to the Joy of the Company which was soon dampt by being inform'd that there was no Grain to be had nor any other Kind of Provision but such as were to be Kild by the Hunters. After we arrived at the Kenhaway we incampt at the Boat yard on the Bank of the River—We made

shift to get diner out of the Old fragments of our Provisions—
not knowing where we should get any More.

May 8th Friday Cloudy and warm, we continued at our incampment
and made shift to Purchace [a] half Bushel of Corn, which we
Parched and Pounded to meal, which we thickened water with
and sweeten'd with sugar and Drank for Diet making a Virtue
of necessity—Purchased a boat 30 feet by 8—being very indif-
ferently Built—

May 9th Saterday—after taking Breakfast we put the said Boat in
the Kenhaway [River]. Loaded it with our Package and
Proseeded down the River. pas'd the mouth of Paint Creek and
Kelly's Creek and Landed at another Boat Yard where we
unLoaded the said Boat and struck camp on the Bank of the
river three miles below the above mentioned Boat Yard where
we were Obliged to wait for the Building of another Boat,[6] 20
by 8 foot—Very bad water on the Kenhaway which may be
alluded to the great quantity of stone Coal—that lays in the
Mountains and in many Places in the Banks of Creeks and
Branches appear Very Visiable some of which I took out of the
Branches that had been washed there and Brought to Camp
which burnt as well as any I ever saw. The Kenhaway River is
very little over two Hundred and Twenty Yards wide. when we
were incampt we were now furnish'd with Corn for ourselves
but not any for our Horses while we Lay by—the Bread we eat
we pounded to meal in a Morter as there were no other nor
Better Conveniency in that Country. We Purchas'd a Poor she
Bear of a Hunter for which we paid Six shillings—began to
cloud up in the evening and rained in the night, was very agreeable to us as the River was very Low for the season and the
Higher the river the sooner we should make our Passage—

May 10th Sunday. Rained 'till 10 Oclock. shaved and shifted myself—
being very unwell since the morning after I arrived at the
Kenhaway. Breakfasted on Cat fish and Bear meat—we Continue at our last mentioned Camp being [a] very Disagreeable
place to me under our Circumstances. Morris the Owner of
the Boat yard showed me a mountain in sight of the sd. Boat
yard Which he inform'd me the Contents were chiefly Coal.

May 11th Monday Cloudy & Cool. we stil continue at our

incampmnent Call'd Kellys Landing. Our diet, chiefly consists [of] pounded meal, Hominy, some milk, and such meat as we can Purchace of Hunters, far from being of the Best Kind. I have made several meals on Diet—which—Nothing but necessity could have reduced me to but comply as chearfully as possible as we have not the smallest Prospect of being better Provided for 'till we can arrive at Lim[e]stone which is a very desirable Port to us at this time and for some time Past, continue with a bad Cold & sore throat—I cannot Help remarking here the workmen who are imploy'd by Morris in Building Boats have no better diet than what I have allready described and that but indiferenty cook'd and when the Hunter Imploy'd by the said Morris fails to Kill game they very contentedly feast on dry bread as corse as small Hominy. they are very diligent in Placing out their Hooks to take fish which is a very Comfortable dish among the said workmen—I have seen Cat fish taken at this Place which would measure five inches between the Eyes but very small to what has been taken in the Kenhaway—

May 12th Tuesday—cloudy and cool—being very unwell and continue at time same disagreable place—

May 13th Wednesday—cloudy and cool—and continue unwell with bad cough and cold—corn 4S[hillings] P[er] bushel Bear Meat 1S. Per £ [pound] Flower 36S. P. Hundred [weight]. Weighed myself and weighed 187 lb. being reduced 18 lb. in fifteen days. Launched our Boat about sun set that we have been under the necessity of waiting for.

May 14th Thursday had some showers of rain this Morning, but Loaded our Boats as Quick as Possible. Set out about Ten OClock which is a very agreeble departure to me from a Place Little better than a Prison—We soon Pass'd Cabin Creek and very bad shoals call'd by the same name—pass'd two other shoals not bad and several Poor cottages on the Bank of the river—came opposite the Burning Spring [a natural gas seepage]. Landed our Boats and Viewed the said spring—set it on fire which Burnt very rapidly—there is something remarkable in this spring there is no water that runs to it nor from it. Perceable boiling up in Lo[w] grounds of the river with far more forse than I ever saw a pot or any other vessel placed on the fire—from thence we Proseeded down the river to Elk river. pas'd Elk shoals about one Hour besun. The Country begins to appear much Leveller. The Mountains almost begins to disappear. The Buffalow fish make a very uncommon noise about the Boats. Continued down to cold river where we Landed about Two Hours in the night & Loged in a Town at Cold river consisting of four Cabbins without chimneys or any Doors. Call'd 30 Miles from Morris's to Cold river—

May 15th Friday Loaded our Boats again and set for Point Pleasant (Cloudy & Like for rain) being call'd Forty Eight Miles. pass'd Pokotalico [Pocataligo: "River of Fat Bison"] Creek & the shoals call'd the red House shoals. had several Hard showers of rain in the evening and this night being as Disagreable night as I ever saw—We arrived at the Point at Cock Crow—Point Pleasant [on the Ohio River] is a most Butiful Place and very rich Land—very few inhabitants and but indifferent Buildings. slept not more than an hour & half—

May 16th Saterday clear and cool and the wind began to rise. The Ohio began to rise very fast which made in favour of us here. I took Breakfast with Colo. [Daniel] Boon[e] and his family being the best I had Eaten for many days and never more fateagued in my life[7]—Here also I got myself my sister Walker & Children and my horse in Colo. Boons Boat—being determined so to do the first Opportunity that Offered—about ten Oclock we set out the Wind Blowing very High we cross'd the Ohio to get under the north shore in order to shun the Wind as much as Possible but before we could reach the said shore the wind continued to rise and the waves likewise that one of our boats not being rightly steared was very near Sinking which Obliged [us] to run to shore fasten our Boats & wait for the winds lying nearly in sight of the Point—and thought to be—dangerous of Indians—here we waited 'till near Two Oclock in the evening before the [wind] began to ly so that we could Venter out in the current of the Ohio—we push'd out about the above mentioned time. The waves being still very High and the wind Likewise we how[ev]er made very good way runing nearly as was supposs'd between—Eight & ten miles an Hour. we put to shore to get water and wait for our Horse Boat which we had nearly two miles the start of—(I ought to have mentioned a Remark that I made on the—Kenhaway River before I had left it but being an Oversight shall hint it here. (id est) being remarkable straight river and Keeping nearly the same width) we then onhitched again the wind lying and having a fine Current. we travelled very fast and agreeable. we fastened our small Boat to Boons not long before dark making no stop whatever. we Continued on our way all night. we past several rivers in the night and being a sleep I took no Memorandum of—especially the Big & Little sandy which makes in on the south side of the Ohio.

May 17th Sunday being a fine clear cool morning. We met a Keel Bottom Boat an[d] Canoe going from Limestone [upriver] to the Point who Hailed us and advised us to Keep near the Middle of the River as they had seen some skins hung out to dry which they supposed that it was Indians not far from the mouth of the Siotha [Scioto] River which we pass'd soon after about Ten O'clock which makes in on the north side of the Ohio. The wind began to rise and cloud up—The Country began now to appear very Broken. We Continued on our way nothing happening to—retard our Passage. we arrived Just above the Mouth of Limestone where we unloaded our Horse boat and fastened the others near the shore about two OClock in the morning for fear the Landing was too crowded with Boats and in case we should miss the right Landing it would be attended with some difficulty to Land—Here I can say that I never felt more satisfaction in finis[h]ing any undertaking than the Present, as a continual uneasiness had hung over me for many days—not so much on my own acct. as my sister and her young and tender family's not doing well.

May 18th Monday Morning Clear & Cool—Soon after Day Break we unhitched our Boats and Run to shore in the mouth of Limestone. unloaded our Boats—being very happy in not having any more Difficulties to incounter on the Ohio—Being informed that Thos. & Wm. Brooks Lived in the Town I took directions where to find the Sd. Mr. Brooks immediately being greatly fatigued and in want of refreshment—and as soon as the sd.

Mr. Brooks knew me he with the greatest civility entertain'd me—and insisted on my tarrying some time with him in town to recrute myself and Horse and as we both stood in great want—I thought [it] Proper to comply with said request—(Mr. Walker and family set out for Mr. Chiles's on the south of the Kentucky River in Mercer County—after making a short tarry in town) After taking a Very agreeable Breakfast with sd. Brooks I shaved and shifted myself—after taking nap of sleep I walked about Town and got Acquainted with several in Town—And Took bed with Mr. Brooks—This being the second night since left Home that have lain with my Breeches off.

May 19th Tuesday Cloudy & Cool—Continued in Town. Nothing very remarkable to be seen without the Boats Coming down the Ohio Loaded with Families—The Town which is erecting at Limestone is call'd Maysville & the Buildings of the sd. Town are very—indifferent chiefly Built with Boat Plank. The situation is on the Banks of the Ohio a Large—Mountain Making down very near the sd. River—Leaves not much ground for the sd. Town—the chief Groath Between the River and Mountain is Large Beach Trees—and the Land appears to be inclined to swamp very disagreable in wet weather—Grain very scarse in Town. Corn selling at [the high rate of] Four Shillings P Bushel—

May 20th Wednesday—Cloudy & Cool within Frost Contin[u]ed in Town making my stay chiefly at Mr. Brooks. Boats coming down the river as many as Eight in a Company Landed this morning.

May 21st Thursday—Cloudy & Cool—I set out soon after Sun rise from Limestone for Washington Town Four miles from Limestone without any Company the Land being very Broken & Appear'd Rich—from Limstone to Washington Very indifferent Buildings. The Houses were erected with hewn Logs[8]— Here I could get nothing to feed my Horse with—took Breakfast & Getting in Company with Two men and one Woman neither of which had any Kind of Arms except myself—We set out for Lexington—pas'd some very good Land on the Road after Leaving the Town of Washington but Broken—cross'd several forks of Licken [Licking] River and not seting down their names as I pass'd them I forgot them—after I came within Seven or Eight Miles of the Blue Lick the Land began to get Very Poor & Broken (we pass'd a small Lick Call'd Mays Lick which is [the] only Station on the Road after Leaving the settlements near Washington to the Blue Lick on the main fork of Licken Call'd Twenty Four Miles and Very dangerous for Indians—) especially near the road which may be Call'd a very great Curiosity from the sine of the Buffalows Travelling to and from the Blue Lick—I stopt at the Blue Lick and had my Horse fed and then Proceeded on our Way (after Viewing the said Lick and tasting the Water) The Land Continued Poor and Very Broken especially the road way for Ten Miles to the south of the Blue Licks after leaving the sd. Lick we had Twelve Miles to Travel before we came to any Settlements—we came to Very good Land of a Mulatto Soil after we had pass'd the above mentioned of poor Land The Land appearing As far as we Travelled this of the above mentioned Soil I put up at a House within a mile & half of Bourbon Town [modern Paris] Very much gaded with my days Travel[9]—

May 22d. Friday Cool with a Killing frost this Morning—Set out Very early (NB the inhabitants Just listing their corn ground & some not cleared their ground)—after crossing Two other forks of Licken Pass'd Bourbon Town which but small and the Land very Broken. here I left my Company and Continued on my way to Lexington without any Company passing some very good Land but to my great Surprise much more Broken than I expected to have seen from the—Carrecter of Kentucky—after Leaving Bourbon I had to ride 'till Twelve OClock before could get any Thing for myself or horse to eat—Which however I had the fortune to be supplied at Briants old Station on Elk Horn [Creek] from thence I proseed to Lexington pasing a Very Beautiful body of Land between the said Station and the Last Mentioned Town through which Town I past between one or two Oclock in the evening—and took directions for Mr. John Watkins's [a kinsman] fifteen miles below Lexington at which place I arrived not long before sun set—Passing very good Land in general this days Travel and of a Mulatto soil—after Acquainting Mr Watkins who I was he treated me very cival.

May 23d Saterday here I shall omit taking notice of the weather
for the Latter part of Jornal. Continued at Mr. Watkins's. went
in the evening to view a cave near the sd. Mr. Watkin's Plantation imploying myself in Perusing history.

*Joel Watkins, once he recovered his health, did his best to explore the
Kentucky settlements and assess their potential. He visited
Harrodsburg, Danville, Boonesborough, Bardstown, and Louisville
and looked with interest upon everything he passed. He attended court
days, weddings, and church services. But he had not come west with
an intention to settle (at least, not yet). On the first day of September,
perhaps by a previously made plan, Watkins turned his face eastward
and returned home.*

Sept 1st Tuesday—This being the mor[n]ing to turn my Course
Hom[e]ward took Breakfast With Walker & Settled my other
Little affairs—took Leave of my friends etc.—Set out for the
Crab Orchard in Company of Messrs. Cheatham & Asherd
who had Waited for my Company two days—in my way to
the Crab orchard the Land appear[e]d Very Well as to soil but
Broken for 9 or 10 miles and from thence to the Crab Orchard
the Land nearly divided between Rich and Poor—We pass'd
through what is Call'd the Bald Hills (i e) No groth on sd.
Hill's except Weeds for 100 Acres together. perhaps the cause
of these Places People have different Ideas [concerning whether
the high praise for Kentucky land was warranted]. We pas'd
Dickses River at Baylors Mill and from thence arrived at the
Crab orchd. at 2 hours besunn in the evening where we Were
informed that a Company had Set out Yearly and [early on] sd.
morning— (this morning being Cool & Somewhat Hasey —
wind blowing hard with some small showers of rain but not
[enough] to lay the dust in the road) after taking some grog
and no company meeting—we proseeded to a Certain Mr.
Ously's about 3 miles from the said Orchard crosing dixes River
in our way to the sd. Place—the Land Level about the Orchd.
some very rich and some very Poor which may be said to resemble manured Places in poor Land changing to Quick from
one to the other. The said Mr. Ousley lives on Lick creek oppo-

site the Mouth of Drak's Camp Creek. these are the Waters of Dickes river and very good Bottom Land and the sd. Creekes severall Bald hills in sight of Ousley's etc. here we put up and Contin[u]ed all night—

Sepr. 2d. Wednesday—cool and cloudy—we Continued at Ousleys all day without seeing anything worth Mentioning etc.

Sepr. 3d. Thursday—(cool and cloudy) we continued at the above mentioned Place 'till after diner. we then took the second trip to the Crab Orchd. in Order to start the next Morning etc. after paying for our Board etc. at sd. Place—we arrived at sd. Crab Orchard at 3 Oclk in the evening—Contd. All night at sd. Place Lodging in and old House—where there were the greatest Plenty of fleas—We had this evening at the sd. Place a Sermon Preach'd by a Baptist who was to be one of our Company the next day etc.

Sepr 4th Friday (clear cool Morning) after feding our horses and fixing ourselves we left the Last mentioned place and came to Inglishes [English's] Station 2 miles from last mentioned place at sun rise. the whole of our Company peraded for the Wilderness which consisted of 26 men & a negro boy Ten Guns and three Holster pistols and one or Two pocket Pistols—soon after sun rise we left Inglishes—Here I shall omit mentioning the soil of the Land I travel thro' Home any more than say it were in general Poor and Broken from last mentioned Place Home passing very Little good Land in comparison to the Poor—We pass'd the Waters of Dixes River taking the Middle trace and from thence fell on the Waters of Little Rockcastle River and from thence to Bigg Rockcastle. fed our Horses and Eat ourselves on a Branch of sd. River—from thence Proceeded onwards. pass'd the Hasel Patch as computed 7 or 8 miles and incampt soon after dark some distance from the Trace. fed our Horses and Placed out Sentories to the Number of 4 Men at a time—clouded up this evening but not to hide the sun.

Sepr 5th Saterday (clear Morning and Cool) We set out about an hour before day pasing several Waters none of our Company Knew 'till we came to Laurel river, Rich Land Creek, the Rackoon [Raccoon] Spring, and stinking creek near which is the flat Lick thro' which the [Indian] war Trace pases, we made several Halts to let our Horses grase and fed and eat ourselves on the Waters of Richland Creek—on the said creek saw Plenty of Fresh Buffalo sign and heard some run thro' a cane Brake—we—Came to the crosing of Cumberland River about an Hour after dark & cross'd incamping nearly on the Bank of said River—saw no Indians nor their sign these two days past—Cum[ber]land River is between Sixty and One 100 yard wide.

Sepr 6th Sunday (Large fog this morning etc.) Set out after day—Pasing Yellow Creek, and Cun[ber]land Mountain and arrived at the new Station two Miles East of sd. Mountain between 11 & 12 Oclock—pasing the sd. station some distance. fed Horses and Eat selves, from thence pas'd Martins Station 5 Miles and put up with an old man etc.

Sepr 7th Monday. (clear Morning) Set out very early. Proseeded onwards Crossing Powel[l]s River which [is] about 30 yds. Wide Waldens Ridge, Powels Mountain, and the Slippery Hill, pasing thro' the Devil's Race Path and down stock creek to—Clintch River, where we made a stop to Eat & feed our Horses, here four of us set out some time after dark to get where we might get some feed for our Horses what We had being Exhausted—We pass'd Clintch River which [is] between 50 & 80 Yds. wide as I cuputed pasing some time after dark. we prosd. up a Branch and from thence to Copper Creek Crossing the same—we came to Copper creek Ridge (which might be call'd a high Mountain) passing the same and Arriv'd at a house at Midnight Where we got fodder for our horses and a house to sleep in 'till Morning being very much Gaded—as well as my Horse etc.—On stock creek I saw what is called the Cucumber Tree with fruit growing on it nearly Red and somewhat Like a Cumr. in shape.

Sepr. 8th Tuesday—Cloudy & Raining some this morning. set out after sun rise—Passing thro' Clintch Mountain in the MacKason [Moccasin] Gap crossing a creek call'd MacKason—arrived at the North Fork of Holstein [Holston] River wh. is—about the size of Clintch—we from thence came to the Block House (which is in the—state of North Carolina & Sullivan County) at 9 Oclock. fed our Horses and Eat Breakft. here I might hint that it is thought there is some danger of Indians 'till a Person gets out of the MacKason gap. two others of our Company we left

the night Past coming up with us at the above mentioned Place—
from thence we prosd. to Fulgersons (within Twelve miles of
Washington Town, in Washington County in the sd. Town the
Court house Stands [modern Abingdon] and put up—Clearing
away about the time we got to the Block House etc.—The Rest
of the Company we Left Overtaking us at Fulgerson's. we all
Participated in our Lodging together, Rained this evening etc.

*Joel Watkins proceeded onward from the Block House. From thence
he was able to find regular lodging and food, but the weather was
cool and rainy. He reached his mother's home on September 14.*

Part Three

A New Era of Peace

By the 1790s, the westward stream of travelers had yet to level off. Indian danger continued during the early part of the decade, forcing the national government to launch military campaigns in both the northwest and southwest. As a consequence, Indian resistance to trans-Appalachian migration virtually ended by 1795. Natural obstacles remained substantial, but the Wilderness Road was easier to follow, and the boatbuilding industry for Ohio River emigrants was better established. Moreover, the extent of uninhabited wilderness had contracted. Small settlements along both routes offered migrants welcome way stations. Crossing the Allegheny Mountains had changed significantly from two decades earlier.

10

Moses Austin, 1796

Moses Austin came from a family of New England merchants. A branch of the family business was located in Richmond, Virginia, and included an important lead mine in southwestern Virginia. Austin supervised this operation, a key industry during the Revolution. Unfortunately, by the closing years of the eighteenth century, the mines were yielding less ore. Austin therefore became interested in the mines located in the vicinity of St. Genevieve on the western shore of the Mississippi River. In 1798, two years after this journey, he removed with his family to this district, then part of Spanish Louisiana. He was the father of Stephen Austin of Texas fame. This selection opens with Austin's departure from the tiny settlement named Austinville at the Virginia lead mines.

On the 8. day of Decemb'r 1796 in the Evening I left Austin Ville on Hors Back takeing Jos. Bell as an assistant and a Mule to Pack my baggage and that night went to Mr. James Campbells who on the morning of the 9 started with me for Kentuckey. Nothing of note took place from Mr Campbells to Capt Craggs where we arrived on the 11th at Eve furnishing ourselves with Blankets &c at [the town of] Abington as we pass.d.
the Morning of the 12 I left Capt Cragg, in Companey with a Mr Wills from Richmond bound to Nashvill in the State of Tennessee. that night I arriv.d at the Block Hous, so Call.d from

being some years past us.d as such but at this time in the hands
of Colo. Anderson, at whose Hous, it was Expected good
accomedations, could be had, more so in Consequence of his
being a friend of Mr Campbells. however, it was with great
Trouble, that he admited us under his Roof, or would allow us
any thing for our Horses and Mules. Colo. Andersons is 36
Miles from Capt Craggs, which, I left by Day light, takeing the
road Through Powells Valle. at this place I parted with Mr
Wills who took the road for Cumberland [in Tennessee] Which
fork.d at this place. the road being Bad and the weather uncommonly Cold, I found it was with hard Traveling that we
reach.d the foot of Wallons ridge that Night. from Andersons,
to Benedict Yancy's is 34 Miles and an uncommon Mount's
road. Fifteen Miles from the Block Hous is Clynch mountain
and the river of the same name. I the same Day pass.d number
of Mountains and ridges, the most considerable of which are
Copper Creek Powells and Wallons, as also several large Creeks
and Powells River. Mr Yancys is the enterence into Powells
Valley. a Wagon road has lately been Open.d into, and Down
the Valley, and Notwithstanding great panes and Expence, the
passage is so bad that at maney of the mountains the waggoners
are oblig.d to lock all the wheels and make fast a Trunk of Tree
Forty feet long to the back of the waggon to prevent it from
Pressing on the Horses. in this manner many waggons have
pass.d on to Kentuckey.

It was late in the Evening of the 13th that I arriv.d at the Hous of
this Mr Yancys, and the badness of the weather, had made Me
Determin, not to go any Further, being then 8 OClock and
snowing fast, however I found it was not so Easy a matter to
bring the old Man and Woman to think as I did; For when I
demand.d or rather request.d leave to stay, they absolutely
refus.d me, saying, that we could go to a Hous six miles Down
the Valley. Finding moderate words would not answer I plainly
told Mr Yancy that I should not go any further, and that stay I
would. Old Mrs Yancy had much to say about the liberties
some Men take, and I replied by observing the Humanity of
Others, and so end.d our dispute. our Horse was strip.d and
some Corn and Fodder obtaind. we soon Found ways and means

to make the rough ways smooth, and takeing out our Provision Bag made a good supper, after which placeing our Blanketts on the Floor with our feet to the fire I sleep.d well.

The 14 we start.d from Mr Yancys and the Day being bad with snow and rain, we stop.d at a Mr Ewings five miles Below Lee [County] Court Hous and Ten from Mr Yancys. at Mr Ewing we reced the *welcome* of Mr and Mrs Ewing at whos Hous we staid, untill the morning of the 15, when after being furnish.d with Every thing we wanted and a Good Piece of Beef to take with us, we took leave of Mr and Mrs Ewing and family and that Night about Sun down Arriv.d at Cumberland Mountain. About ½ a Mile before you pass this mountain you come into the road from Hawkins [County, Tennessee] Courtt Hous and Knox Vill, which is said to be the Best road. after passing the Mountain which we did this Night, we stop.d a[t] Mrs. Davis's who keeps Tavern Down the mountain, and met with very good accomedations. Powells Vally has lately been made a County by the name of Lee, takeing all the Country from Washington County to the Kentucky line. The Court Hous is About Thirty miles up the Vally from the pass of Cumberland mountain at which place is a Small Town of Six or Ten Houses and Two Stores. Powells Vally is, I am inform.d about six miles Broad and 60 in length. its good land but so Inclose.d with Mount'ns that it will be always Difficult to Enter with waggons. When the Vally becomes well improv.d it will be an Agreeable place but at this time its thinly settled and Small farms.

On the 16th by Day light our Horses being ready we took our leave of Mrs Davis, who I must take the liberty to say may be Justly call Cap'n Molly of Cumberland Mountain, for she Fully Commands this passage to the New World. She soon took the freedom to tell me she was a Come by chance her mother she knew little of and her Father less. as to herself she said pleasure was the onely thing she had in View; and that She had her Ideas of life and its injoyments &c &c. a Mr Hay from Knox Ville Joined us this Day. the weather still continued Cold and the road which had been much broak up was now hard frozen. however we arrived by Dark at Ballingers Tavern miles from Cumberland Mount'n at this place I meet with a number of

Gentl'n from Kentucky and a Doct Rosse from the Illinois with whome I had much conversation respecting that Country. our Horses suffer.d this Night being Oblig.d to make them fast to a Tree and feed them on Cane, but the Accomedations for ourselves was good Considering the Newness of the place.

the 17 leaving Ballingers we Travel.d that Day over an unpleasant road passing several large waters and Cumberland River. we came at Night to a small Hutt on Little Rock Castle [River] 30 miles from Richland or Ballingers. at this Place our Accomedations was abominable bad. the hous was about 12 feet square and the Night which was distressingly Cold oblig.d all that was stop.d at the Place to take shelter in the Hutt, in all women and Children include.d 17 in Number,—nor can a more filthy place be immagin.d. this Night our Horses Suffer.d much. a few Oats was all that the place afford.d. after takeing a supper from our Provision Bagg we took some rest on our Blanketts and at Day light, started on our Journey and in the Evening arriv.d at the Crab Orchard and took up our quarters at a Mr Davis, 23 Miles from Rock Castle, makeing in all 90 miles from Cumberland Mountain to the Crab Orchard.

The Crab Orchard, has long been a place of Note and it being the grand Gateway into Kentucky I expected to have found a Hous of Entertainment at which a Traveller could have recruted himself but I was disappointed. the accomedations at Davis.s is bad and nothing agreeable in or about the place. The Country from Cumberland *Mountn.* to Langfords which is Ten Miles before you come to the Crab Orchard, and which is know[n] by the Wilderness, is a Disagreeable broken Mounto. Country but some good lands, and will be in time Sufficiently settled to furnish Travellers, but can Never be a desireable Country. Its now settled with 18 families, who are but a remove from Indians in their manners or moreals. Much Work with many Bridgs may make a good road, but its not to be expected for many years altho the road has been lately opend for waggons and much work don on it. much more must be don to make it Tolerable.

on the 16 [sic] between Cumberland Mounto. and Ballangers I pass.d Capt Sparks with a Company of United States Troops from Fort Detroit on his way to Knox Ville About 100 in all, the Troops made a good apperence, was well Cloth.d. and good-looking men. I cannot omitt Noticeing the many Distress.d families I pass.d in the Wilderness nor can any thing be more distressing to a man of feeling than to see woman and Children in the Month of Decembr Travelling a Wilderness Through Ice and Snow passing large rivers and Creeks without Shoe or Stocking, and barely as maney raggs as covers their Nakedness, with out money or provisions except what the Wilderness affords. the Situation of such can better be Imagined then discribed. to say they are poor is but faintly express'g there Situation,—life *What is it, or What can it give,* to make Compensation for such accumulated Misery. Ask these Pilgrims what they expect when they git to Kentuckey the Answer is Land. have you any. No, but I expect I can git it. have you anything to pay for land. No. did you Ever see the Country. No but Every Body says its good land. can any thing be more Absurd than the Conduct of man, here is hundreds Travelling hundreds of Miles, they Know not for what Nor Whither, except its to Kentucky, passing land almost as good and easy obtain.d, the Proprietors of which would gladly give on any terms, but it will not do its not Kentuckey its not the Promis.d land its not the goodly inheratence the Land of Milk and Honey. and when arriv.d at this Heaven in Idea what do they find? a goodly land I will allow but to them forbiden Land. exausted and worn down with distress and disappointment they are at last Oblig.d to become hewers of wood and Drawers of water.

19 I arrived in companey with Mr James Campbell at Mr C. Campbells 12 Miles from the Crab Orchard who reced us Kindly, and at whose Hous I stade untill the 20th the Weather beeing so Cold as to render it almost impossible to Travel. Mr Hay part[ed] with me this Day takeing the road for Lexington and Jos. Bell went to a little Town Call.d Stanford.[1]

21 I took leave of Mr C. Campbell and famely to whome I am much indebted for there politeness and about Twelve arriv. d at the Town of Stanford where I meet with a Number of the former inhabitents of New River and that Night stay.d with a Mr Nath[a]n Forbus. The Town of Stanford is the County Town of Lincorn [Lincoln] and it beeing Court Day I had an

oppertunity of seeing a Number of Gentlm and Isaac Shelby late Gov[erno]r to whome I had letters [of introduction].[2] little can be said in favour of the Town of Stanford. it Contins about 20 Hous of Loggs excep a Brick and Stone Hous, has Three small Stores a Tan Yard and Four Taverns, the Land in and about the Town is good and some large improvements.

22. I arriv.d about 12 0 Clock at the seet of Isaac Shelby, Esqr with whome I dined and from whome I reciv.d letters [of introduction] to M' Argotee at Frankford [Frankfort] and that night reach.d the Town of Danvill. Govr Shelby has a large and well improvd farm a plain but neet Stone Hous and is said to be a man of Great Welth. the Town of Danvill is 12 Miles from Stanford but 20 the way I went. I stay.d at a Mr Smyths Tavern and on the Morning I left Danvill for Harrodsburg, 13 Miles from Danvill at which place I arriv.d on the same Day at 12 OClock. Danvill is a well laid out place and the streets are Broad crossing each Other at right angles Situated on a level spot of ground, but badly Built Contaning about 36 Houses the most of which are loggs. the lands Near Danvill are good and when well improv.d will be an agreeable Country.

I found the 23rd so Cold that I Concluded to stay the remander of the Day a[t] Harrodsburg and on the 24. leaveing Harrodsburg I arriv.d at Frankford that Evening being 31 Miles. Harrodsburg is a small place said to be the oldest place in the State is Elevated something above the surrounding Country and there beeing a large quantity of Land Clear.d appeard more pleasent then any place I see in the State. the Houses are about 20 in Number and Mostly of Stone. the Court Hous is of Stone and a good building. Harrodsburg is the County Town of Murcer [Mercer]. the Country from Danvill to Frankford is level but Not good Land as I expected. Frankford is the Seet of [the state] Government and is Situated on the Kentuckey River which at this place is about 160 Yards over. the Town stands on a flat spott of ground and has some good Buildings. the State Hous is a good Convenient Hous but not Elegant. the Other Publick Buildings are not worth Notice. the Town Contains about 6o Houses in all Eight of which are Brick and Stone. Whicker keeps the best Tavern and the accomedations are good.

The situation of Frankford cannot be call.d pleaseing it beeing incircled with high nobs and Hills at Every point, its the County Town of Frankling [Franklin]. Mr. Argotee beeing from home I had to wate his return and on the 27 I finish.d my business with him takeing letters [of introduction] to Monsieur Zeno Trudeau Commandant of St. Louis in the [Spanish] province of Louisiana. passing the Kentuckey river on the ice I took the road for Louis Ville at which place I arriv.d on the Evening of the 28. the Night of the 27 I lodg.d at a small Town called Shelby [modern Shelbyville] which place I shall always remember, from the uncommon behavior of the LandLady Mrs. C—. the Town of Shelby is small and like all the Towns in Kentuckey badly built. about 20 Houses and Two Stores, the Land from Shelby to the Ohio is not of the Best nor is the Country as well Settled as I expect.d. in short it may be call.d a Wilderness. From Frankford to the Town of LouisVille is 52 Mile and the Country uncommonly level. The Ohio is a Noble River and its almost impossible to bring yourself to beleave You are so far from the *Atlantic*. Louis Ville is the County Town of Jefferson is situated immediately on Banks of the Ohio. the situation is beautiful and I think this place may in time be of Consequence altho its now an inconsiderable V[i]llage. Louis Ville has about 30 Houses but there is not an Elegant Hous in the place. the Court Hous is of Stone and built with some Taste. at this place I see a Number of Indians from the Nations over the Ohio, Piankishas Delawares and Wyatenas. Notwithstanding Louis Ville is the landing place of all Boats that Come Down the Ohio and Bound to any place below the Falls in consequence of which there is a great resort of Companey yit there is Not a Tavern in the place that deserves a better name than that of Grog Shop. Louis Ville by nature is beautifull but the handy work of Man has insted of improving destroy.d the works of Nature and made it a detestable place.

Austin proceeded to Vincennes in future Indiana, a town of some 200 houses, and then toward his ultimate destination. The winter weather made the trip, sometimes in snow three feet deep, extremely difficult.

After much struggle, Austin reached St. Louis and then went north to visit the lead-mining district near St. Genevieve, where he settled a few years later. He returned to Austinville via Natchez, Nashville, and Knoxville.

11

Francis Baily, 1796

Englishman Francis Baily was twenty-two years old when he decided to make an extended tour of the young United States. He embarked for New York in 1795, but the ship was driven off course by storms and landed in Antigua. After spending a short time there, Baily sailed to Norfolk, Virginia, quickly proceeding north through Baltimore and Philadelphia to New York. City life being somewhat familiar, Baily devoted little space to this period in his journal. The core of his journal, published in England posthumously, is the account of his voyage from Pittsburgh down the Ohio River, disembarking at several points for closer observation, to New Orleans. He then returned overland through Natchez and Knoxville to the seaboard states. At several points he inserted references to other works, such as that of Andrew Ellicot (included later in this volume), which was not published until 1803. These references indicate that Baily enhanced his original journal after returning home, adding information for the benefit of his British readership.[1]

This selection follows Baily's unusually difficult descent of the Ohio from Pittsburgh to the Cincinnati area. Although western travel was less dangerous by 1796, his experiences illustrate that nature remained untamed. Baily's misfortune, however, is fortunate for posterity. The delays Baily suffered allowed him the leisure to compose detailed and extremely rich journal entries.

October 17th, 1796 . . . Pittsburgh is pleasantly situated at the junction of the Monongahela and Allegany rivers; the union of which two forms the beautiful river Ohio. The southern bank of the Monongahela is near 300 feet high, and almost perpendicular; the top of which subsides into a level country. The town, which is situated in north latitude 40° 25' 50" is built on a beautiful plain at the point of the two rivers, which plain extends a considerable way along the banks of both, and at a small distance from them is terminated by the high country. This appearance is very common in the western parts of America, and arises from the general surface of the ground being so much higher than the beds of the rivers. Innumerable excavations are formed by every little running stream, which disfigure the face of the country very much.

The town, which contains about four hundred houses, is laid out nearly on Penn's plan, though the streets do not cross each other at right angles; but those which are near the river are so formed as to run parallel to it.[2] It was first settled about 1760, and is famous for being the subject of dispute between France and England in 1756, and in part hastened the rupture between the two countries. Louisiana and Canada being then in the hands of the French, they wished to unite these two countries by a chain of forts, and with that view they surprised and took a fortified post which the Virginians had established on the forks of these rivers: here they erected a fort, which was called Fort Du Quesne. To reduce this, and expel the French from this part of America, was the object of General Braddock, whose defeat is well known to every one conversant with the history of this period. [George] Washington had been sent to attack this post some months prior to this, but his attempts were unsuccessful. On the approach, however, of General Forbes, in 1758, the French retreated down the Ohio to their settlements on the Mississippi, and left him in possession of place, the name of which he changed to Fort Pitt, in honour of the Premier.[3] The English demolished the block fort which the French had erected, and raised a regular fortification at the point of the town, consisting of five bastions, with a ravelin facing the Ohio, all of which is now in ruins; for, though a fort here was absolutely necessary at the first settling of the country, and is still kept up, yet it is nothing more than a *block* fort. These *block* forts are laid out upon the same principles as other forts, but instead of having either a glacis, covered way ditch, rampart, or parapet, they consist of nothing more than very thick planks of wood, fourteen or fifteen feet high, set upright in the ground, with holes bored in them at certain distances, through which the garrison present their muskets; and they are much better calculated for a defence against *Indians,* than the European method of constructing them, as well as being less expensive.

From the period we have been mentioning to the close of the American war, the inhabitants of this country had to settle their plantations and reap the produce of them amidst continual attacks of the Indians, who never ceased, night or day, to harass and distress them. Every farm-house was then a fortification, and was so built, that it might be defended against the Indians, let them attack on which side soever they chose. The upper part of the house projected considerably beyond the lower, and holes were bored in the floor, through which they might fire down upon the enemy, if they should approach to set fire to the house. These houses are called block-houses, and are still to be seen in many parts of the country, a monument of usurpation on the one hand, and of predatory warfare on the other. A person in travelling this country will often hear the sad story of sons and daughters being shot within a few yards of the house, whilst following the plough or tending the cattle, by Indians, who perhaps had been lying in wait for weeks for an opportunity of destroying the encroachers on their property. Truly may this country be said to have been established in blood, as there are very few of the first settlers but have felt the effects of Indian revenge in the loss of some part of their family. But to return to Pittsburgh.

Soon after the close of the American war, when the United States found itself at peace with all the Indian tribes, this town, from its peculiar situation, being the depot for every thing passing down the Ohio, (the navigation of which had been considerably increased since the infant state of Kentucky had been settled,) began to rise considerably in importance; and at present may challenge any of the western counties of Pennsylvania for its size and commerce. Through this town is the great channel of emigration to those countries lying on each side of the Ohio, between the Wabash and Tenessee rivers: and here, after coming in shoals across the Allegany mountains, either in waggons or afoot, they stop to supply themselves with boats to carry them down the river. These boats, which may be more properly termed rafts, are built without one particle of iron in their composition; they are generally from 30 to 40 feet long, and about 12 feet broad, and consist of a framework fastened together with wooden pins, which constitutes the bottom of the boat, and to this is fastened a flooring, which is well calked to prevent leaking; the sides are about breast high, and made of thin plank; and sometimes there is a rude kind of covering, *intended* to keep the rain out. These boats draw very little water, not enough to sink the framework[4] at the bottom under the water, and are generally furnished with a pair of oars, not so much to expedite their progress, as to keep them from the shore when they are driven towards it by the current; and there is a pole projecting from the stern, to steer them with. When they are going down the stream, it is immaterial which part goes foremost; and their whole appearance is not much unlike a large box floating down with the current. The article of boat-building forms one of the chief employments of this town. The common charge for boats of this kind is a dollar, and sometimes 1 ¼ dollars, for 12 square feet, that is, as to her bottom: thus a boat 40 feet long and 12 feet wide would cost 40 dollars; at 1 dollar per 12 feet. Ironmongery forms another considerable article of commerce in this town, but it is chiefly of the coarser sort, such as is used for mills, ploughs, and the various articles of husbandry. There is a great quantity of iron near this place, which is brought down the Monongahela river; and as to coal, it abounds very much all over the western country, and lies so near the surface of the ground, that the waggon wheels often cut into it on the roads: it is of an excellent quality, and extends for *some hundred miles* over the country. The inhabitants lay it in at about 3 [shillings] ½ [pence]d sterling per bushel.

The waggons which come over the Allegany mountains from the Atlantic states, (bringing dry goods and foreign manufactures for the use of the back-country men,) return from this place generally empty; though sometimes they are laden with deer and bear skins and beaver furs, which are brought in by the hunters, and sometimes by the Indians, and exchanged at the stores for such articles as they may stand in need of.

At the tavern where I put up, there was a young Indian who was on his return to his own tribe; he came in with the army of the United States at the close of [the] last war with the Indians, when they were defeated by General Wayne [at Fallen Timbers in 1794], in which action his father and uncle bore a conspicuous part, and in which they were the leading men. I remembered seeing him about a twelvemonth back at Philadelphia, when he first arrived: he talked English very well, but was very shy when any one spoke to him, as all the Indians are, though upon a better acquaintance he would be facetious, and sometimes would be ridiculously antic. He mentioned a fact, which is scarcely credible, but which was confirmed by several officers then in the house, and who were in the engagement:—that immediately on the motion of General Wayne's army to attack the Indians, he ran with all the haste imaginable, to give his countrymen the first notice of their approach, and absolutely passed over the distance of ninety miles in twenty-four hours! To however great lengths the powers of the body or the mind may be carried, yet this seems to stagger our faith, and to cause us to doubt whether he might not be deceived with respect to the distance.

The width of the Monongahela river at its junction with the Allegany is 1,089 feet; and the Allegany is nearly the same width. When I arrived there the water was so low that cattle waded across both rivers; though, when the rains come down, they nearly overflow the banks, which are about thirty feet high. It having been very dry for some weeks prior to our arrival there, we were obliged to wait some time before the river was high enough for us to venture down; for in low water on the Ohio, there are a number of rocky shoals which extend the whole width of the river, and over which the water is driven with great impetuosity, causing it to ruffle and roar like a milltail, which makes it dangerous for boats going down at this season of the year, till the water has risen high enough to cover these obstructions. These places, which are very numerous till you arrive at Tart's Rapids, are called by the inhabitants "Riffles;" I suppose, a corruption from the word "ruffle," as the water is violently agitated in those parts.

The principal part of the inhabitants in this place are either store-keepers or engaged in some handicraft. The houses (which are mostly of wood) are generally well built for a new-settled place; though they have lately taken to building them with brick, of which there are great quantities made near the town. A new town-hall which they were building will add much to the beauty of the place.

M. Laches [La Chaise],[5] a general in the French army, who boarded in the same house with us, intending to proceed down the Ohio in a small skiff which he had purchased, we agreed to go down a little way with him, to see whether the river was deep enough to take our boat down or not. Accordingly, about twelve o'clock we started, and, I must confess, I felt myself highly delighted on first entering this beautiful stream: a stream which, after running near 1500 miles, and receiving several others almost as large as itself, empties itself into another still larger, where it is considered as a *mere rivulet*.

We had not proceeded above two or three miles, before we came to one of those riffles I have been speaking of, and just above which I observed several boats made fast to the shore, fearing to venture over it. We made towards that part of the river where the commotion[6] was the greatest, and, our skiff being light and narrow, we were carried through without sustaining any accident. It is impossible to pass these places without some momentary sensations, which such a conflict of the rocks and waters naturally excite; otherwise, the rapidity of the motion with which you are carried through the stream is far from being unpleasant; and, under the guidance of a person who understands the navigation of the river, you may wholly divest yourself of fear for your personal safety.

We proceeded about thirteen or fourteen miles down the river, having passed over six of these riffles in so short a distance; and here we put ashore about an hour before sunset, at a farm-house we saw on the banks. Here we stopped, intending to pass the night; and accordingly we went a little way into the woods, and killed some squirrels for our supper, and bringing them home, the old gentleman of the mansion, whose name was Woollery, furnished us with some turnips, pumpkins, and other necessaries, and we soon had a dish of excellent soup. Whilst this was getting ready, the general (who had brought his violin with him, on which he plays exceedingly well) struck up a tune, which soon brought in the old gentleman's family, among whom were three or four pretty daughters. Seeing such a party collected together, a dance was immediately thought of, and a dance was soon commenced, not much in the style either of Bath or Paris, but sufficiently pleasing to drive away the gloom inspired by the surrounding wilderness, and to banish all idea of separation from civilized society.

The general was a very pleasant man, and kept us agreeably entertained the whole evening. After supper, some blankets were spread on the floor before the fire, (the only bedding which is to be expected in this part of the country; and not always *that,* unless you take it with you), and we all laid down and slept very soundly till morning. As it was the first time that I had ever experienced this new kind of *couch,* it was some time before I could compose myself to sleep; but so far does custom influence our dispositions and conduct, that it will be seen in the sequel I have often preferred this mode of sleeping when I have had the choice of a feather bed. In the morning, to our regret, we parted with the general, he proceeding down the river, and we endeavouring to make the shortest way by land through the woods to Pittsburgh. We took some breakfast before we started, and then, loading our guns, we struck into the woods, and in the afternoon we found ourselves upon the banks of the river, about three miles below Pittsburgh, where we had observed the boats the day before. We went aboard one of them, and, getting some refreshment, reached town in the evening, having in the former part of our route missed our road, which carried us some miles out of our way.

Thursday, November 24th, 1796.—The river having risen within these few days, in consequence of some rain which had lately fallen, we started from Pittsburgh this afternoon, about three o'clock; however, we did not proceed above four miles down, as the stream was very slow, and we were afraid to venture in the night in consequence of the riffles, which were not completely covered; therefore, seeing some other boats near the shore, we made towards them, and joined them for that evening. I thought it a very pleasant sight to see so many boats floating down the stream at the same period. The late dry weather had prevented all navigation for some time, and the vast body of emigrants and storekeepers who were bound to Kentucky made them take this advantage of proceeding on their voyage. Accordingly, as soon as the river was reported to be navigable, all the *Kentucky boats* (as this flat-bottomed craft is termed) were in motion, and eager to pursue their route. As the gentleman who travelled with me was going to establish a settlement on the Miami river, he had got every article that he thought would be necessary in his new habitation; therefore, we were not so badly accommodated as some of the boats were, who went sometimes most miserably supplied, with scarcely a covering to the boat or a blanket to lie down on, and barely a pot or a kettle to dress what provisions they might chance to meet with. We had laid in a sufficient quantity of beef, mutton, flour, bacon, and what other provisions we thought we might want, and we had three or four good feather beds and plenty of bedding; and as it was very cold weather, we stopped every crevice we conveniently could, and made ourselves a very comfortable habitation and as we might now and then meet with a plantation on the river side, where we might get milk, or eggs, or butter, we had not the prospect of a very unpleasant voyage, especially as we expected to reach our place of destination before the winter set in. However, our views were disappointed in this respect, as we were frozen up ere we had proceeded half the distance, our boat carried off by the ice, and ourselves reduced to great straits for provisions in the midst of a wilderness.

Friday, November 25th, 1796.—By daylight we started in company with another boat. The stream was very dull, we therefore kept our men constantly rowing, and then could not proceed above two miles and a half an hour. At eleven we came to Woollery's, where we put the boat ashore to bring off the old gentleman to pilot us over a very bad riffle just below his house. When we had got him aboard, we reminded him of the pleasant evening we passed at his house, which he seemed to remember with much satisfaction. After we had passed over the riffle we gave him half a dollar, (which is a fee they generally expect,) and set him ashore again. We stopped this night opposite the mouth of Big Beaver Creek, on the western side of which creek there is a new settlement formed, called Fort Mackintosh. We sent the men ashore to cut down some wood; for the wind was very high, and the weather very cold; the effects of which we found the next morning;—

Saturday, November 26th, 1796;—for we observed several large pieces of ice floating down the river, some of which obstructed our passage very much this day; and we observed several boats ashore, which were afraid to proceed any farther till the ice had passed off a little. About one we passed the Pennsylvania [state] line, which crosses the river from north to south, extending as far northward as lake Erie. The wind was very high to-day, which, together with the quantities of ice, which seemed to increase, determined us to wait till the weather should prove more favourable before we proceeded farther. Accordingly, the next morning,—

Sunday, November 27th, 1796,—having proceeded about two miles farther on the river, we observed two other boats made fast to the shore, and accordingly joined them; and as there was a plantation within a short distance of the place, we got supplied with what little necessaries we might want; and amused ourselves by shooting in the woods during the short time we were here, which was till

Wednesday, November 30th, 1796,—when, the river having cleared itself of a great quantity of ice, we determined to proceed. Accordingly about eleven o'clock we started, and, in spite of all the obstructions which the ice was continually throwing in our way, we managed to get eleven miles this day. The next morning,—

Thursday, December 1st, 1796—we got fast upon a riffle near Brown's Island; but as it was a sandy one, we got off without any danger, on lightening the boat. A little after three we passed

Buffaloe Town and Creek. Buffaloe Town (which I believe is also called Charlestown) a new settlement, containing about thirty or forty houses, very pleasantly situated on the banks of the Ohio, and just at the mouth of the Creek, on the eastern side of it. It was about two miles below this town where we stopped this night. The next day,—

Friday, December 2nd, 1796,—we met with a disaster which threatened us with very disagreeable consequences; but from which we were happily relieved, without experiencing any material loss. It was about two o'clock in the afternoon; the river was very full of ice, and we were floating along at a slow pace, when, about a mile above the town of Wheeling, (where there was a riffle), we got aground, and all our endeavours to get her off were ineffectual, and no remedy was left but to unload the boat. Accordingly we loaded a little skiff which we had with us, and sent her down to the town; and this we repeated twice before it grew dark; but our endeavours to get her off were still ineffectual, and we were obliged to remain in this situation all night,—in the middle of the river, the stream running with great rapidity and bringing down with it vast quantities of ice, which came against us with great violence, and with a noise like thunder, and threatened at every repeated stroke to stave the sides of the vessel. In order to break the force of the ice, we nailed a plank on the stern, and fixed the oars out at the after part of the boat; so that the ice might be cut in two and separated ere it struck us. This had the desired effect, and we the satisfaction of seeing daylight appear without experiencing any other loss except that of sleep; and early in the morning,—

Saturday, December 3rd, 1796,—we sent another skiff-load down to the town; and a *flat*[boat] coming down the river about breakfast time, we got the men to stop, and we then unloaded the boat sufficiently to let her float down to the town, which place we reached about ten o'clock. The stream was so rapid from the place where we ran aground down to the town, that one man in the skiff could not oppose the current with a pair of oars; and it was with difficulty that two could accomplish it.

Wheeling is about a hundred miles down the river from Pittsburgh, and may contain about fifty houses. It was settled some few years back by Mr. Lane [Ebenezer Zane], who has a house in the town built with stone. Lane is related to some Indian families by intermarrying with them; and some of them were visiting at. his house when we were there. There is a creek runs from east to west at the south end of the town; and on the north side of the creek, on the banks of the river, there is a block fort, in which are about five or six men. A number of these forts are established at different places on the Ohio, and were of use formerly, when the country was first settled, to keep off the incursions of the Indians; but, on account of the frontier settlements of Kentucky and the northwestern territory, these surrounded colonies do not stand in need of any farther support.

Wheeling, like Buffaloe, is situated on a bottom about fifty or sixty feet[7] above the bed of the river, and surrounded at the back by very high hills. There has been a road lately *blazed*[8] on the north side of the Ohio, which reaches from Limestone, in the state of Kentucky, to Pittsburgh; and it crossed the Ohio at this place, which renders it a town of great resort when the roads are passable. These roads are seldom travelled but in parties; and they are obliged to take their provisions with them, and also blankets for their bedding; in which manner they travel somewhat like our gypsies. There was a party of Kentucky merchants collecting when we were there, and they were to start in a day or two. If a person intending to go through the wilderness does not know of a party going, it is not unusual for him to advertise in some of the provincial papers; and sometimes the parties themselves will advertise, in order that others may join them; but the best and most usual way is to stop at the last town (such as Wheeling) through which they must pass, and then join them as they go through.

Wednesday, December 7th, 1796.—After laying in a fresh stock of provisions at this place, and repairing the little damage we experienced from the ice, we pushed off from the shore, and continued our progress down the river. We had stayed near five days at Wheeling, during which we were in doubt whether we should proceed any farther or not till the river should rise, and get a little clearer of ice. This morning we found it had risen about five inches, in consequence of some rains which we sup-

posed had fallen near the heads of the river; and this determined us to continue on. Mr. Bell, a Kentucky merchant, lay at
Wheeling with his boat at the same time that we did; and we
both started together. We went about twelve miles down the
river this day; and in the evening put to, on the southern shore
of the Ohio, opposite a small settlement, called Grave Creek,
from the number and size of some ancient mounds which are
found in that place, and which are supposed to have been burying mounds. Of these we shall have occasion to speak hereafter. The next morning,—

Thursday, December 8th, 1796,—we floated about six, and at
twelve we put ashore, to inquire concerning a bad riffle at
Capteen Island, which we understood was difficult to pass.
Seeing a bit of a hut on the shore, we made our boat fast to
some trees on the banks and went to inquire about it. We
stopped here near two hours. The person whom we met with
there was just come down the river, and was forming himself a
plantation; he had made himself a miserable hut, and was erecting some kind of shelter for the few cattle he had brought with
him. About two o'clock we left him; and, passing Capteen Riffle
in safety, we proceeded about nine miles down the river this
day. Here we put ashore at a plantation which was inhabited
by Mr. Daily, an Irishman. He informed us that the Ohio was
frozen up about five miles, and that it would be impossible for
us to proceed. The weather had been very cold for several days,
and the river had continued to fall; so that we determined to
moor our boat in some place of safety, where she might not be
exposed to the logs and large trees which are continually drifting down the river, and there to wait for a change of weather.
Accordingly, the next day,—

Friday, December 9th, 1796,—Heighway and myself walked down
the banks of the river, about five miles, to a place called Fish
Creek, and, to our sorrow, found it completely blocked up with
ice, and frozen over for several miles down, so that it was absolutely impossible to proceed. We observed four or five boats
on the opposite shore, who were in the same predicament with
ourselves. Having satisfied ourselves in this respect, we returned
home to our boat, and the next day,—

Saturday, December 10*th*, 1796,—we dropped down the river about a mile to a place which we had observed yesterday in our walk, and which we conceived more secure from the bodies drifting down the river, than the one we were in. Having moored ourselves, as we conceived, in a place of safety, and having every prospect of passing the winter in this situation, we began to apply ourselves to the laying in of a good stock of provisions. Mr. Bell's boat was with us; and another boat which was proceeding down the river had joined us; and we all lay moored together; so that there were fourteen or fifteen of us in company: and we every day sent out some of them into the woods with their guns to hunt for deer, turkeys, bears, or any other animals fit for food. We had a good quantity of flour, and of Indian meal with us; so that as long as our gunpowder lasted (of which we were very sparing) we had not prospect of suffering a great deal from hunger; which, in a country like that, surrounded with plenty, would have been truly shocking.

There was a plantation or two in the neighbourhood, one of which, I mentioned, belonged to Mr. Daily, but they could render us no assistance, nor furnish us with any article we wanted; they were, in fact, in the same destitute situation in which we were— obliged to depend upon their guns for subsistence; and if they gathered a crop of corn in summer, it was generally gone before the winter was over, or at least reduced to a very scanty pittance. There was also a settlement about nine miles off, called Grave Creek; but it was impossible to get to it by water, and the road by land to it, through the woods, was very bad, and in this weather even dangerous. However, as I had a great desire to see the [ancient] curiosities which are in that place, I could not refrain from going over there; accordingly, getting Mr. Daily to be my guide, we set off one afternoon (*December 16th*) to see them. The sun had shone beautifully bright all that day, and it was about two hours high when we started. We at first traversed over a flat bottom on the banks of the river, and then, ascending a very steep and high hill, we were carried along the ridge of it till we came within about a mile of the place. As this hill carried us above the level of the surrounding country, every break through the trees presented to us a *sea of woods,* whose tops, just tinged by the setting sun, displayed one of the most beautiful sylvan scenes I ever remember seeing; at the same time, every now and then the Ohio opened to our view, whose gentle stream, covered with the drifting ice, formed a fine contrast to its umbrageous shores. We had scarcely proceeded half our journey before a bear with three cubs crossed the road at some distance before us. She did not observe us, neither did we attack them, as we had but one gun in company. They were making towards the river, and Mr. Daily informed me that it was most probable they would find shelter in the rocks on the shore for that night, and in the morning cross it; however, when we got to Grave Creek, we sent some persons after them; but I never heard whether they took them or not. Within about a mile of Grave Creek, we had, from the point of the hill we were just descending, a fine prospect of the rough buildings which compose this settlement; and the smoke ascending through the thick woods, which was beautifully tinged by the setting sun, heightened the effect of the scenery. Here too we had another view of the Ohio, which had just shaped its course round a point of land not a great distance from us, and whose bed might be traced (though unseen) by the dark cavity which was observed amongst the tops of the trees, which extended as far as the eye could reach. My attention was taken off from this beautiful prospect, on which I dwelt some time with pleasure, by the roughness of the path which carried us down the hill. It was at least five or six hundred feet high from the level of the river, and nearly perpendicular; at least so much so that there were steps cut in the ground in many places like a pair of stairs, and I often turned round with my face towards the ground, as if I were going down a ladder, fearful that my foot might slip had I proceeded otherwise. However, with regret, we descended the dark valley below in safety, and soon arrived at the settlement, where we slept that night; and in the morning I went out to see the curious remains of antiquity with which this place abounds. They consist of circular and square entrenchments and mounds, which are scattered at different distances for ten or twelve miles along the banks of the Ohio. One of the principal circular entrenchments and mounds is on the very spot where the settlement is built; and three of the principal mounds also are within a hundred yards of the same, one of which is near one hundred feet high; and has trees growing on it to the very top, some of which must be very old; at least they appear of the same size and age with those which grow in the surrounding valley. With respect to the entrenchments, they are about breast high, and appear, from their situation, &c., to have been intended for, and used as, fortifications; and these mounds (from which the settlement takes its name) seem to have been graves, either used as public burying places, or thrown up for those dead who might have fallen in some engagement near the place. I was informed that one of these mounds has been opened, and that it was found to contain human bones,[9] which (if true) confirms the opinion. There are three mounds at this place, the principal of which I have mentioned as far exceeding the others in size and height. I walked up to the top of it, and found that it took exactly one hundred steps to reach it; and each of these steps I computed to rise me about a foot, so that the mound was at least one hundred feet high. The top of it was sunk in the middle, which (if it really has been a burying-place) may arise from the dissolution of the dead bodies beneath. I walked round the top of it, and found it took me about seventy steps, which, allowing two and a half feet for a step, makes the diameter of the top, at a rough calculation, between fifty and sixty feet. On a tree rising from the middle of the hollow on the top of the mound there were a number of names carved by those whom curiosity had drawn to visit this place. As to the entrenchments, what remained of them was perfectly circular; but in many parts the ground had been torn up either by the cattle, or to plant their corn.

Having satisfied my curiosity with respect to this place, we set off in the afternoon, and, striking through the woods, reached our boat in the evening.

We continued at this place about a fortnight, anxiously expecting every day that the river would break up, and thereby give us an opportunity of proceeding on our route. Some heavy rains which had fallen within these few days gave us reason to hope for this favourable event. But, alas! how vain are the expectations of men, and how short-sighted in all their views! The event, as we had fondly imagined, did take place, but with circumstances that rendered our situation still more unpleasant and dangerous.

It was on *Tuesday,* the 20*th* of *December,* that our spirits seemed to be more than commonly high at this prospect of escaping from our imprisonment. We had even been a little more lavish than common of the rough fare which we met with in these uncivilized parts. The snow was upon the ground, and the weather severely cold, the thermometer standings at seventeen degrees below zero. The noise of the Ohio, bound in its wintry chains, was heard no more; and the rude blast, whistling through the trees, strongly marked out to us our separation from an inhabited country. Our boat was firmly frozen up by the ice, close to the shore, and we had the precaution to fasten her with strong chains to some large trees on the banks, lest the ice (when it broke up) might carry her away; we had also cut down a large tree just above the boat, (which was not perfectly separated from the stump,) in order to break the force of the ice floating down the stream, and which, coming against our boat, might endanger it. Having taken these precautions we went to bed soon after sunset, and about one o'clock the next morning,—

Wednesday, December 21st, 1796,—we were awakened out of our sleep with a noise like thunder, and, jumping out of our beds, we found the river was rising, and the ice breaking up. All attempts would be feeble to describe the horrid crashing and tremendous destruction which this event occasioned on the river. Only conceive a river near 1,500 miles long, frozen to a prodigious depth (capable of bearing loaded waggons) from its source to its mouth, and this river by a sudden torrent of water breaking those bands by which it had been so long, fettered! Conceive this vast body of ice put in motion at the same instant, and carried along with an astonishing rapidity, grating with a most tremendous noise against the sides of the river, and bearing down everything which opposed its progress!—the tallest and the stoutest trees obliged to submit to its destructive fury, and hurried along with the general wreck! In this scene of confusion and desolation, what was to be done? We all soon left

the boat in order every one to provide for his own personal
safety; but seeing that the precautions we had taken the day
before prevented the ice from coming upon us so soon as it
otherwise would have done, and that there was a chance, though
at great risk, of saving some, if not all, the things from the
boat, we set to, as earnestly as we could, to unload her. There
were near eleven tons of goods in her, the principal of which
were implements of husbandry, designed for Mr. Heighway's
plantation; the rest consisted of articles of barter, intended for
the Indians, and of provision and other necessaries during our
journey. We, in the first place, took care to secure these last
mentioned; and then we set about getting out the others, some
of which were very bulky, weighing upwards of five hundred
weight. We had not proceeded in this undertaking above a quarter of an hour, when a large sheet of ice came against our boat,
and, with a tremendous crash, stove in one side of her! We saw
it coming, and happily escaped from the boat before it reached
us. She was immediately filled with water, but as she was near
the shore, and almost touched the bottom, (the water being
very low,) she was not immediately covered. The river was rising at a very rapid rate, and as we knew that if we once lost
sight of her, we should never see her more, and as we saw that
there was still a chance of saving something more from the
wreck, (though at the risk of our lives,) which might tend to
make our situation more comfortable whilst we were obliged
to stay here, and not leave us utterly bereft of every neceasary,
we determined upon making one more effort; therefore, jumping into the boat, up, to our middle in water, we continued to
work near three hours, amidst vast fields of ice, which were
continually floating by us, and whose fury we would escape
when they made towards us, on being warned by one of our
party, whom we had set on the banks to watch. In this manner
did we persevere, till we had got most of the things out of the
boat, in one of the coldest nights ever remembered in this country: the thermometer[10] was at 17° below zero, and so intense
was the cold, that the iron chain which fastened our boat had
the same effect on our hands as if they had been burned with a
hot iron. Farther, whilst we were in the boat this last time, the

moment we raised our legs above the water, (in walking,) our stockings froze to them, before they were put down again, as tight as if bound with a garter! In such a situation and in such severe weather, it is a wonder we had not perished; and possibly we might, had not the river, which was now rising rapidly, completely covered our boat, and obliged us to desist from our attempts. Thus went our boat!—and thus went every hope of our proceeding on our journey! Thus were all our flattering prospects cut short, and none left but the miserable one of fixing our winter habitation on these inhospitable shores!

It was still dark when this event happened, and this, added to the desolation which was making around us, whose power we could hear but not discern, heightened the effect of our forlorn situation. Some women who were of our party had kindled a fire on the banks; and when we saw that no more could be done, we took our blankets, and clearing away the snow, lay ourselves down before it, and, overcome with fatigue, gave ourselves up to rest. Some of our party were so affected by the intense cold, and by so long exposure in the water, that their feet were frostbitten; others had their legs swelled up in large knots as big as an egg. As to myself, I felt no ill effects from either.

When morning approached, a scene the most distressing presented itself to our view. The river was one floating wreck! Nothing could be discerned amidst the vast bodies of floating ice, (some of which were as big as a moderate-sized house,) but trees which had been torn up from the banks, and the boats of many a family who had scarcely time to escape unhurt from such an unlooked-for event, and whose whole property (perhaps scraped together to form a settlement in this distant territory) was now floating down, a prey to the desolating flood. Canoes, skiffs, flatts, in fact, everything which was opposed to its fury, was hurried along to one general ruin.

As daylight advanced, we had also an opportunity of seeing in what situation we stood ourselves; and here, instead of finding any ray of comfort or hope, we observed our misfortunes increasing upon us, for the bank where we lay was full fifty feet high and nearly perpendicular; so much so, that it could not be ascended or descended without great difficulty. There happened to be a little bit of a level where the boat was, and where we placed the things we had preserved from the wreck; but the water was rising so rapidly, that it had almost covered this place, and we were under the necessity (worn out as we were) of carrying them still higher up the bank, or they would have shared the fate of our vessel. This was a most laborious undertaking, and to have hauled them to the top of the bank, would have taken us up some days; we were, therefore, under the necessity of hauling them up *one by one* about two or three feet at a time, and lodging them behind the trees which grew on the bank, and which prevented their rolling back into the river; and this we were obliged to continue to do till we saw the river had ceased rising; and then we left them for a day or two, in order to rest ourselves from our fatigue, and to fix up some kind of habitation to protect us from the inclemency of the weather.

Having thus happily escaped from this danger, and saved most of our property from the flood, we set about erecting a covering under which to lodge it; and this we did with a number of blankets and some coarse linen which we had brought with us: it was a rough sort of building, but such an one as answered our purpose in the situation we were in. We made it by fixing two poles in the ground, about ten or twelve feet asunder, and laying another transversely at the top of them. This was the front of our tent, and was left always open. The back and sides were formed by straight poles leaning against the horizontal one which was placed transversely across, and over them were thrown blankets, &c. This secured us in a measure from the rain, which ran off almost as fast as it fell; and, in order to keep off the cold, we kept a large fire constantly burning in the front of our tent; and thus circumstanced, we endeavoured to make ourselves as comfortable as we could, consoling ourselves, that it might have been worse with us; and that even now we were not so badly off as many[11] of those who had descended the river this season. Here we found full employment for some time in drying our goods, which had got wetted when the ice stove the boat. Some of the packages were so much frozen as to take three days standing constantly before the fire, ere we could get out their contents to dry them. This took us up near three weeks, during which time we had got into more comfortable lodgings. For in the neighbourhood of this place we had found a log-house, which appeared to have been used for the purpose of keeping fodder for cattle. It was open on all sides between the logs; but this we soon remedied, by lining the whole with the blankets and coarse linen which before we had covered our tent with. We also built up a chimney in it, and had our fire wholly within doors; so that now we began to look a little more in order, though there was no flooring to the house, neither was there any window, for all the light we had came down the chimney, which was large and wide, or in at the door; however, this was a *luxury* with which we could easily dispense, considering the hardships we had gone through; therefore, hauling all our goods to this place, and stowing them under this roof, we may, not improperly, be said to have commenced *house keeping*. This was on the

24*th December*; and as it was above a mile from the place where we were, we made a sledge for the convenience of dragging our goods to the house; otherwise, we should never have been able to have accomplished it. We had four horses aboard with us, which expedited us in this undertaking very much.

December 25th, Christmas Day—Two of our party being ill with the fatigues we had undergone on the 21st, the task of superintending the conveyance of our goods devolved upon me. We had been employed at it the whole of yesterday; and as soon as daylight approached this morning we began the same career again, nor did we cease this routine, except to take the scanty pittance we had saved from the wreck, till the setting sun and our own weary limbs told us it was time to close the scene once more. I could not think of the happy moments which were enjoyed in my own country on this auspicious day, and perhaps by those whose remembrance is the most dear to me, without contrasting them with my present situation. Here am I in the wilds of America, away from the society of men, amidst the haunts of wild beasts and savages, just escaped from the perils of a wreck, in want not only of the comforts, but of the necessaries of life, housed in a hovel that in my own country would

not be good enough for a pigstye, at a time too when my father, my mother, my brothers, my sisters, my friends and acquaintance, in fact, the whole nation, were feasting upon the
best the country could afford. I could not but picture to myself
the fireside of my own home, where I saw them all assembled
round; a beam of happiness perhaps glistening in every face,
save when after dinner I was remembered in their glasses; then,
perhaps, a sigh broke out from some of them, and the conversation might turn upon "where I was," and "what I was doing;" but this dying away, I should soon be forgotten again,
and they would return to spend the day in mirth and happiness. Ah! little do they think of the hardships I have undergone, or of those which seem to continue to press us. Little do
they think that, while they are partaking of all the bounties of
nature, that I am suffering the contrary extreme through want;
and would gladly partake of the refuse of their table, or thank-
fully receive what they would give a common beggar at the
door. Methought, if I could but make my appearance in the
midst of them at this time, that I should scarce be remembered
by them, my long beard, my rough and tattered clothes, and all
together would puzzle them at first to conceive what *stranger*
was come amongst them; at least, I think they would begin to
chide the servant for admitting so uncouth a visitor before they
would recollect or discover who I was.

Our meal this day was the most scanty we have had for some time.
We had some apples on board our boat, of which, together
with some coarse Indian meal, we endeavoured to make an
apple pudding; it was a rough kind of a one, but such as it was,
it constituted our *only food* for this day. To be sure, we were in
the midst of plenty, for there was abundance of deer and turkeys in the woods; but we were too much engaged in the confusion of our wreck to spare the time to go after them. However,
finding our stock of provisions diminishing very fast every day,
we were obliged, for our own preservation, to seek after them.
Accordingly, we took it by turns to go out every morning with
our gun and shoot whatever we could find; and many a time
would we lay ourselves down at night without a prospect of
anything wherewith to break our fast the next morning, save

what our guns might procure us the next day; yet even in the midst of this apparent distress, we were very happy. We all enjoyed one of the greatest blessings of Providence, which is *a good state of health;* and as to the rest, we were strangers to all those artificial wants which man in a civilized state has brought upon himself. Those which we stood in need of were easily satisfied; and the very means which we took to satisfy them was one of our chief pleasures, and afforded us the greatest amusement. All that we wanted was the *necessaries* of life, the mere food we eat; and the getting of this constituted our chief diversion. Whether it were the novelty of the thing which attracted us, or the scenery of the country, and the sublimity of its views, so very different from what we had been used to in the *old* country, I know not; but certain it is, there is something so very attractive in a life spent in this manner, that were I disposed to become a hermit, and seclude myself from the world, the woods of America should be my retreat: there should I, with my dog and my gun, and the hollow of a rock for my habitation, enjoy undisturbed all that fancied bliss attendant on a state of nature. Often, when I have wandered across the woods in search of game to carry home to my companions, have I been lost in contemplation raised by the grandeur and novelty of the scenery around me. Happy men! cried I, who, ignorant of all the deceits and artifices attendant on a state of civilization, unpractised in the vices and dissipation of degraded humanity, unconscious of artificial and unnecessary wants, secluded from all those pomps and ridiculous ostentations which serve to enslave one half of a nation for the gratification of the other; unshackled with the terrors which fanaticism and superstition inspire; enjoying equally the free blessings which nature intended for man, how much, alas! how much I envy you! Could I but renounce those habits which education and custom have endowed, how cheerfully would I join your lot, which men (more barbarous) have branded with the name of savage, but where are found health, happiness, and independence, three of the greatest blessings the Divine Being can bestow upon man! 'Tis true the arts and sciences have not found their way amongst you, but it is much to be doubted whether they bring with them their boasted advantages. Great pleasure may be derived from the pursuit of them by some of their votaries; but how few, alas! how few are they, in comparison to the bulk of mankind! And it will ever remain an undetermined problem whether human happiness has kept pace with the progress that has been made in the arts of civilization;—whether man has not given up the innocence, happiness, and independence he enjoyed in a state of nature, for the vices, misery, and oppression which are evidently too glaring in an improved state of society. In the former situation, his wants are few, and those wants easily satisfied; and if at any time, through accident, he be reduced to great distress for provisions, he takes without repining, in fact with thankfulness, the scanty pittance which Providence has allowed him: his happiness and his independence go together, and the latter is not to be taken away but with his life. In the other situation, view the contrast, and for the truth of it, read the history of man from the earliest ages to the present time.

Thursday, January 5th,1797.—We had by this time got all our things hauled to our new habitation. We found the greatest difficulty in getting them up the bank, which (as I observed before) was upwards of fifty feet high, and nearly perpendicular. When I have been helping the men up with some of the heavier packages, our feet have slipped from under us, and the package (freed from its support) has come trundling down the bank, and with difficulty been saved from falling into the river again; and this sometimes when we had nearly reached the summit of the bank, so that we had all our labour to go through again; it often reminded me of our fellow-labourer in the regions below, as described by Homer in his Odyssey:—

I turn'd my eye, and as I turn'd, survey'd [. . .]"
A mournful vision! the Sisyphian shade;
With many a weary step, and many a groan,
Up the high hill he heaves a huge round stone;
The huge round stone, resulting with a bound,
Thunders impetuous down, and smokes along the ground.

Book XI

However, we lost very little this way, and we had the satisfaction of observing things a little more in order; and, if I may so speak, of being *pretty well settled;* but this afternoon an event happened which had nearly cost dear. By some accident or another our little habitation caught fire, and the whole roof (which was thatched) was in flames ere we knew anything of the matter; our confusion was very great, as may be naturally conceived, when it is recollected that all our necessaries and provisions, in fact everything which tended to render our situation at all tolerable, were under that very roof which we now had the mortification to see enveloped in flames. To make the matter worse, it was impossible to get at the water in the river, owing to the steepness of the banks, and the thickness of the ice near the shore; but, as good luck would have it, there was a spring not a great way off, to which we sent all the vessels we had for water; and by throwing wet blankets upon the roof, and as much water as we could get, we happily extinguished it without any further inconvenience than having thrown us into a terrible confusion and alarm. Had the flames got the better of our exertions, our situation would have been deplorable indeed; we should then have been deprived at once of every means to render our forlorn situation at all comfortable; for it would have been almost impossible to have saved any (or very few) of the things which were in the house; for there was but one narrow entrance, and our packages were too bulky to be easily moved, and the house, being of wood, would soon have been destroyed. We suppose the accident must have happened from some sparks falling on the roof from the chimney.

I had observed before that there were two other boats with us when our accident happened. on the 21st ult[imate] These two boats did not receive any material injury; for, being small, and placed below us, our boat broke off in a great measure, the force of the drifting ice, and they were still farther protected behind a bush of willows which grew just within the water; these boats therefore went on down the river when the ice had cleared off a little, and left us by ourselves. Circumstanced thus as we were, we were under the necessity of getting another boat to carry us on; but ere we could come to any resolution of

this kind, or determine where we could get it accomplished, we
had the mortification to see the river freeze over once more,
and close up as fast as ever. However, this did not prevent us
from getting a boat ready against it should break up again.
Accordingly, two of the men who accompanied us being pretty
good mechanics, we dispatched them off to Grave Creek, across
the woods, where they might have the advantage of a saw to
saw the planks for the boat, (for as to all other tools we had
plenty of them with us,) and where they might have the assistance of more hands if required. Accordingly, about the middle
of this month (January) they set out for Grave Creek, taking
with them all the tools which they have occasion for in their
undertaking; and they set about felling some trees immediately,
and soon put their work in a state of forwardness. But what
relieved us most in our present distress, was their meeting with
a supply of gunpowder, which, though small, was very accept-
able to us, as we were reduced to our last charge, and were in a
great dilemma what to do, as we depended on our gun for our
daily food.

Whilst they were getting the boat ready in this manner, we would
occasionally take our guns and go over to see them, and encourage them in their undertaking. These two men had lately
come from England, and Mr. H., meeting with them at Philadelphia, gave them currency £50 for their service for two years;
and they were now going down with him to help him to form
his settlement on the Miami river; they had got their wives
with them, which, together, with another person and Mr. H.
(seven in all), formed. our whole company. But, what is very
remarkable, and what may never happen to seven other people
who were travelling near four thousand miles from their country, we happened to be all English. This made it very pleasant,
as in this distressing situation in which we were, even to talk of
England afforded us pleasure; and it was a conversation in which
we could all *feelingly* join; for in the wilds of America, all dis-
tinctions of rank are necessarily laid aside.

Those hours of the day which were not engaged in hunting, we
used to employ in some useful or amusing manner; for even in
this lonely place, if there is any disposition to be active, there

are abundant opportunities of exercising both the body and the mind. In the first place, then, seeing a number of sugar-trees in the neighbourhood, and this being the right season of the year for it, we set about making some sugar. This was an article we wished for very much, as we had both tea and coffee with us, but could not make use of them for want of this article; and in this we happily succeeded far beyond our expectations. The sugar maple (the *Acer Saccharinum* of Linnaeus) grows in great abundance in all the western parts of the middle states of America. The upper counties of the state of New York, and the western counties of the state of Pennsylvania, and all the parts bordering on the Ohio, produce these trees in the greatest abundance. They are generally found on the richest land, and frequently in stony ground, and mixed with the beech, ash, cherry, elm, oak, cucumber, and other trees; though some-times they will cover six or seven acres in a body, with very few trees of any other sort interspersed with them. When they are found in this manner, they are called sugar groves, which is a term applied to any place of this kind where the process of making sugar from the trees is carried on.

It has been observed that springs of the purest water are in great plenty where these trees abound, so that it is almost a sure index of a desirable[12] situation for a plantation. I have seen them from six inches to near three feet diameter, though two feet is the common size for a full-grown tree; and their height is from 100 feet upwards. In the spring, ere they show a single leaf, they put forth a beautiful *white* blossom. The colour of the blossom distinguishes it from the *Acer Rubrum*, or the red maple, which puts forth a blossom of a red colour. The method of getting the sap from these trees, (for it is from the sap that the sugar is made), is by making an incision into the substance of the tree; and this is generally done either with an axe or an augur, though the latter is the preferable method. If it penetrate but a quarter of an inch, it is sufficient to cause the sap to ooze out at the incision, though not in any great quantity; and any incision made in this way to obtain the sap, is called *tapping* the tree. It is remarkable, that the trees are not at all injured by tapping; on the contrary, the oftener they are tapped, the more syrup and of a better quality is obtained from them: in this respect they follow a law of animal secretion. A single tree has not only survived, but flourished, after forty-two tappings in the same number of years (See "Amer. Phil. Trans.").[13] The effects of a yearly discharge of sap from the tree in improving and increasing the sap, are demonstrated from the superior excellence of those trees which have been perforated in a hundred places by a small woodpecker. The trees after having been wounded in this way distil the remains of their juice on the ground, and afterwards by the action of the sun and the air on the juice, whilst trickling down the tree, it turns the bark of a black colour; and this blackness is always a sure sign of a good tree; for, owing to the causes above mentioned, the sap of these trees is much sweeter to the taste than that which is obtained from that which have not been previously wounded, and it affords more sugar. The wood of the sugar-maple is exceedingly inflammable, and is preferred on that account by hunters and surveyors when they make a fire in the woods. Its ashes afford a great quantity of potash, exceeded by few, or perhaps by none; of the trees that grow in the United States. The tree is said to arrive at its full growth in about twenty years, though its existence is supposed to be as long as the oak or any other tree.

The most preferable method of tapping the trees, and which is the one we practised, is to bore a hole with an inch augur, and about an inch deep, in a declined direction, so that there may be a kind of cup formed for the sap to lie in; then to bore another hole with a gimlet in a horizontal direction, about the size of a quill, to enter at the bottom of this hollow cup, in which a reed or any hollow instrument may be inserted, to carry the sap from the body of the tree, and to cause it to fall into a trough placed underneath. If the tree be large, three or four taps may be inserted in one tree. If the weather be very favourable, the sap will run in a small stream from the end of the reed, but generally it will only drop in very quick succession; and it will be found necessary every two or three days to make the tapping a little deeper, in order to increase its produce.

The season for tapping is very early in the spring, and may be

easily determined by making an incision through the bark with
an axe; for if it be the season, the sap will almost immediately
follow the axe. Warm days and frosty nights are the most
favourable to a plentiful discharge of the sap; and in this case
the discharge is always suspended during the night, and re-
newed again as soon as the sun has warmed the trees, and then
continues running all day till sunset; when, if the weather be
cold, it ceases, but if otherwise, it will continue running all
night; and, in this case, it is said to indicate a change of weather;
in fact, we generally[14] found it so. The quantity obtained from
a single tree depends, in a great measure, upon its size, as well
as upon the weather, varying according to these circumstances
from a pint to five gallons. Mr. Low informed Mr. Noble, (see
"Amer. Phil. Trans.,") that he obtained near twenty-three gallons of sap in one day (April 14th, 1789) from a single tree
which had been tapped for several successive years before. Such
instances, however, of a profusion of sap in single trees are
very uncommon. I have been informed, that a moderate-sized
tree will yield during the season, which is about six weeks,
from forty to fifty gallons of sap, from which may be made
about six or seven pounds of excellent sugar. The method we
took to preserve the sap and make the sugar, and which is the
method generally pursued in this western country, is to place a
rough wooden trough (made out of any of the trees which grew
in the neighbourhood) under each tap. These troughs may hold
about a gallon; and if the trees run fast, we go three or four
times a day and empty the sap from these troughs into a large
kettle which we carry round; and after having gone round to
all the trees, (which is no great distance where there are plenty
of them,) we place this kettle over a fire, which is made nearly
in the centre of the sugar-grove, and boil it down till it becomes
pretty thick; then if the white of an egg, a little lime, or any
other article of this kind which is used by sugar refiners, be put
to it, and it be suffered to stand for twenty-four hours, all the
gross particles will fall to the bottom, and the pure liquor may
be poured off into an iron vessel, which must be suffered to
boil over the fire till it be fit to grain, which is easily, determined by trying whether it will rope betwixt the finger and

thumb: if it will, it must then be taken off, and stirred incessantly till the grain can be felt, when the whole process is over, and your sugar is made. And in this manner did we make as excellent and as well-tasted sugar as any I ever tasted in my life. It has a flavour which distinguishes it from the West India sugar, and which, in my opinion, is very pleasant; and in point of colour I think it surpasses it. It takes about six or seven gallons of sap to make a pound of this sugar, and the sap should not be kept longer than twenty-four hours before it is boiled.

The season of sugar-making is a very busy time in those parts where these trees are plenty; it furnishes employment for every branch of a family; and that, happily, at a season when they are not otherwise employed on their plantations. It employs them night and day; for in the daytime they are busily employed in collecting the sap as it runs from the trees, and during the greater part of the night in boiling this sap down to its proper consistency. The children are equally useful in this office with the men; for whilst the latter are doing the laborious part of the undertaking, the children are employed in graining the sugar, and watching the kettles. However, though the process of sugar-making is so simple and easy, yet I never could find any sugar down the river but what was coarse, and of a dark brown colour, and so hard, that it looked like a lump of bees' wax. I mean such as is offered for sale; for people on their own plantations must be negligent indeed, if they do not produce sugar of a better quality than that.

During the little time we were here we made near 20 lbs. of sugar, which (considering the earliness of the season, and the few trees we had tapped, and the inconveniences we lay under) was very considerable. Another mean too, of employing our time (at least that of H. and myself) was by surveying, and laying out imaginary tracts of land. We had got a Gunter's chain with us, and also a compass, out of which I made *circumferenter*, and with this we used to survey and make plans of the country; and with this, by measuring a line on the banks of the river, we found by trigonometry the width of the Ohio where we were to be 1,208 feet; and we had an opportunity of verifying this calculation, by actual measurement, when the river froze over again.

H. had also some books with him, which was another source of
amusement during those times when the weather prevented us
from going out, or after our return home; but in this we were
limited for time; for when the sun set all our means of reading
departed, as we had no candles. This had one good effect upon
us, that it obliged us to rise with the sun, in order that we
might accomplish all we had to do by daylight. We *did* make a
few candles out of the fat of some deer and some bears we had
killed; but we were obliged to be very saving of them, and use
them only when there was an absolute necessity, though we
kept up such an excellent fire, that there was little occasion for
a candle to see our way about our hovel. Thus, when the sun
was set, all our *employment* had ceased for the day; but not
our *amusement,* for we would then shut the door of our miserable hut, to keep out the chilling blast which whistled round it,
and, all assembled round the enlivening fire, we would endeav-
our to keep each other in spirits by talking of Old England.
Then it was we would compare our present situation with what
we once enjoyed; then would the presence of each of us recal to
mind some of the difficulties we had lately undergone, and induce us to reflect on the dangers which we had providentially
escaped; and thus, by some kind of converse, we would endeavour to pass away the evening as pleasantly as our situation would allow, till at last our watches would summon us to
rest; then, laying our blankets and what bedding we had down
before the fire, we would sleep soundly and securely till the
morning. I have oftentimes, when lying down to rest, thought
how very little would suffice for man, if he were disposed to be
happy therewith. If any person, when I set out on my journey,
had informed me of the circumstances I was to pass through,
and had related to me the situation I was now in, I should have
thought it either impossible to have borne it, or that I should
have been completely unhappy and miserable therein. But so
soon does the mind of man accommodate itself to the trials
which it is to undergo, that I declare I did not indulge one
unpleasant thought, not feel myself at all unhappy, except when
I reflected on my separation from my friends, and how anxiously they would wish to be informed how and where I was.

In other respects we passed our time as merrily as if we had been at our own home, conscious that we could not impute to our own conduct any part of our present sufferings.

January 31st, 1797.—The river, which had been frozen up now near five weeks, broke up again this day, with a repetition of all those destructive circumstances which attended it the last time; and we had the anxiety of beholding once more its ravages. It is to be observed that the cause of the last breaking up was owing to some partial rains which fell in the upper country, and which caused the river to rise about ten or twelve feet; and when that passed off, it fell again to the depth it was before. But this was now the time of year when it was expected that the melting of the snow in the upper countries would not only break up the ice, but cause the river to rise to the level of its banks, as is customary at this season; for all the rivers in this back country are extremely low in winter, so as even to allow cattle to cross; and then their banks, which are from forty to sixty feet, appear like walls on each side. But no sooner does the melting of the snow cause the streams to swell, than the rivers assume a different appearance, and not only rise to the top of their banks, but sometimes overflow them; and these streams come down in so rapid a manner, as to cause the rivers to rise ten, fifteen, and even twenty feet in twenty-four hours. Nothing can differ more than the contrast in the appearance which the same river makes at these two different seasons. In the former instance we see a broad channel from a quarter to a mile wide, bounded on each side with high banks, and with scarcely water enough in it to cover its bottom, and in many places confined to one narrow stream, and flowing with a dull and lazy current. In the latter, we see this same channel completely filled with water, and in many places overflowing its banks, and rushing amongst the trees which grow thereon, and flowing with a rapidity of five and six miles an hour, and causing every object which is floating thereon to be carried along with an astonishing celerity. This is the difference of the two seasons; and this last was the one which was now beginning to open upon us, and of which this breaking up of the ice was the prelude. For the same waters which caused the ice to break up, raised the river to such a degree that in the course of a few days it had nearly reached the top of its banks; and the same river to which about a week before we had to descend above seventeen yards, now flowed at our feet. We were happy to see this change in the weather, as it flattered us with a prospect of a speedy escape from this wilderness. We accordingly made another visit to our men who were engaged in building the boat; and, expediting it as much as possible, we had the satisfaction of seeing her launched on *Friday, February* 17*th,* and the next day,—

February 18*th,*—we brought her down to the place where we lay. This boat was thirteen feet wide and forty feet long, and boarded up at the sides and covered over at the top all the way, except at a place in the front, which was left for the horses, and for the men to row. It was about nine o'clock in the evening when she arrived. We had just laid ourselves down before the fire, when we heard a noise not far from the house, which at first startled us, not thinking what it might be; but on going out, we congratulated ourselves at seeing a light on the river, from whence the noise proceeded, and we soon found that the men had brought our boat down. We went to welcome them; and, after having made her fast we set before them what provisions we had got by us, and after making them detail the account of their proceedings, we lay down to rest, and before daylight the next morning,—

February 19*th,*—we got up, and proceeded to load the boat. This took us up the whole day, so that it was next morning,—

Monday, February 20*th*, 1797,—about ten o'clock in the forenoon, when we pushed off from the shore, and, bidding a final adieu to our old habitation, proceeded down the river on our journey. On taking leave of this spot, I could not but admire the marks of civilization we had left behind. We had cleared a piece of ground, fitted up a comfortable house, cleared out a spring that was in the neighbourhood, and left a sledge and other things behind us, which would clearly point out to a traveller on that road, that it could not be the work of the Indians alone. The association of ideas had induced in us an attachment to this infant settlement of our own, and we kept our eyes constantly fixed on it, till a cruel bend in the river snatched it from our sight for ever. We anchored (or rather fastened our boat to the shore) about the middle of Long Reach this evening. Long Reach is the most beautiful place I ever saw in my life: the river at this spot preserves one straight course for fifteen miles, and is agreeably interspersed with a number of islands through its whole length. It runs nearly in a westerly direction, and the setting sun at the extreme end, reflecting itself in the smooth water, and beautifully tinging the distant trees, rendered it at once one of the most sublime views I ever was witness to. The river looked like a little sea of fire before us; and, by the rapidity and smoothness of its current, seemed to be silently hurrying us on towards it. I regretted then, more than ever, the want of the pencil, and had the mortification of soon seeing it vanish from my presence for ever, except when faintly recalled by the aid of memory. We had come thirty miles to-day, and the next morning,—

Tuesday, February 2lst,—about five o'clock, we started and came to Muskingham [Marietta][15] about one. Muskingham, so called from the river of that name, at the mouth of which it is built, consists of about one hundred houses agreeably situated on the eastern point where the Muskingham joins the Ohio. The western bank of the Muskingham rises into a very high country, forming a kind of amphitheatre from the town. The river itself is 150 (Imlay says, 200; Hutchins, 250) yards wide at its mouth;[16] and in the Ohio, just above the town, there is a long island which divides the Ohio, and when the streams join again, makes it appear very broad from its banks; so that it is not much unlike three rivers falling into one current. About a quarter of a mile from the town are the remains of an old fort, near which are some [ancient] graves nearly similar to those at Grave Creek, and from the fort to the river there is a covered way. The roads were so exceedingly bad when we were there, that I could not possibly get to them, but we could see the graves from the river. This is said to be the first settlement made by the Americans on the western side of the Ohio in what is called the north-west territory; it was formed in the year 1787 (see Imlay, p. 20), and has been progressively increasing to its present size ever since, though now the emigrants seem disposed to go farther down the river.

A view of Marietta in the late eighteenth century. Source: Georges-Henri-Victor Collot, *A Journey in North America* (Paris: Printed for Arthus Bertrand, Bookseller, 1826).

We stopped here about an hour to get provisions, and then proceeded[17] on our route. We did intend to put ashore about sundown, not wishing to float all night; but the stream was so rapid, that we did not dare to venture near the shore, for our boat would have been dashed in pieces against the trees which now appeared to *grow out of the water*, though, when the river was low, they were only on the sides of the banks; and not finding any eddy into which we might row to stop the rapidity of her progress, we were under the disagreeable necessity of continuing on the river all night, which, unfortunately for us, proved one of the most tempestuous I ever experienced. The sun had scarcely set, ere the atmosphere began to be overcast, and to threaten us with a violent storm; the wind also began to increase, which rendered our situation very precarious, as these boats are very dangerous in windy weather. However, as we could not make the shore without subjecting ourselves to greater danger, we were determined to meet the worst; and, in order to be ready in case of any accident or probability of danger, we all kept watch this night, and were continually on the look out. About eight o'clock the wind began to get pretty high, and the rain seemed to descend in torrents. The night was exceedingly dark, so that we could not tell in what part of the river we were, save when the lightning broke through the clouds, kindly informing us of our situation, and seeming to roll in volumes along the stream; this, mixed with the most tremendous thunder I ever heard, resounding from the echoing woods, rendered it one of the grandest, though at the same time the most awful, sight the imagination can conceive. This continued through the whole of the night, though the wind had, fortunately for us, considerably abated; and we had the satisfaction of seeing the dawn advance, and usher in one of the finest mornings the eyes ever beheld. About the middle of the night I was witness to one of the strangest scenes imaginable; both the novelty and the horridness of it will make so indelible an impression upon my mind that I shall never forget it. We were surprised at seeing a light at some distance before us, apparently on the banks of the river. On our nearer approach to it, we observed this fire to move in different strange directions, and for some time puzzled our imaginations in conceiving what it could be. At first we thought it might be some kind of *ignis fatuus*, produced from the particular situation of the country, which appeared to be swampy; but on our coming opposite to it, we saw distinctly the appearances of human beings nearly naked, and of a colour almost approaching to black; and each of these beings furnished with a couple of firebrands, which they held in each hand. There might be about a dozen of them, and they had got a large fire blazing in the middle of them, and were dancing round it in the wildest confusion imaginable, at the same time singing, or rather muttering, some strange incoherent sounds. Their peculiar appearance, whose effect was heightened by the contrast of the tempestuousness of the night, and the rolling of the thunder and lightning around us, put me in mind so much of the descriptions which are given of the infernal regions, that for the moment, I could not help considering them as so many imps let loose upon the earth to perform their midnight orgies; though it proved to be nothing more than a few Indians, who, disturbed by the inclemency of the weather, could not sleep, and were innocently diverting themselves with singing and dancing round their fire.

February 22nd—This morning, about nine o'clock, the wind began to increase again, and in the course of half an hour got so high, that we were obliged to make towards the shore, and fasten our boat to some trees on the banks. We were now ninety-four miles from Muskingham, where we were yesterday at one o'clock, having come that distance in about twenty hours, which is near five miles an hour. We went ashore here with our guns, to see if we could get any provisions, and soon brought home a couple of turkeys. We proceeded a few miles into the country, and found plenty of game and some excellent land. We also tried for some fish in the creeks we met with: we caught but few, and those of no excellent quality. We observed plenty of wild fowl, but did not think it worth while to kill them. We stopped here till three o'clock in the afternoon, when, the wind having abated, we pushed off from the shore, and, proceeding on our route, came to the Great Kanaway [River].[18] about seven o'clock, sixteen miles from where we stopped. There is a settlement on the eastern side of this river consisting of about twenty houses, and very appropriately called Point Pleasant; for though it was nearly dark when we arrived there, yet we saw enough of it to pronounce it a most delightful situation. We put ashore here to get some fodder for our horses, and some necessaries for ourselves; and about one o'clock in the morning (the night being remarkably serene and pleasant) we ventured to proceed on our journey.

About four miles below [the] Kanaway is a settlement formed by some French people, called Galliopolis, and near which there is an island; and about ten miles farther is another island; which are the only two islands (excepting three very near Limestone) between the Great Kanaway and Cincinnati, a distance of 200 miles. At half-past nine we came to Guyandot [Guyondotte] river (forty miles). It is but a small stream, though in high water navigable for batteaux. At twelve we came to [the] Big Sandy (twelve miles). This is the boundary of the state of Kentucky; so that, having passed this, we may consider ourselves in that famous country so celebrated by Imlay and others. At five we put ashore for the night, not wishing to proceed farther on account of the weather.

The next morning, *Friday, February 24th*, we started by daylight, and at nine we came to Tigent's [Tygert's] Creek, which is thirty miles from Big Sandy; and at ten we came to Sciota river, (five miles,) at the mouth of which, on the western side, there is a settlement of about eighteen or twenty houses.[19] Here the water had risen so high, that it had overflowed the banks, and the poor inhabitants of this settlement were in the greatest distress, endeavouring to save what little property they had in their houses from the desolating fury of the flood, and putting it on board canoes and rafts, and taking it to some place in the country where the water could not reach them. We would have offered them some assistance, but we did not discover their situation till we were opposite to them; and, going with the rapidity with which we did, it would have been impossible to have stopped our boat till we had got three or four miles below them; and then we could not have got at them, as our boat could not bear against the stream. At half-past one we were obliged to put ashore on account of the wind. The next morning,—

Saturday, February 25th,—starting about seven, we passed the salt works about eight, situated at the mouth of Saltlick Creek. This is twenty-one miles from the Sciota river, and consists of a few houses, where there are some salt works carried on from a neighbouring lick. These licks, of which there are a great number all over this western country, are nothing but salt springs, but have this peculiar circumstance attending them (from whence they derive their name) that the [impregnated] ground in their neighbourhood is *licked* up for a considerable distance by the deer, buffalo, and other wild animals, who frequent them at certain seasons of the year; and in such astonishing quantities, that a lick is easily found out by the road which is made by the frequent passing and repassing of these animals. Nay, Imlay says (page 323) that so great is the number of buffaloes and other animals that resort to these licks, that it fills the traveller with amazement and terror; especially when he beholds the prodigious roads they have made from all quarters, as if some leading to some populous city. The vast space of land around these springs is desolated as if by a ravaging enemy, and hills reduced to plains; for the land near these springs is generally hilly. At half-past nine we came to Graham's station, on the Kentucky shore (eight miles); it may contain about twenty houses; and at ten we came to an island, to the north of which the Little Sciota [River] comes in (two miles). About twelve we came-to, on account of the wind; went a shooting on the shore; saw plenty of deer and turkeys, but had no sport. We were now got into the neighbourhood of a settled country, and the wild animals were all very shy.

Sunday, February 26th, 1797.—About six o'clock this morning we started, and in about half an hour came to two islands close to each other, and about half-past nine came to Limestone (nineteen miles from Little Sciota). Limestone is called the landing place to Kentucky; and is generally made the resort of all the emigrants who are bound to the interior of this state. Here they land their goods and their domestic implements, whether of husbandry or of the household, and transport them to their distant settlement, in waggons which they either bring with them, or hire at this place.[20] It may contain from thirty to forty houses, situated on the western side of the mouth of a creek, and at the bottom of a hill. There is a place about a mile above (which we passed by) called the upper landing. This was a settlement formed prior to that of the town, and was meant for its site. Here a number of boats stop to unload, owing to there being convenient warehouses and cranes; but it has greatly fallen to decay lately. Limestone appeared to us a very dirty place when we came to it; the houses are chiefly log houses, and presented a much more pleasing prospect on our approach from the water than when close to it. Provisions of every kind were very dear when we were there, owing to the number of boats lately come down.

This may be said to be the first settlement in Kentucky, or rather the first place where the country begins to assume a settled appearance; and from this place, as far down as Louisville, at the [Ohio River] falls, which is 203 miles, the whole southern bank of the Ohio assumes a civilised appearance, and, from the agreeable mixture of woods and plantations, forms a number of most enchanting views.

We did not stop at Limestone above three or four hours, but, wishing to pursue our journey, we pushed off from the shore about one, and after going about twenty miles, were obliged to put-to again on account of the wind.

Monday, February 27th.—We started again, at six o'clock, and about half-past three we came to Columbia [near Cincinnati], our long-wished-for port, having, through unforeseen difficulties and unavoidable delays, been six months on our journey.

Baily's companion, Mr. Heighway, had joined several others in purchasing "about thirty or forty thousand acres of land" about forty miles up the Little Miami, where he intended to begin a town. They had bought this land for $1.25 per acre and were selling it to settlers for two dollars, with town lots priced at six dollars. Baily found living conditions not only rustic but filthy. After all the suffering to reach his destination, Baily "could not help smiling as I lay abed at the miserable hole I had got into." Moreover, the return journey east, he knew, would bring more challenges. To his great credit, Baily resolved to maintain a positive outlook and discover all that he could about the western settlements of America. On his return to England, Baily became a prosperous stockbroker.

12

David Meade, 1796

Virginia planter David Meade came from a privileged background.[1]
He was educated in England and elected to the House of Burgesses in
1769. Meade had also traveled extensively in America prior to his
journey to Kentucky. Although he had inherited a plantation in
Nansemond County, Virginia, he relocated to a new 600-acre planta-
tion in Prince George County, also in Virginia, in 1774. Meade re-
sided there until his departure for Kentucky in 1796, where his son
had, on his father's behalf, already purchased more than 300 acres of
prime land, superior in quality to his larger Virginia holdings. Mov-
ing an established planter household was no simple task. Horses ran
away; wagon wheels broke under the strain of mountain travel, and the
heavily laden boats became stuck on submerged obstructions. Before
reaching Redstone, three of Meade's numerous slaves had already found
opportunities to run away. Most of all, the migration of such a large
household was expensive. Meade, however, seemed more concerned
about maintaining his genteel posture than in the outflow of money.

The selection written by Meade is not in the form of a journal, but
a detailed letter to his sister, Mrs. Ann Randolph, wife of Richard
Randolph, in eastern Virginia. The letter, however, was written soon
after Meade's arrival in Kentucky and closely follows either a journal
or some sort of daily record. One of the more interesting aspects of
Meade's migration is that, in addition to his family, he was transport-
ing a number of slaves, and several comments indicate that their jour-
ney was more arduous.

Lexington, September ye 1st 96 My dear friend & Sister—In the short letter which I wrote you by Mr. O. Byrd I promised you that I would avail myself of the return of Judge Fleming to give you a more particular account of our present circumstances & the prospect we have before us of our future establishment, but will begin first with a narrative of our progress towards this Country and arrival at Lexington to which I may subjoin for the information of your sons particularly Brett & Ryland (who are the most likely to be interested by such information) the observations either phisical or moral, agricultural or commercial which I have made since we entered the western Country. You have long since been acquainted with our movements as far as our brother Richards in Frederick [County]—from thence we took our departure the 8th day of June & went no farther than Winchester [the county seat town].

9th traveled only sixteen miles & put up at a Dutchmans.[2]

10th continued our journey, crossed big Cacapon [creek], and notwithstanding heavy rains which had fallen the preceding evening (which made it most agreeable to ferry over) and showers this afternoon added to very rough roads, we advanced about twenty miles this day and put up at John Kieners a Saxon.[3]

11th forded little Cacapon. crossed the So. Branch Mountain, ferried over the So. Branch & got to Frankford upon Paterson's Creek in the evening having advanced this day sixteen miles, the roads remarkably good for a Mountainous Country—one of the large wheels of our baggage Waggon gave way this afternoon near Springfield, a small Hamlet (within five or six miles of Frankford) where we left it to be repaired.

12th waited for the baggage until twelve o'clock—which being repaired was advancing to join us when the wheel gave way a second time. it became now necessary to put new spokes in it all around. we therefore left it at Frankford for repair and proceeding on our journey, crossed the No[rthern]. Branch of Potowmack [Potomac River], entered Maryland, and arrived at Gwins an excellent Tavern at the foot of the Alleghany Mountains in the Evening, having traveled this day not quite twelve miles.

13th the hired Waggons joined us at about half after eight this morn. our baggage Waggon left at Frankford for repair the day before had advanced within a mile of us when one of the Iron axle trees gave way & we were detained several hours until it was repaired. fortunately for us a smiths shop was near. we advanced only six miles this day to Stidgers a German—our fare here was very tolerable, but the civility of the people & their attention to us made our stay here very agreeable.

14th the Iron axle tree of our Baggage Waggon again gave way in the same place this morn, but so near Stidgers where is a good smith that it was well mended. & we proceeded on our journey a quarter after two in the afternoon—and got to Tomlinsons at the little meadow—eleven miles on in good time. these repeated disasters of the baggage Waggon were really disheartening. Sally [Meade's wife] however preserved very good spirits.

15th advanced to Simkins's eleven miles eight miles of which is the worst road I had ever seen particularly the ascent & descent of Negroe Mountain the former rocky the latter almost entirely free from stone, but rendered bad by the number and depth of the ruts. here one of our hired Waggons overset without injury to any person or thing altho' there were several little negroes at the top of it.

16th a heavy rain this morning prevented our seting out before ten o'clock—two miles from Simkins's we crossed the line of Maryland and entered Pensylvania—six miles further the principal branch of the Yohogana [Youghiogheny] River, at this place called the great crossing & got with ease to Hall's eleven miles from Simkins's—the last mile of this days journey is steep & rough with stone, the rest tolerable.

17th purposing to get as far this day as Union or [also called] Beeson Town we set out earlier than usual the distance is twenty-one miles. the big meadows are about half way, memorable for the defeat & capture of the American Hero [George Washington] by the French before the declaration of War in 56[4]—here near the road was intered the body of Brad[d]ock the rash British General slain in the same War. to the Laurel ridge the roads are pretty good, but the ascent of the Mountain is rough and descent four miles the most so of any we have ever seen. from the laurel hill is extensive & beautiful views of the Country watered by the Monongahala river. from the foot of the Alleghanys to Union Town is two miles entirely free from stone. the Town is pretty well built, handsomely situated and well watered, the growth of timber for some miles about the town is altogether white Oak, and very beautiful.

18th David [Meade, Jr.], Geo. Royster & Upton went early this Morn to Redstone old fort for the purpose of procuring Boats and the rest of the Company followed at half past twelve. the roads not being good and the Country hilly we did not arrive at Redstone until eight in the Evening.

19th waiting for our hired Waggons we employed ourselves in making preparations for our voyage some [illegible] roofing was put to the Boat intended for our white family⁵—we this day had for dinner Pearch of the western waters—one of them weighed after being cleaned more than 6 1/2 lb—a few days afterwards in the Ohio we purchased one weighing 20 lb—

everything being in readiness we at nine o'clock June ye 20th embarked in two Boats all our Company, goods and carriages—the Horses we left under the care of Geo. Royster to be conducted by him & two negroe boys to Wheeling about a hundred miles below Pittsburg. the river being very low & continuing to fall fast, our floating houses moved very slowly. those vehicles are generally twelve feet wide & of various lengths. the two we had were 40 & 34 long—of the forty near two-thirds covered with a roof of boards put on in the featheredge way. this divided into two apartments formed a very comfortable habitation for our family which was increased by the addition of a Mr. Lee, a gentleman from Hagerstown in Maryland who requested a passage as far as Wheeling where he has a Store—-about five in the afternoon of this first days voyage in passing a narrow stony bar, our boat stuck upon it—by considerable exertion with all hands out into the water we however got off in about a quarter of an hour,—the other boats went clear, warned by our disaster. after sunset we ran upon a log, not one of those call'd in these waters a Sawyer, but one firmly fixed in the sand or mud at bottom. the danger now appeared to be greater than when we were a little before on the bar, but we had again the good fortune to get clear in a short time without any other injury than having had our fears excited on account of delay, the river continuing to fall fast.

21st we this day stuck upon shoals of large stone which made bars from one side to the other of the river—two or three times without injury to our boats. Just below the confluence of the Yohogany & Monongahala we took in a [local] Pilot to conduct us thro' Braddocks Riffle or Ripple as all the shoals in the western Rivers are call'd, where there are falls or rapids. this called Braddock's is the most considerable in the Monongehala & most difficult & dangerous to pass. it is about twelve miles [upstream] from Pittsburg. notwithstanding the precaution used in hireing a Pilot both boats stuck at different parts but were got under way—without injury or much delay—our voyage the rest of this night as well as the preceding was without obstruction.

22nd arrived at Pitt (as it is usually called in these parts for brevity) about nine o'clock this Morn. & stayed there until three in the afternoon (the whole time employed in procuring stores) when we continued our Voyage now down the Ohio. from this time the scenes presented to our view in the whole course of our passage were entirely different from what my imagination had ever represented to me & by which I had hitherto been misled. whether or not the Idea I had formed of the lands lying immediately upon the river was grounded upon representations of those who had navigated it I will not positively say, but why should I have supposed it so different from what it is unless I had been told that the famed Ohio in its passage of so many hundred miles to unite with the Misissipi watered for the most part a Mountainous & ruggid Country—but so very different is the truth that from Pittsburg (where indeed the lands are extreamly broken but not Mountainous) the Country on each side of the river as you recede from that town become more & more level & in the whole course of the river as far as we have navigated it no very high lands or distant mountains are to be seen. On the contrary the Ohio here & there mildly murmuring in more places almost sleeping—but generally gently sweeping thro' the finest & most extensive valey perhaps in the world—on one side or the other of the river, are extensive low grounds, or bottoms as they are here called, a great part of the distance on both sides—but always on one side or the other—so extreamly rich, that (in the judgment of those individuals of our Company who were frequently on shore) the most indifferent of it is better than the best upon [Virginia's] James River below the Falls [at Richmond] has ever been, this eulogy of the Ohio Country may seem to my friends to be but the effusions of an imagination always rather disposed to be visionary but now warmed by the novelty of the scene,—that it is not the case, cannot at this time be proved & I shall submit to you & others the credit of such facts as I may advance upon the evidence of my opinion, and they will be established with, or rejected by you, as you may think my judgment cool or intemperate. the first impressions which the scenes I have witnessed made upon my mind are not likely ever to be removed, for as often as I contemplate the subject, I feel convictions of the propriety & justness of them, firmly persuaded that the River Ohio waters the finest and most extensive rich Country on this Globe, founding my belief on what I have heard from others but much more upon what I have seen with my own eyes. it is natural enough for me to anticipate with pleasure the future g[r]andeur of these western regions, it requires no preternatural spirit of prophesy to foresee what in the nature of things must inevitably come to pass (unless nature should violate he[r] own laws which is impossible) an immense population on the banks of the Ohio—Cities, Towns & Villages never out of the travelers view and more of them than are at present or ever can be hereafter on the banks of the Rhine or Danube, in ten or at most fifteen years, there will not be a tree left on the bank of the Ohio but such as may be intended for ornament—before that time the voyage from Pittsburg will [be] taken by people of fortune for pleasure—already it is agreeable. there was but one day during our passage to Limestone (so astonishing has been the progress of population) that we did not procure from on shore both morn and afternoon Milk & Cream. settlements are made daily. we saw many where the belted Trees[6] were yet alive & many where the patches of Corn were not more extensive than your Garden. little more than eighteen months ago [before the army's victory at Fallen Timbers] there was danger in landing upon either shore. when we came down some of our company went on shore ten times a day. we had a punt constantly plying between our boats & the land sometimes on one side sometimes on the other—I myself (cautious as I usually am & at that time rendered so to a degree of timidity by the discharge which I had) went several times to land & generally on the Indian Shore [modern Ohio] where I sometimes walked a mile or two in the woods along the bank & at some distance from it. on the eve of this day about dark in passing a Riffle or rapid both boats stuck fast, but were extricated with much exertion in half an hour. we however secured our boats to the shore a little below for the night, having been informed that there was another more difficult of passage about three miles below us.

23rd. at sunrise got under way, being here thirteen miles from Pitt. passed the difficult rapid call'd the dead riffle & between eleven & twelve passed by the mouth of big Beaver Creek twenty-eight miles from Pitt. Fort McIntosh is within a quarter of a mile below on the same side where is likewise a Ferry. this day passed several Creeks and George Town where is a Ferry. continued to drop down the river all night.

24th passed thro the Mingo bottom and by the mouth of Buffiloe Creek where is a Hamlet of several well looking two story log houses & two of brick not finished. at half after two in the night we moored our boats at Wheeling twelve or fourteen miles below Buffiloe.

25 Wheeling is a small Hamlet in situation & population very like Buffiloe but the houses are not so good. Col. [illegible, probably Zane] who resides here is building a pretty two story small brick house. our horses had been at Wheeling two or three days before us. we now embarked them but were obliged to take them out again, the horse boat proving so leaky that it became necessary to caulk the lower seam almost all round, we in consequence remained where we were all night, and did not proceed on our voyage until after sunup the next morn.

26th passed the mouths of several Creeks this day & continued our course all night.

27th this morning at eight near forty miles from Wheeling we entered the eighteen mile reach, continued droping down all night and on the

28 at nine in the morn arrived Marietta, mouth of the Muskingum, about ninety miles below Wheeling. here the wind riseing at S.W. and blowing fresh we lay by until ye evening & landed our horses to pasture. at seven o'clock got the horses on board again & moved down. we had advanced only two miles when thunder sq[u]all all coming up we brought our boats too on the Harrison shore for the night which proved very tempestuous with unceasing rain, some part of the time very heavy.[7] upon this occasion our old dining room carpet did us good service. it had been drawn over the chamber part of our cabbin in a [illegible] rain whilst we lay at Wheeling.

29th this morning after the rain was the first since we embarked at Redstone without a considerable fog on the river. twelve miles from Muskingum passed the mouth of little Kenahwa [River] nearly opposite to which is a settlement called [Belpre] which continues on the bank of the river several miles. here we saw a Mill in the river upon boats,—continued moving all night.[8]

30th passed the [illegible] falls this afternoon. at two o'clock piloted a very obliging Piroguean who had kept company with us from Muskingum. this good man was from grove [Grave] Creek on the Virginia shore twelve miles below Wheeling and was bound to Cincinnati the capital of the N. W. territory with seventeen or eighteen barrels all of them flour but one of Maple sugar in a very long Canoe or as they are called on the Ohio Pirogues—the falls are the most considerable rapids in the River except the great rapids of Louisville—continued as usual moving on all this night.

July 1st at eight this morning arrived at Point pleasant, the mouth of the great Kanawha,—here we were so fortunate as to purchase the carcass of a large Doe just brought in by a hunter. this proved a very reasonable acquisition, for our black people were at short allowance of both meat & bread; we had found provisions of kinds for man as well as horse scarce & very dear ever since we left Winchester. we had purchased every article at [expensive] Tavern prices, our grain had uniformly cost us a shilling per gallon. nor did we find it otherwise in Kentucky. Indian Corn between Limestone & this place included has been, & yet is, five shillings a bushel—Oats the same until a plentiful new crop has reduced them to eighteen pence—our Doe was the cheapest provisions we had hitherto met with, being only two pence a pound, a price which would have been thought high at any time before this Summer,—we left point pleasant after a short stay having had very little inducement to land there other than that of sending our horses on shore to graze for an hour or two, but which had at this time been like to cost us much vexation for by the negligence of the Boys set to look after them they [got] out of the liments of the Hamlet at this place and we were in danger of not recovering them for several days,—fortunately for us, however, a man was coming along the road towards the point, stoped & stayed them until our people got up & drove them back—four miles below point pleasant is the French settlement, Gallipolis, on the opposite shore. it consists of a long string of small log huts built adjoining each other with some two story frame houses of but indifferent appearance—that this settlement is not in a flourishing state is not to be wondered at. it had been made several years back at a time when (probably) there was rather a cessation of hostilities with the Indians than a regular ratified peace, and the poor people have had every [sic] since until within eighteen months to contend with all the evils which could be brought upon them by war, and that with a savage enemy. You may judge what must have been the wretched situation of those people (some of whom were genteel and many very excellent artists) when you are informed of those tactics in this western country on the frontiers or any exposed places—whilst part of the company (of whom perhaps are the women & small boys) are cultivating the ground, the men & youths with their Riffles walk round the field all the time to prevent a surprize by the Savages—under such unfavorable circumstances the French settlement of Gallipolis could not thrive. many valuable workmen in different arts withdrew to other parts more safe from Indian depredation—those who remained have met with another discouragement in addition to those which have been

mentioned—their title to the land was more than questionable—
they were (to the discredit of the American character) shame-
fully cheat'd—however Congress has befriended them so far as
to secure to them the property in a small part of the lands immediately about their Town.[9] here David & Geo. Royster went
on shore & procured a few stores in part of which was a large
loaf of the best bread we had heretofore seen in the western
Country. continued moving downwards all this night and
on ye 2nd passed the big and little Sandy, the little Scioto, and
about dawn of Day on ye 3[r]d passed the big Scioto near fifty
miles above Limestone. at about eleven this Forenoon we met
three large keel Boats rowed by naked Copper colored men—
of very savage appearance and working with prodigious exertion. I had little doubt [to] what race of men they belonged &
notwithstanding my reason assured me that there was nothing
like hostility to be expected from them my fears were all awakened and I will confess that I did not feel altogether easy until
they were out of sight which was in a very short time for they
plied their oars with a degree of agility and force unknown on
James River [in Virginia]—I observed that white men were at
the Helm of each Boat from which circumstance I formed the
conjecture that they were Indian traders & that being at peace
with the Indians they had hired some of them to navigate the
Boats—the number of copper color'd men were probably over
twenty in all the boats we ha[i]led each other as we passed at
the distance of about a hundred & twenty yards but we did not
understand what they said either in questioning us or in reply
to us, but we should do them the justice to say that they behaved with savage civility for we could distinguish a sound
articulating how do mistress—a small distance below where
we met the Boats and thirty miles above Limestone are salt
works where David landed and was informed that Boats we
had seen were from the Illinois Country bound to Pittsburg
loaded with Furs & Lead, and that the people who navigated
them were a mongrel race between French & Indian—they are
said to make excellent watermen,—
a little after sunrise on the 4th of July being the day on which
Independence was declared, the great festival of America, we

grounded our Boats or floats on the shores at Limestone—which receives all the little consequence it professes from its having been heretofore the only tolerable safe place for emigrants to land at and is at present perhaps not far from its highest point of prosperity for there are now much more convenient places a little above—at best it is but a trifling Hamlet scarcely equal to Wheeling—a great part of the day was spent in debarking everything in our boats & purchasing for the journey [overland to Lexington]—at five o'clock in the evening we set out with very poor horses and tattered Carriages. we had hired only one Waggon which could carry only part of our baggage. the rest we stored at Limestone,—we found no little difficulty in ascending a very high hill (call it mountain) beginning at the back of the Hamlet which stands on a narrow slip of low ground. it was nearly dark when we reached [the town of] Washington. only four miles from the landing in the course of this short journey [slave] Henry in a drunken frolic (his passion for which he continues to indulge more freely than ever) deserted us, going off before my face in the woods—he was the next morning taken up at Limestone & together with David's [slave] Pointer who had likewise absconded, and were both found tied & confined in a warehouse—the poor drunken Henry joined us the next evening—we have from necessity employed him to wait upon us in the house ever since having no other male house servant than the little Boy Dian—we now feel very sensibly the loss of Baddow, as we did during the continuance of our journey the want of so good a Postillion as Syphax—Washington is the second town in Kentucky for population. it at present consists of one long street & stands upon waveing ground which will prevent its ever appearing to advantage—the houses are partly of logs & partly framed. there are some stone houses tolerably well built & sizeable upon the whole I do not think it a handsome town—the Country in the vicinity is extreamly fertile but more waveing than any other part of Kentucky I have yet seen—we found very good quarters at Washington in a two-story log tavern. the next morning not very early—

e 5th we proceeded on our journey and without meeting with any but petty disasters of the minor class. we got that night to a mean Cabbin on Johnsons fork of the Licking [River]where our horses found much better fare than we did. Sally & the Girls [Meade's wife and daughters] had now become such veteran travelers that they were willing to make a sacrafice of some part of their own comfort to the good of our horses.

6th we moved onwards to a Cabbin within six miles of Paris (Bourbon Courthouse). the distinction between a log house & Cabbin is that the former has a shingled roof—whereas the other has a roof of slabs put on without nails & secured by long poles or rather logs stretched length-ways of the roof to keep the slabs or boards down. in these Cabbins many opulent and some Genteel people live in them even at this time & I am told that they are by the latter made more than barely comfortable—we have not yet met with any in this stile—from Johnson's Fork a visible change in the quality of the soil takes place. hitherto it was all fine, it was now changed to Oakland and what is here call'd poor to the Blue lick on the main Fork of the Licking about six miles—but of this there is great part that would be thought good with you & little very bad. within this distance of Kentucky poor land are several good plantations on the road. the knobs about the Blue licks are so extreamly sterile that a few trees only are to be seen upon them & a very thin herbage. the cause of this appearance probably is, that the earth in the immediate vicinity has been so strongly impregnated with salt that the surface of the earth has been licked off by the Buffiloe & other wild animals—at these Licks about fifty bushels of salt is daily made from different springs, not all the property of one person. I was informed that there is water enough for two hundred bushels daily—this place is memorable in the annals of Kentucky for the many that have been killed at it by the Indians & one or two considerable defeats[10]—after breakfasting here we continued our journey for about six or seven miles thro' a drought or narrow valley rising all that distance the land being of inferior quality but much of it very good. the lodging this night was much worse than the night before, for it was the filthiest Cabbin we had heretofore been in.

7th we were on the road by times this morning and got to Paris in good time for breakfast. this village is very thriveing & well built, more of Brick & Stone than of Wood—of the former are several large well-looking houses, of the number a new Courthouse not complete of stone—we arrived this evening before sunset at Lexington all well—it was difficult for our friend Charles Byrd (who had been joined by David a few hours before our arrival) to procure any kind of private quarters—he however did succeed in geting the two upper rooms of a two story framed house where after remaining about seven or eight days we removed to better lodgings in a more agreeable part of the Town which we have taken for three months at the rate of Fifty five pounds per annum. we here have the upper & garret rooms of a two story brick house—two large apartments & a closet on each floor—the population of Lexington is unusually great for the extent of it which in the latter respect does not exceed my expectations, but if we take a retrospective view of it to a point of time not more than seven or eight years back it must astonish. here are now very many (I will not say elegant) handsome brick houses—and some few of stone—framed houses likewise & many of logs but chiefly two storys high— of the inhabitants are several genteel families, chiefly from the northern States. many new houses are now building, more of them of brick than of timber.[11]

The remainder of Meade's letter, which continues at length, describes Lexington and central Kentucky in positive terms. His intention was clearly not only to satisfy his sister's curiosity but to encourage her family to likewise consider relocating to the new west. He believed that if his sister's husband Richard Randolph was, like he had been, thoroughly frustrated with making his tidewater plantation thrive, "I assert that with his great activity & skill in husbandry brought into action—two or three thousand pounds [money] and the Negroes which he at present possesses, would enable him to live as well here (if not better) upon that fine estate, . . . & he would here be more in the way of procuring lands for his Children." Meade remained in rented quarters in Lexington until a residence suitable for a transplanted Virginia planter's family could be constructed on his tract of land. His determination to maintain a genteel life somewhat distinguished him from the majority of early Kentucky settlers, who expressed a greater inter-

est in long-term prosperity, as when he had commented critically on the genteel settlers content to reside in cabin quarters while getting established.

As Meade was to discover, however, a genteel posture involved considerable expense.

13

Andrew Ellicott, 1796

Andrew Ellicott, born in 1760, was already a prominent surveyor by the time of his trip down the Ohio River in 1796. He went as an official agent of the United States government to survey the southern frontier and help establish the actual boundary between the United States and Spanish Florida. Ellicott had previous public service as Virginia commissioner for extending the Mason-Dixon Line in 1784 and a few years later in surveying the boundary between Pennsylvania and New York. President Washington personally appreciated Ellicott's contributions in executing L'Enfant's plan for the District of Columbia. He was therefore well qualified to locate and mark the northern boundary of Spanish Florida. Ellicott's scientific inclinations included gathering climatic data, a distinctive feature in his journal entries. Ellicott's entries also reflect an advantage unavailable to most western travelers: official credentials and government aid.

This selection from Ellicott's journal is drawn from his report, published in 1800 with maps and extensive observations. It begins with his arrival at Pittsburgh on September 28, 1796, having departed from his home near Philadelphia on the sixteenth, and follows his journey as far as Louisville.

[September] 28th, Cloudy: left Greensburgh at seven o'clock in the morning, and rode to Col. John Irwin's and took breakfast, from thence to M'Nair's and dined. Left M'Nair's in a heavy rain, which continued till I arrived at Pittsburgh.—Thermometer 60° in the morning, rose to 68°.

The morning after my arrival at Pittsburgh I waited upon Major Craig, and found that he had two boats ready, one of them flat-bottomed, commonly called a Kentucky boat, the other a second hand keel-boat. These being insufficient he was requested to procure another, which he did in a few days, it was likewise a second hand one. After leaving Major Craig, I waited upon Col. Butler, and presented an order from the secretary of war for a military escort: he gave me assurances, that the men should be ready by the time the waters were sufficiently high to descend the river. The waggons with our stores, instruments and baggage arrived on the 3rd of October.

On the 4th I examined the state of the instruments, and found that some of them were injured by the jolting of the waggons; repaired them on the 5th. On the 6th, found the water in the Alleghany river 68°; that in the Monongahela 64°; and a few paces within the coal-pit, the temperature of the water was 51°.

On the 16th, there was a small rise of the water, and the three boats were sent off, but had not waters to proceed more than three miles. On the 20th, Gen. [James] Wilkinson, and his family arrived, and he very politely gave his boat up to me;[1] it was a second hand one, but the cabbin was new and spacious. The 21st and 22nd, were spent in making some repairs to the boat, and on the 23rd, I went on board of it, and proceeded down the river to the others, and made such a distribution of the loading, that each vessel drew about the same water.

During my stay at Pittsburgh, the fogs were very heavy, every morning except two, and on those days we had rain.—The thermometer was at no time below 48° nor above 71°.

The town of Pittsburgh continues to improve, the situation is favourable, being on a point of land formed by the confluence of the Alleghany and Monongahela rivers, from which circumstance it enjoys a considerable trade.

24th, Got under way about 10 o'clock in the forenoon, but the water was so low, that it was with difficulty we made eight miles.—the thermometer rose to 76°. The morning was very foggy.

25th, Left the shore at sunrise. The large boat was stopped for want of a sufficiency of water, three times in the course of the day; but by the exertions of about thirty men, she was brought along. Fog in the morning—Thermometer rose from 53° to 71°.

26th, Got under way early in the morning. The large boat was so much injured by dragging her over the stones, that the men had to keep lading out the water all last night: proceeded with great difficulty down to a small town, opposite to the mouth of little beaver [creek]. The large boat did not arrive. Fog in the morning—Thermometer rose from 42° to 70°.

27th, The large boat arrived early in the morning, but so much injured that we had to unload her, stop the leaks and make some repairs; reloaded about 4 o'clock in the afternoon, and proceeded a short distance down the river, to get clear of the town, where some of our men got intoxicated, and behaved exceedingly ill. This will generally be found the case in all small, trifling villages, whose inhabitants are principally supported by selling liquor to the indiscreet and dissipated in the neighbourhood, and to the imprudent traveller. Fog in the morning—Thermometer rose from 41° to 69°.

28th, Left the shore early in the morning; the fog was so thick that when our boats were within twenty yards of each other, they could not be discovered by any of the persons on board. We made about sixteen miles this day. The water had but little motion.—Thermometer rose from 39° to 61°.

29th, Got under way very early in the morning: but little fog; the atmosphere had been so full of smoke ever since we left Pittsburgh that it was but seldom we could see across the river distinctly, but it was carried off this morning by a smart north west wind.

The buildings on the river banks, except in the towns, are generally of the poorest kind, and the inhabitants, who are commonly sellers of liquor, as dirty as their cabbins, which are equally open to their children, poultry and pigs. This is generally the case in new settlements; the land being fresh, produces with little labour the immediate necessaries of life, from this circumstance the habit of industry is diminished, and with it the habit of cleanliness.

Encamped in the evening opposite to the Mingo bottom which is rendered memorable for the inhuman murder of the Indians of that name, who resided on it, either by, or at the instigation of Capt. Cresup, Harman[,] Greathouse, and a few others. This outrage was followed by a war of retaliation, which continued for many years with a cruelty scarcely to be equalled in the annals of history.[2]

The evening became calm, and the atmosphere again loaded with smoke, occasioned by the dead leaves and grass, over a vast extent of the country being on fire, which during the night, illuminated the clouds of smoke and produced a variegated appearance beautiful beyond description. Our smoky weather in spring and autumn, is probably the effect of fire extending over the vast forests of our country.

Our people were much fatigued by dragging our boats over the shoals.—Thermometer rose from 39° to 57°.

30th, Detained till one o'clock in the afternoon by the commissary who was endeavouring to procure some meat; but being disappointed we proceeded down the river to Buffalo, where we were again disappointed. Buffalo is a decent village, and is situated on the east side of the river, just above the mouth of a rivulet of the same name. Left Buffalo in the evening, and proceeded about three miles and encamped. The morning was very smoky.—The thermometer rose from 30° to 51°.

31st, Our commissary went on a few miles before us, and purchased three beeves, we followed between seven and eight, in the morning; it was then so smoky, that we proceeded with difficulty. Encamped about four miles above Wheeling. Several of our men were indisposed with sore throats, owing probably to colds contracted from their frequent wettings [in getting the boat over the shoals].—Thermometer rose from 36° to 47°.

November 1st, About one o'clock in the morning we had a furious gale of wind; it appeared, as if nature was making an exertion to free the atmosphere from the astonishing quantity of smoke, with which it had been filled for so many days. Stopped at Wheeling and took the latitude, and then proceeded to the mouth of Grave Creek and encamped. Went to view the amazing monuments of earth, thrown up many ages ago by the aborigines of the country, for some purpose unknown to us. One of those monuments is more than 70 feet high: it has a cavity or depression on the top, in which a large oak tree was growing. The atmosphere again becomes smoky in the evening.—The thermometer rose from 30° to 52°.

2d, Found that one of our soldiers had deserted after being detected in stealing liquor: made search for him but to no purpose. Got under way at ten o'clock, but our progress was much impeded by dragging our boats over the shoals. Encamped at five in the evening. Cloudy with an appearance of rain most of the day, but cleared off in the evening.—Thermometer rose from 29° to 50°.

3d, Got under way about 7 o'clock in the morning, and continued down the river till sun down. The large boat was impeded by a strong head wind, and did not overtake us till eight o'clock in the evening. Cloudy in the morning but no fog, clear at night.—Thermometer rose from 36° to 55°.

4th, Set out early in the morning, but our progress was impeded by head winds. Encamped at sunset. The large boat did not overtake us. Cloudy with thick smoke all day.—Thermometer rose from 35° to 56°.

5th, Left the shore before sunrise, and proceeded down the long reach: at the lower end of it the water was so shoal, that we were two hours employed in dragging our boats over the gravel, and then encamped. The large boat still behind. The fog was so thick in the morning, that for four hours, when in the middle of the river, we could see neither shore; some appearance of rain in the evening.—Thermometer rose from 33° to 49°.

6th, Left the shore at seven o'clock in the morning.—Thermometer rose from 37° to 51° a strong head wind all day, and but little smoke or fog.

7th, Set off at sunrise, and arrived at Marietta about eleven o'clock in the forenoon. Unloaded the boats to stop the leaks, and make some repairs. Smoke as in the morning.—Thermometer rose from 25° to 56°.

8th, The men were employed in repairing the boats. Viewed the amazing works thrown up many ages ago by the Indians.[3] They are the most regular of any I have seen. Some smoke and fog in the morning.—Thermometer rose from 31° to 52°.

9th, Our men still employed in repairing the boats. Our large store boat arrived in the evening. The smoke was so thick all day that we could not see over the river.—Thermometer rose from 34° to 53°.

10th, The boats were repaired, and loaded by one o'clock in the afternoon, we then proceeded down the river.

Marietta is a handsome town, standing on a high bank, on the west side of the Ohio river, just above the mouth of the Muskingum. The annual rise of the water has sometimes inundated the lower part of the town. The latitude by a mean of four good observations appeared to be 39° 24' 21'.

During our stay, we were treated with great politeness by Col. Sproat, and a sensible young gentleman by the name of Tupper, a son to the General of that name. I paid a visit to Gen. [Rufus] Putnam, who had lately been appointed Surveyor General of the United States, and presented him with one of my pamphlets upon the variation of the magnetic needle. He did not return the visit, neither did I hear from him afterwards. The fog and smoke was so thick till ten o'clock in the forenoon, that we could not distinguish one person from another the length of one of our boats. Encamped at sun down.—Thermometer rose from 34° to 56°.

11th, Left the shore at seven o'clock in the morning. Passed the little Kanhawa [River], and afterwards a miserable village by the name of Belle Prae, next a floating mill, and lastly, the mouth of little Hockhocking [River].[4]

The ordinary streams of water in that part of the western country, so universally fail in the summer, and beginning of autumn, that the inhabitants are under the necessity of having recourse to floating mills, or to others driven by the wind, or worked by horses to grind their corn. Those floating mills are erected upon two, or more, large canoes or boats, and anchored out in a strong current. The float-boards of the water-wheels, dip their whole breadth into the stream, by which they are propelled forward, and give motion to the whole machinery. When the waters rise, and set the other mills to work, the floating ones are towed into a safe harbour, where they remain till the next season. Although floating mills are far inferior to permanent ones driven by water, they are nevertheless more to be depended upon than wind mills, and may be considered preferable to those worked by horses. The lessening of manual labour and that of domestic animals, is a subject at all times, and in all countries, which merits the attention of the moralist, the philosopher and legislator. The effect produced by either the wind, or water, is not attended with any expense, and while those elements are directed to the execution of some valuable purpose, manual labour, and that of domestic animals, may be employed in a manner equally beneficial to the community, and more to their ease, safety, and convenience.

Encamped opposite to a miserable village called Belle Ville: made 24 miles this day.[5] Fog in the morning, and smoky all day.—Thermometer rose from 37° to 66°—Water in the river 45°.

12th, Left the shore at daylight. Dragged our boats over several shoals, and encamped at sun down. Very smoky all day.—Thermometer rose from 37° to 55°.

13th, Got under way very early; had to drag our boats a considerable distance over the shoals, with which one of them was much injured. Encamped about sun down, and caught a number of fine cat fish, one of them weighted more than 48 pounds. Very smoky all day.—Thermometer rose from 27° to 52°.

14th, Were under way at daylight, and arrived in the evening at Point Pleasant, a small and indifferent village on the east side of the river, just above the mouth of the great Kanawha. We were politely treated by Mr. Allen Pryor of that place. Near to where the village now stands, was fought the memorable battle between a detachment of Virginia militia, (commanded by Col. Lewis) and the Shawnee and Delaware Indians [in 1774]. The engagement continued several hours, and the victory was a long time doubtful, and alternately appeared to favour each party; courage, address and dexterity equally characterized both; but the Virginians remained masters of the field.[6]

We had a light shower of rain in the morning, and two in the evening. The atmosphere yet filled with smoke.—Thermometer rose from 41° to 62°.

15th, Arrived at Gallipolis about eleven o'clock in the forenoon. This village is situated on a fine high bank, on the west side of the river, and inhabited by a number of miserable French families. Many of the inhabitants that season fell victims to the yellow fever, which certainly originated in that place, and was produced by the filthiness of the inhabitants, and an unusual quantity of animal, and vegetable putrefaction in a number of small ponds, and marshes, within the village. Of all the places I have yet beheld, this was the most miserable.

There are several Indian mounds of earth, or barrows, within the vicinity of the village. Detained the remainder of the day in procuring meat. The smoke yet continues.—Thermometer rose from 40° to 62°.

16th, Left Gallipolis at eight o'clock in the morning. About two in the afternoon, one of our boats went to pieces in a body of strong rough water, and it was with difficulty conveyed to the shore without sinking. Encamped at sunset. A strong north wind all day, which carried off the smoke.—Thermometer rose from 37° to 52°.

17th, Left the shore at daylight: got fast on a shoal, which extends across the river when it is low, by which we were detained two hours in drawing our boats over it: detained again from one, till two o'clock in the afternoon in passing another shoal. Shortly afterwards, two black men belonging to a boat we fell in with in the morning, were drowned in attempting to go to the shore in a canoe. We sent some of our people to aid in finding them, one was taken up but could not be revived. Light showers of rain in the evening.—Thermometer rose from 27° to 63°.

18th, Left the shore before sunrise, got fast, and were detained for more than one hour. Passed the mouth of Sandy Creek, which is one of the boundaries between the states of Virginia and Kentucky. Encamped just before dark. A heavy fog in the morning, the afternoon remarkably clear.—Thermometer rose from 43° to 64°. Water in the river 46°.

19th, Set off before day, got fast on a log where we remained till near sunrise. The fog was so thick, that we could neither discover sand-bars nor logs, till it was too late to avoid them. The fog disappeared about ten o'clock in the forenoon: reached the mouth of the Big Scioto [River] a short time before noon, and took the sun's meridional altitude, by which the latitude appeared to be 38° 43' 28'N. The waters of the Scioto have a strong petrifying quality. We collected several fine specimens.[7] Proceeded down the river, and encamped after sunset.

Cloudy, with thunder and lightening in the evening, accompanied by a shower of rain. The atmosphere again filled with smoke.— Thermometer rose from 43° to 65°.

20th, Left the shore at daylight, had a sharp thunder gust between six and seven o'clock, in the morning. At ten o'clock, I left the boats, and went on shore with my skiff to view the salt works, which are about one mile from the river, in the state of Kentucky, and collected the following information, *viz.* that 300 gallons of water, produce one bushel of salt: that they had 170 iron kettles, and made about 30 bushels of salt per day, which sold for 2 dollars cash per bushel, or 3 dollars in trade, *as they term it* [meaning barter]. The salt lick, or spring, is situated in the bed of a small creek, which when high overflows it. The back water from the river also inundates the lick, or spring, when high, together with all the works. From these causes, they were not able to carry on the business more than eight months in the year. But the greatest difficulty they found, was with the *bitter water*, which I supposed was what the manufacturers of salt in England, call bittern, and drains from the salt after it is granulated, and stowed away in the drales to dry. However I asked the manager for an explanation, who replied, "Bitter water is mixed with the salt water, and separated from it in this manner. After boiling the water, till the salt will just begin to crystallize, it is laded out into troughs, or vats, and let stand for some time, and the bitter water which assumes a dark brown colour, floats on the top of the salt water, and is skimmed off, and thrown away, and if this separation was not made, the salt would not properly granulate, but become tough, and form a hard mass of a bitter taste, and quite useless: and if the bitter water was evaporated, it would leave a hard mass of matter, of a disagreeable, and nauseous taste, but as it was useless, they had none of it by them." He likewise informed me, that the bitter water was very injurious to cattle, by inflaming the skins of such as frequently drank it, that the same effect was often experienced by their workmen, and that in a few hours it would destroy the quality of leather. The lick, or spring, does not appear to have been much frequented either by buffaloes, or deer, and the cattle in the neighbourhood are not remarkably fond of it. The temperature of the water in the spring was 60°.

Returned to the river, and followed the boats, passed two villages, one in Kentucky by the name of Preston, the name of the other I did not learn. Overtook my company about sunset, and encamped. Cloudy in the evening.—Thermometer rose from 45° to 70°. Water in the river 50°.

21st, Set off before day, and arrived at Limestone about ten o'clock in the forenoon. It is a miserable village; left it in about an hour. Encamped at dark. Cloudy, with mist, and light showers all day.—Thermometer rose from 39° to 42°.

22nd, Rain, and hail from four till ten o'clock in the forenoon, when a heavy fall of snow began, and continued till night. The weather was so extremely bad, that we could not proceed.— The thermometer was 42° in the morning, 33° at noon, and 25° at eight o'clock in the evening.

23rd, Clear morning, and hard frost, cleared our boats of ice and snow by ten o'clock in the forenoon, and proceeded down the river. Encamped at sunset.—Thermometer rose from 19° to 27°.

24th, Got under way at eight o'clock in the morning. About eleven o'clock in the forenoon my boat struck the root of a lodged tree in the river, and was so much injured by it, we had to put in to shore and stop the leak, which detained us till noon. The river was much lower than it had ever been known, since the first settlements commenced in that country, and it was with the greatest difficulty we made any progress on that day, being obliged to drag our boats over several shoals, of considerable extent, the weather at the same time being so cold, that the men's clothes froze stiff almost as soon as they came out of the water. Encamped after sun set on the east side of the river, opposite to a village called Columbia.—Thermometer rose from 14° to 25°. Water in the river 40°.

25th, Proceeded to Cincinnati, where we arrived about ten o'clock in the forenoon, and found ourselves under the necessity of procuring another boat, in place of one which was rendered useless by dragging it over rocks, stones, and shoals, and repairing the one I had from General Wilkinson. The waters were so low that no boats but ours had reached that place from Pittsburgh since the preceding August, and the season was then so far advanced that no others could be reasonably expected. Our success was owing to the number of people we had with us, and whose quiet submission to unusual hardships does them great credit. A clear day.—Thermometer rose from 20° to 25° and fell to 14° at nine o'clock in the evening.

26th, A clear day.—Thermometer 3° below 0 at sun rise, rose to 21° but fell to 9° at ten o'clock in the evening. Water in the river 33 ½°.

27th, A clear day.—Thermometer 7° at sunrise, rose to 25°. The water rose this day about 2 inches.

28th, A little fine snow last night.—Thermometer rose from 15° to 37°. In the evening the water appeared to have risen about one foot.

29th, A fine pleasant day, and the snow began to melt. The boat being repaired, and another procured, we left Cincinnati in the evening. The water had risen about three feet.—Thermometer rose from 35° to 46°.

Cincinnati was at that time the capital of the North Western Territory: it is situated on a fine high bank, and for the time it has been building, is a very respectable place. The latitude by a mean of three good observations is 39° 5' 54° N. During our stay, we were politely treated by Mr. Winthrop Sargeant, secretary of the [territorial] government, and Captain [William Henry] Harrison who commanded at Fort Washington.

30th' Floated all night, and passed the mouth of the Great Miami early in the morning. The river in much better order for boating. Rain and snow all day. Encamped in the evening.—Thermometer rose from 26° to 37°. Water in the river 35°.

December 1st, Left the shore at daylight. Snow and rain the whole day. Encamped about dark.—Thermometer 37° all day.

2d, Set off at daylight. Stopped and took breakfast at a small village just above the Kentucky river. Made but little way on account of a strong head wind. Encamped at dark. Cloudy all day.—Thermometer continued at 29°.

3d, Got under way at daylight but made little way on account of

head winds. Encamped at dark.—Thermometer rose from 23°
to 30°. Water in the river 33°.

4th, Set off at daylight, and proceeded down to the rapids, and
encamped. The water was so low that the pilots would not be
answerable for the safety of the boats in passing the falls.—
Thermometer rose from 28° to 35°.

5th, Concluded to risk the boats, rather than be detained till the
rise of the waters, and sent all the people, who were either
afraid of the consequences, or could not swim, round by land,
and a little after noon, all the boats were over, but not without
being considerably damaged: the one that I was in, had nine of
her timbers broken. Squalls of rain and snow, all the afternoon.—Thermometer rose from 24° to 29°.

6th, Spent at work upon our boats. Squalls of snow all day.—
Thermometer rose from 21° to 28°.

7th, Finished repairing our boats. Cloudy great part of the day.—
Thermometer rose from 18° to 26°.

8th, Detained till evening by our commissary, who was employed
in procuring provisions. Set off about sun down.

The town of Louis Ville stands a short distance above the rapids
on the east side of the river. The situation is handsome, but
said to be unhealthy. The town has improved but little for some
years past. The rapids are occasioned by the water falling from
one horizontal stratum of lime-stone, to another; in some places
the fall is perpendicular, but the main body of the water when
the river is low, runs along a channel of a tolerably regular
slope, which has been through length of time worn in the rock.
In the spring when the river is full, the rapids are scarcely perceptible, and boats descend without difficulty or danger.—Thermometer rose from 22° to 29°.

*Andrew Ellicott and his crew proceeded down the Ohio and Missis-
sippi rivers to New Madrid, Natchez, and New Orleans and then on
to conduct their survey.*

Notes

Preface

1. John Mack Faragher, *Women and Men on the Overland Trail* (New Haven: Yale University Press, 1979); Julie Roy Jeffrey, *Frontier Women: The Trans-Mississippi West, 1840–1880* (New York: Hill and Wang, 1979); Wallace Stegner, *The Gathering of Zion: The Story of the Mormon Trail* (New York: McGraw Hill, 1964); John D. Unruh Jr., *The Plains Across: The Overland Emigrants and the Trans-Mississippi West, 1840–60* (Urbana: University of Illinois Press, 1982); Malcolm J. Rohrbough, *Days of Gold: The California Gold Rush and the American Nation* (Berkeley: University of California Press, 1997). The number of published personal diaries are legion (and the unpublished are even more numerous and not to be overlooked). To read a few in their entirety is highly recommended.

2. Thomas L. Purvis, "The Ethnic Descent of Kentucky's Early Population: A Statistical Investigation of European and American Sources of Emigration, 1790–1820," *Register of the Kentucky Historical Society* (hereafter cited as *RKHS*) 80 (1982): 253–66; Lee Shai Weissbach, "The Peopling of Lexington, Kentucky: Growth and Mobility in a Frontier Town," *RKHS* 81 (1983): 115–33; Elizabeth A. Perkins, *Border Life: Experience and Memory in the Revolutionary Ohio Valley* (Chapel Hill: The University of North Carolina Press, 1998), 28–29 and 56–59; Ellen Eslinger, *Citizens of Zion: The Social Origins of Camp Meeting Revivalism* (Knoxville: The University of Tennessee Press, 1999), 79–84. On early American literacy, see William J. Gilmore, *Reading Becomes a Necessity of Life: Material and Cultural Life in Rural New England, 1780–1835* (Knoxville: The University of Tennessee Press, 1989); Joseph F. Kett and Patricia A. McClung, "Book Culture in Post-Revolutionary Virginia," *Proceedings of the American Antiquarian Society* 94 (1984): 97–105. On the general circulation of information among potential emigrants, see Hazel Dicken-Garcia, *To Western Woods: The Breckinridge Family Moves to Kentucky in 1793* (Rutherford, N.J.: Fairleigh Dickinson University Press, 1991).

3. United States Department of Commerce, *Historical Statistics of the United States, Colonial Times to 1970*, Part I (Washington, D.C.: Bureau of the Census, 1975), 24–37.

Introduction

1. These two speculative undertakings, as well as several less ambitious plans for British expansion, challenged French claims to the American interior and helped

fuel the French and Indian War. See Thomas Perkins Abernethy, *Western Lands and the American Revolution* (New York, London: D. Appleton-Century Company, Inc., for the University of Virginia Institute for Research in the Social Sciences, 1937); Jack M. Sosin, *Whitehall in the Wilderness: The Middle West in British Colonial Policy, 1760–1775* (Lincoln: University of Nebraska Press, 1986); Richard White, *The Middle Ground: Indians, Empires, and Republicans in the Great Lakes Region, 1650–1815* (Cambridge: Cambridge University Press, 1991).

2. Among the western explorers were dozens of anonymous men known as "long hunters" from the colonial backcountry who would hunt for months at a time as part of a small group. Robert L. Kincaid, *The Wilderness Road* (Indianapolis and New York: The Bobbs-Merrill Co., 1947), 67; Thomas L. Connelly, "Gateway to Kentucky: The Wilderness Road, 1748–1792," *RKHS* 59 (1961): 109–32; Lucien Beckner, "John Findley, Pathfinder of Kentucky," Filson Club Historical Quarterly (hereafter cited as *FCHQ*) 43 (1969): 206–15. The literature on Daniel Boone is enormous, but a good place to start is John Mack Faragher, *Daniel Boone: The Life and Legend of an American Pioneer* (New York: Henry Holt and Co., 1992).

3. William Allen Pusey, *The Wilderness Road to Kentucky: Its Location and Features* (New York: George H. Doran Co., 1921), 9–10; Thomas Speed, *The Wilderness Road: A Description of the Routes of Travel by Which the Pioneers and Early Settlers First Came to Kentucky* (New York: Burt Franklin, 1886); Kincaid, *Wilderness Road*, 67–76; Beckner, "John Findley"; Faragher, *Daniel Boone*, 76–78.

4. Randolph C. Downes, *Council Fires on the Upper Ohio: A Narrative of Indian Affairs in the Upper Ohio Valley until 1795* (Pittsburgh: University of Pittsburgh Press, 1940); Lucien Beckner, "Eskippakithiki: The Last Indian Town in Kentucky," *FCHQ* 6 (1932): 355–82; William C. Sturtevant, ed., *Handbook of North American Indians: Northeast* (Washington, D.C.: Smithsonian Institution, 1978); Gregory Evans Dowd, *A Spirited Resistance: The North American Indian Struggle for Unity, 1745–1815* (Baltimore: The Johns Hopkins University Press, 1992); Michael N. McConnell, *A Country Between: The Upper Ohio Valley and Its Peoples, 1724–1774* (Lincoln: University of Nebraska Press, 1992); White, *Middle Ground*. European diseases had exerted a devastating effect on aboriginal people all along the Atlantic coast, so that by the late eighteenth century many native groups were amalgamations of once-distinct peoples. To speak of "tribes" is therefore often, though not always, inaccurate.

5. Faragher, *Daniel Boone*, 89–96; Neal O. Hammon, *My Father, Daniel Boone: The Draper Interviews with Nathan Boone* (Lexington: The University Press of Kentucky, 1999).

6. Robert McAfee, interview by Lyman C. Draper. Lyman C. Draper Collection, Wisconsin State Historical Society, Madison, Wisconsin, 14CC102 (microfilm ed.).

7. Humphrey Marshall, *History of Kentucky*, 2 vols. (Frankfort: George S. Robinson, 1824), 1:32–35; Faragher, *Daniel Boone*, 128–29; Neal O. Hammon, "The Fincastle Surveyors at the Falls of the Ohio, 1774," *FCHQ* 47 (1973): 14–28. Floyd worked as deputy under Joseph Preston, surveyor for Fincastle County, Virginia's westernmost county, which included Virginia's uninhabited transmontane territory on the "western waters." These were the only legal Kentucky claims. Governor Dunmore limited his exceptions to the famous Proclamation Line to accommodate several prominent friends, including George Washington, who had military warrants

from the French and Indian War. Floyd settled his family in Kentucky in 1783 and established Floyd's Station on Beargrass Creek. There, he commanded the Jefferson County militia and served under George Rogers Clark on two campaigns but was fatally wounded in an Indian ambush. See Hambleton Tapp, "Colonel John Floyd, Kentucky Pioneer," *FCHQ* 15 (1941): 1–24 and Anna M. Cartlidge, "Colonel John Floyd: Reluctant Adventurer," *RKHS* 66 (1968): 317–68.

8. Boone and Stoner's swift and risky 800-mile mission became part of the Boone legend, with justification. Faragher, *Daniel Boone*, 100–101.

9. Shawnee rights had already been compromised by the Iroquois in the Treaty of Fort Stanwix in 1768. The Iroquois claim was based on their defeat of the Shawnees in the early eighteenth century. As both the Iroquois and the British were aware, but allowed self-interest to ignore, the Shawnees did not acknowledge Iroquois rights to cede their territory. The paper concession signed at Fort Stanwix merely eliminated Iroquois claims to the upper Ohio Valley. As a result, the Shawnees, Delawares, and their allies mounted formidable resistance to American settlement of the Ohio Valley. On Dunmore's War, see Reuben Gold Thwaites and Louise Phelps Kellogg, eds., *Documentary History of Dunmore's War, 1774* (Madison: Wisconsin State Historical Society, 1904), and Randolph C. Downes, "Dunmore's War: An Interpretation," *Mississippi Valley Historical Review* 21 (1934): 311–30.

10. Draper Coll., 48J10–11. Such praises were no exaggeration. Bluegrass land was, and is, some of the continent's best real estate. The problem for Kentucky settlers would be gaining secure title, something that wartime Virginia mismanaged. See Patricia Watlington, *The Partisan Spirit: Kentucky Politics, 1779–1792* (Chapel Hill: The University of North Carolina Press for the Institute of Early American History and Culture, 1972), 24–26; Joan Wells Coward, *Kentucky in the New Republic: The Process of Constitution Making* (Lexington: The University Press of Kentucky, 1979); Perkins, *Border Life*. Historians Stephen Aron, *How the West Was Lost: The Transformation of Kentucky from Daniel Boone to Henry Clay* (Baltimore: The Johns Hopkins University Press, 1996) and Fredrika Teute, "Land, Liberty, and Labor in the Post-Revolutionary Era: Kentucky as the Promised Land," (Ph.D. diss., Johns Hopkins University, 1988), have portrayed Kentucky as fraudulent because approximately half of all Kentuckians failed to become landowners by 1800. A period of tenancy, however, was a common step toward eventual land ownership throughout America and the failure to immediately acquire title to Bluegrass land did not necessarily constitute failure to contemporaries. See Perkins, *Border Life*, 126–28; and Ellen Eslinger, *Citizens of Zion*, 69–77.

11. Kentucky was not the only region to suffer the attention of Britain's Indian allies. The entire backcountry from Pennsylvania to Georgia required militia support and precious materiel. The suffering and loss were extreme and many people returned to the "old settlements" to await safer times. Many others ventured to Kentucky only long enough to claim land for future settlement. In order to reduce civilian casualties the federal government would prohibit territorial settlement until Indian claims had been extinguished through conquest or treaty.

12. Kathryn Harrod Mason, *James Harrod of Kentucky* (Baton Rouge: Louisiana State University Press, 1951). Harrod, it should be noted, was hardly alone in his ambitions. A group led by the McAfee brothers was also making claims in the vicinity, as well as less well-documented others. See Robert McAfee Papers, Draper Coll., 14CC102–104

13. The Cherokees were not the sole native claimants, as the Henderson proprietors knew but chose to ignore. Furthermore, Virginia considered this territory part of its dominion on the basis of its original charter. As Humphrey Marshall, one of Kentucky's earliest historians stated, "Whether the gentlemen of this association were ignorant of the Virginia charter, or supposed it gave no pre-emptive rights of purchase from the Indians; or whether they were encouraged to this act of aggression . . . by the increasing difficulties and beginning of war, between Great Britain and her American subjects, is not certainly known." Marshall, *History of Kentucky*, 1:13–14.

14. Speed, *Wilderness Road*, 25; Archibald Henderson, "Richard Henderson and the Occupation of Kentucky, 1775," *Mississippi Valley Historical Review* 1 (1914): 341–63; Neal O. Hammon, "The First Trip to Boonesborough," *FCHQ* 45 (1971): 108–112. The historical literature on the Transylvania venture is extensive, due in large measure to its association with Daniel Boone. The best place to start is still George W. Ranck, *Boonesborough: Its Founding, Pioneer Struggles, Indian Experiences, Transylvania Days, and Revolutionary Annals*, Filson Club Publications, no. 16 (Louisville: John P. Morton and Co., 1901).

15. "Felix Walker's Narrative of his Trip with Boone from Long Island to Boonesborough, in March 1775," in Ranck, *Boonesborough*, 163. In Kentucky, the "cane" (*Arundinia macosperma*) was thought to mark the best land. Also, it played a valuable role as fodder for livestock at a time when land had yet to be cleared for pasture because it remained green even in winter. Its dense growth also provided good cover for escape from Indians. To blaze a trail through it, however, not to mention then keeping the path open, posed arduous work. See McHargue, "Canebrakes in Prehistoric and Pioneer Times in Kentucky," in Eugene L. Schwaab, ed., *Travels in the Old South, Selected from the Periodicals of the Times*, 2 vols. (Lexington: The University Press of Kentucky, 1973) 1:31; John A. Jakle, *Images of the Ohio Valley* (New York: Oxford University Press, 1977), 57–58; and Perkins, *Border Life*, 74.

16. Speed, *Wilderness Road*, 27; Marshall, *History of Kentucky*, 1:30; Charles Gano Talbert, *Benjamin Logan, Kentucky Frontiersman* (Lexington: The University of Kentucky Press, 1962). Benjamin Logan came to Kentucky as an experienced pioneer of western Virginia. Despite Logan's modest family background, his military abilities and other leadership qualities led to positions of public trust in Kentucky. Logan's Station was located about one mile from the modern town of Stanford. It was about eighteen miles southeast of Harrodsburg and thirty-five miles southwest of Boonesborough. Another spur near the end of Boone's route was followed by early Tennessee settlers, turning south at the Rockcastle hills. See Speed, *Wilderness Road*, 63–64, and Malcolm Rohrbough, *The Trans-Appalachian Frontier: Societies and Institutions* (New York: Oxford University Press, 1978) 15–16.

17. Kentucky constituted the westernmost part of Virginia. The Virginia legislature, prompted by the Transylvania challenge, established it as Kentucky County in 1776, voided the Transylvania Company's claims in 1778, and provided for land acquisition in 1779. At the time Kentucky was admitted as the fifteenth state in 1792, it comprised nine counties. See William Waller Hening, *The Statutes at Large, Being a Collection of all the Laws of Virginia from the First Session of the Legislature in 1619*, 13 vols. (Richmond: printed for the author by George Cochran, 1823) 9:257, 9:358, 9:571–72. Generous rights were granted to settlers with claims prior to 1776, but thereafter Kentucky land had to be purchased. It was up to the purchaser to

locate vacant land, have it surveyed and recorded in court—a cumbersome process that later produced innumerable lawsuits. See Neal O. Hammon, *Early Kentucky Land Records, 1773–1780*, Filson Club Publications, 2nd ser., no. 5 (Louisville: Filson Club, 1992); and George Morgan Chinn, *Kentucky Settlement and Statehood, 1750–1800* (Frankfort: Kentucky Historical Society, 1975), 209–22. The Kentucky fiasco convinced the national government of the need for a more orderly and less privatized process for land claims in the federal territories.

18. Gilbert Imlay, *A Topographical Description of the Western Territory of North America, Containing a Succinct Account of the Climate, Natural History, Population, Agriculture, Manners and Customs* (London: 1792; Dublin, Ireland: printed for Waller James, 1793), 142. Redstone, modern Brownsville, was often referred to as Redstone Old Fort due to its origins as a fortification.

19. Most histories of the Wilderness Road focus on establishing the original route. See, for example, Speed, *Wilderness Road*, and Charles A. Hanna, *The Wilderness Trail, or The Ventures and Adventures of the Pennsylvania Traders on the Allegheny Path, with Some New Annals of the Old West* (New York and London: G.P. Putnam's Sons, 1911). The premier description is probably Pusey, *The Wilderness Road to Kentucky*. Pusey not only studied maps and travel accounts, but also added field observations. Pusey has been enhanced by the meticulous study of early court records by Neal O. Hammon, "Early Roads into Kentucky," *RKHS* 68 (1970): 91–131.

20. Joseph Martin played a pivotal role in western defense during the Revolution and the lingering border unrest. Virginia commissioned him superintendent of Indian affairs in 1777, a post he held until 1786. Martin held a similar appointment from North Carolina between 1783 and 1789. His fortified outpost about twenty miles east of Cumberland Gap was the single settlement between Anderson's Block House and the Crab Orchard in Kentucky for many years. Martin later served in the Virginia Assembly and as a brigadier general of the Virginia militia. See William A. Pusey, "General Joseph Martin, an Unsung Hero of the Virginia Frontier," *FCHQ* 10 (1936): 57–82.

21. J.F.D. Smyth, *A Tour in the United States of America, Containing an Account of the Present Situation of That Country: The Population, Agriculture, Commerce, Customs, and Manners of the Inhabitants*, 2 vols. (London: printed for G. Robinson, J. Robson, and J. Sawell, 1834) 1:120.

22. James Taylor, "Autobiography of Gen. James Taylor of Newport, Kentucky," typescript copy, Reuben T. Durrett Collection, Regenstein Library, University of Chicago, Chicago, 2. Taylor traveled through the area in 1792. Rev. David Barrow Diary, entry dated 23 May 1795, Draper Coll., 12CC165. On the expensive nature of Pittsburgh, see Georges-Henri-Victor Collot, *A Journey in North America*, 2 vols. (Paris: Printed for Arthus Bertrand, 1826; reprint ed. Firenze: O. Lange, 1924), 1:33. Collot's observations date from 1794. See also Francois A. Michaux, "Travels to the West of the Allegany Mountains in the States of Ohio, Kentucky, and Tennessee," in Reuben Gold Thwaites, ed., *Early Western Travels, 1748–1846*, 32 vols. (Cleveland: The Arthur H. Clark Co., 1904), 3:162.

23. A. Lee, "Journal of Arthur Lee," quoted in John W. Harpster, ed., *Pen Pictures of Early Western Pennsylvania* (Pittsburgh: University of Pittsburgh Press, 1938), 157; John Pope, *Tour through the Southern and Western Territories* (Richmond: printed by John Dixon, 1792), 17. See also John May, *Journal and Letters of*

John May, of Boston, Relative to Two Journeys to the Ohio Country (Cincinnati: Robert Clarke and Co., 1873 for the Historical and Philosophical Society of Ohio, 1873), 34.

24. Andre Michaux, "Journal of Andre Michaux," in Thwaites, ed., *Early Western Travels*, 3:32; Michaux, "Travels to the West," 3:157–58; "Extract from the Journal of a Trip from Philadelphia to New Orleans by Way of the Mississippi and the Ohio, 1799," attributed to merchant Louis Tarascon, entry dated 8 September 1799, Filson Historical Society, Louisville, Ky. See also Richard C. Wade, *The Urban Frontier: Pioneer Life in Early Pittsburgh, Cincinnati, Lexington, Louisville, and St. Louis* (Chicago: The University of Chicago Press, 1959, reprint edition), 10–13.

25. Collot, *Journey in North America*, 1:32–33; Lyman C. Draper, ed., *Narrative of a Journey Down the Ohio and Mississippi in 1789–90* (Cincinnati: Robert Clarke and Co., 1888), 23; Michaux, "Travels to the West," 3:166. Most boats were also outfitted with a small brick or sand hearth for cooking on board. Some sort of crude shelter or cabin was another common feature. A broad oar served as a rudder. See also Leland D. Baldwin, *The Keelboat Age on Western Waters* (Pittsburgh: University of Pittsburgh Press, 1941), 44–47; Archer B. Hulbert, *Waterways of Westward Expansion: The Ohio and Its Tributaries* (Cleveland, Ohio: Arthur H. Clark Co., 1903); Michael Allen, *Western Rivermen, 1763–1861: Ohio and Mississippi Boatmen and the Myth of the Alligator Horse* (Baton Rouge: Louisiana State University Press, 1990), 66–67. Keelboats were usually square, with a shallow draft, but unlike flatboats, provided with a heavy timbered base to better absorb shocks.

26. Clement L. Martzolff, ed., "Reminiscences of a Pioneer," *Ohio Archaeological and Historical Quarterly* 19 (1910): 192; John Hedge Interview, Draper Coll., 12CC117; Beverley Bond Wood Jr., ed., "Memoirs of Benjamin Van Cleve," *Quarterly Publication of the Historical and Philosophical Society of Ohio* 17 (1922): 19; Mrs. Pierce Interview, Draper Coll., 13CC7; "Early Settlement of the Ohio Valley: Letters from Capt. Laurence Butler to Mrs. Joseph Craddock," *The Magazine of American History* 1 (1877): 42. A rich portion of Lyman C. Draper's extensive collection of materials on the late-eighteenth-century frontier consists of pioneer interviews conducted by Presbyterian minister John D. Shane that were conducted mainly during the 1840s. Shane was primarily interested in the military aspects of settlement but collected much other information on pioneer life. He did not record interviews verbatim, but his detailed notes are sometimes so vivid that the reader can almost hear the subject's rocking chair creak. The most thorough analysis of Shane's work is Elizabeth A. Perkins, *Border Life*.

27. *The Pittsburgh* (Penn.) *Gazette*, 10 November 1787 and 10 May 1788. Bayard also advertised his boatyard in Philadelphia (see *The Pennsylvania Journal*, 20 August 1788). See also the *Pittsburgh Gazette* advertisements of Alexander Craig's boatyard opposite Pittsburgh dated 8 November 1788 and that of Duncan, Berryman and Company at Elizabethtown on the Monongahela River, dated 20 June 1789. On the seasonality of travel, see Perkins, *Border Life*, 156–58.

28. Imlay, *A Topographical Description of the Western Territory*, 146; William M. Kenton Statement, Draper Coll., 8S18; Christian Schultz, quoted in W. Wallace Carson, "Transportation and Traffic on the Ohio and the Mississippi before the Steamboat," *Mississippi Valley Historical Review* 7 (1920–21): 30. See also Baldwin, *Keelboat Age*, 52–53. Some flatboats were accompanied by canoes as tenders, allow-

ing easy access to shore. Americans used both British pounds and dollars during this period.

29. John Taylor, quoted in Speed, *Wilderness Road*, 54; B.B. Wood, "Memoirs of Benjamin Van Cleve," 16; Imlay, *A Topographical Description of the Western Territory*, 146; Tarascon, "Extract from the Journal," entry dated 8 September 1799.

30. Tarascon, "Extract from the Journal," entry dated 10 September 1779; Lucien Beckner, ed., "A Sketch of the Early Adventures of William Sudduth in Kentucky," *FCHQ* 2 (1928): 43–44; Otto A. Rothert, ed., "John D. Shane's Interview with Colonel John Graves of Fayette County," *FCHQ* 15 (1941): 240. See also "Journal of J. Gregg in Kentucky, 1796," entry dated 3 April 1796, typescript copy, Reuben T. Durrett Collection, University of Chicago.

31. Michaux, "Travels to the West," 3:33; Tarascon, "Extract from the Journal," entry dated 10 September 1799; Michaux, "Travels to the West," 3:171–72. On the urban rivalry between Pittsburgh and Wheeling, see James M. Callahan, "The Pittsburgh-Wheeling Rivalry for Commercial Headship on the Ohio," *Ohio Archaeological and Historical Publications* 22 (1913): 40–54.

32. Interview No. 25, Draper, Coll., 13CC82; "Unfinished Autobiography of John Rowan—A Sketch of His Youth—Written in 1841 at Federal Hill, Ky.," in Willard Rouse Jillson, *Tales of the Dark and Bloody Ground: A Group of Fifteen Original Papers on the Early History of Kentucky* (Louisville: C.T. Dearing Printing Co., 1930), 91–92.

33. Benjamin Hardesty Interview, Draper Coll., 11CC169; Lucien Beckner, ed., "John D. Shane's Notes on an Interview with Jeptha Kemper of Montgomery County," *FCHQ* 12 (1938): 153; "Diary of Major Erkuries Beatty, Paymaster of the Western Army, May 15, 1786 to June 5, 1787," *The Magazine of American History* 1 (1877): 175. See also Lucien Beckner, ed., "Shane's Interview with Benjamin Allen, Clark County," *FCHQ* 5 (1931): 67; "Some Particulars Relative to Kentucky," in Schwaab, *Travels in the Old South*, 1:55; "Autobiography of Gen. James Taylor," 6. See also J. McClure Interview, Draper Coll., 12CC153; Eleanor Duncan Wood, "Limestone, a Gateway of Pioneer Kentucky," *RKHS* 28 (1930): 151–54.

34. Lewis Condict, "Journal of a Trip to Kentucky in 1795," *Proceedings of the New Jersey Historical Society* 4 (1919): 117; Collot, *Journey in North America* 1: 97. See also Andrew Wood Statement, Draper Coll., 7S113.

35. G. Glenn Clift, *"Second Census" of Kentucky, 1800* (Baltimore: Genealogical Publishing Co., 1982), v.

36. Donald F. Carmony, ed., "Spencer Records' Memoirs of the Ohio Valley Frontiers, 1766–1795," *Indiana Magazine of History* 55 (1959): 338; Benjamin Hardesty Interview, Draper Coll., 11CC169; Ned Danaby Interview, Draper Coll., 11CC164. According to Hardesty, the lack of human presence at Limestone induced a number of Ohio voyagers to continue to Louisville, despite its longer approach to central Kentucky by several days. Some effort was made to maintain the road from the Lower Blue Licks to Bryant's Station (one of the earliest and larger stations). From Bryant's, emigrants could follow buffalo traces farther into the interior. See Mrs. William H. Coffman, "Big Crossing Station, Built by Robert Johnson, Recorded in John D. Shane's Interview with Pioneer Ben Guthrie," *FCHQ* 5 (1931): 9; Beckner, "Interview with Jeptha Kemper," 153. A periogue was a style of large canoe, usually burned out of a log.

37. Ned Danaby Interview, Draper Coll., 11CC164. The town of Washington grew around a station built by frontiersman Simon Kenton in 1784 and quickly surpassed Limestone in population. Paris was the seat of the more densely settled Bourbon County, established in 1786. As this instance reveals, road building was burdensome for frontier communities. Also, additional manpower had to be devoted to a militia guard to protect the road workers.

38. Beckner, "Shane's Interview with Benjamin Allen," 67. The Allens reached Strode's Station in Clark County, where former neighbors had settled, in merely three days, but the family left most of their goods in storage at Limestone, probably enabling them to travel more quickly. The Allen story did not, however, end happily. A short time later, Mr. Allen was killed while hunting with young Benjamin, who was captured by Indians but who soon managed to escape.

39. Carmony, "Spencer Records' Memoirs," 341. William Sudduth was in the fort and also mentions this incident in his memoirs. See Beckner, "Early Adventures of William Sudduth," 46; Coffman, "Big Crossing Station," 8; Samuel Potts Pointer Interview, Draper Coll., 12CC247.

40. Tarascon, "Extract from the Journal," entry dated 27 September 1799.

41. James A. Jacobs, *The Beginning of the U. S. Army* (Princeton, N.J.: Princeton University Press, 1947); Francis Paul Prucha, *The Sword of the Republic: The United States Army on the Frontier, 1783–1846* (Lincoln: University of Nebraska Press, 1969), 17–40; Rohrbough, *Trans-Appalachian Frontier*, 48–52.

42. Robert L. Reid, *Always a River: The Ohio River and the American Experience* (Bloomington and Indianapolis: Indiana University Press, 1991), 135; Julia Perkins Cutler, *Life and Times of Ephriam Cutler Prepared from His Journals and Correspondence* (Cincinnati: Robert Clarke and Co., 1890), 22; Condict, "Journal of a Trip to Kentucky," 116; Martin R. Andrews, *History of Marietta and Washington County, Ohio, and Representative Citizens* (Chicago: Biographical Publishing Co., 1902); Samuel P. Hildreth, *Pioneer History: Being an Account of the First Examination of the Ohio Valley and Early Settlement of the Northwest Territory* (Cincinnati: H.W. Derby and Co., 1848); E.C. Daws, "The Beginnings of the Ohio Company and the Scioto Purchase," *Ohio Archaeological and Historical Society Publications* 4 (1895): 1–19; Andrew R. L. Cayton, *The Frontier Republic: Ideology and Politics in the Ohio Country, 1780–1825* (Kent, Ohio, and London: The Kent State University Press, 1986).

43. *Pennsylvania Gazette*, 19 September 1792; Michaux, "Travels to the West," 3:35; Tarascon, "Extract from the Journal," entry dated 15 September 1799. See also John L. Vance, "The French Settlement and Settlers of Gallipolis," *Ohio Archaeological and Historical Society Publications* 3 (1890–91): 45–81; Theodore Thomas Belote, *The Scioto Speculation and the French Settlements at Gallipolis* (New York: Burt Franklin, 1907) 45–81; John Francis McDermott, "Gallipolis as Travelers Saw It, 1792–1811," *Ohio State Archaeological and Historical Quarterly* 48 (1939): 283–303.

44. Condict, "Journal of a Trip to Kentucky," 119 and 118; Michaux, "Travels to the West" 3:35; Tarascon, "Extract from the Journal," entries dated 20–22 September 1799; Wade, *The Urban Frontier*, 22–25.

45. B. B. Wood, "Memoirs of Benjamin Van Cleve," 16 and 40; Pope, *Tour through the Southern and Western Territories*, 18; William Brown quoted in Speed,

Wilderness Road, 57–59; Michaux, "Travels to the West," 3:33; Tarascon, "Extract from the Journal," entry dated 10 September 1799; Michaux, "Travels to the West," 3:171–72; Cutler, *Life and Times of Ephriam Cutler*, 21; James Hedge Interview, Draper Coll., 12CC17; Beckner, "Early Adventures of William Sudduth," 46; Beckner, "Shane's Interview with Benjamin Allen," 67; "Journal of J. Gregg," entry dated 13 May 1796; Webb Interview, Draper Coll., 13CC75; John Taylor quoted in Speed, *Wilderness Road*, 54. The length of the trip and its level of difficulty predominate most emigrant diaries and memoirs, overshadowing comments on the landscape or personal matters.

46. John May to Samuel Beall, 15 April 1780, Beall-Booth Family Papers, Filson Historical Society; William Brown quoted in Speed, *Wilderness Road*, 19–20; "Autobiography of Allen Trimble," *The Old Northwest Genealogical Quarterly* 9 (1906): 212.

47. John Taylor quoted in Speed, *Wilderness Road*, 54.

48. Wade Hall, ed., "Along the Wilderness Trail: A Young Lawyer's 1785 Letter from Danville, Kentucky to Massachusetts," 61 *FCHQ* (1987): 288–95; John Taylor quoted in Speed, *Wilderness Road*, 54; "Personal Narrative of William Lytle," *Quarterly Publication of the Historical and Philosophical Society of Ohio* 1 (1906): 3; Cutler, *Life and Times of Ephriam Cutler*, 21; Beckner, "Early Adventures of William Sudduth," 43 and 45; William Brown quoted in Speed, *Wilderness Road*, 19; Lyman C. Draper, ed., *Narrative of a Journey Down the Ohio and Mississippi in 1789–90* (Cincinnati: Robert Clarke and Co., 1888): 23; "Letters from Capt. Laurence Butler," 42; "Journal of J. Gregg," entries dated 28 April 1796 and 2 May 1796.

49. Chester Raymond Young, ed., *Westward into Kentucky: The Narrative of Daniel Trabue* (Lexington: The University Press of Kentucky, 1981), 44 and 47.

50. Otto A. Rothert, ed., "John D. Shane's Interview with Pioneer John Hedge, Bourbon County," *FCHQ* 14 (1940): 180; Beckner, "Early Adventures of William Sudduth," 44–45. Lucien Beckner, ed., "Rev. John Dabney Shane's Interview with Mrs. Sarah Graham of Bath County," *FCHQ* 9 (1935): 227; Carmony, "Spencer Records' Memoir," 338. See also Herman Bowman Interview, Draper Coll., 13CC170.

51. Wymore interview, Draper Coll., 11CC130. (Raids were less common in winter, when snow made the trail easy to follow.) Beckner, "Interview with Mrs. Sarah Graham," 236; Isaac Hite to Abraham Hite, 26 April 1783, Filson Historical Society, Louisville, Ky.; Hall, "Along the Wilderness Trail," 289. See also William Fleming to Ann Fleming, 25 Sept 1779, Fleming Family Papers, Filson Historical Society, Louisville, Ky.

52. "Autobiography of Gen. James Taylor," 17; *Kentucky* (Lexington) *Gazette*, 1 November 1788. Other examples for 1788 can be found in the issues dated 12 April, 3 May, 17 May, and 29 November, indicating a regular stream of eastward travel. "Letters from Capt. Laurence Butler," 46.

53. Beckner, "Early Adventures of William Sudduth," 46; B.B. Wood, "Memoirs of Benjamin Van Cleve," entry dated 21 Aug 1792, 40; Speed, *Wilderness Road*, 66; Lewis Collins, *History of Kentucky*, 2 vols. (Louisville: Richard H. Collins, 1877), 2:113. See also letter of Charles Scott to the governor of Virginia, 2 April 1791, Draper Coll., 14S9–10.

54. Hall, "Along the Wilderness Trail," 292; Jane Stevenson Interview, Draper Coll., 13CC136; Hickman, "A Short Account of My Life and Travels," Reuben T.

Durrett Collection, University of Chicago, Chicago, 13; Condict, "Journal of a Trip to Kentucky," 122; F.F. Jackson Interview, Draper, Coll., 15CC66.

55. Smyth, *Tour in the United States*, 1:317, 318, 320, 322, and 232.

56. William Brown quoted in Speed, *Wilderness Road*, 19–20.

57. "Autobiography of Allen Trimble," 207–8.

58. Michaux, "Travels to the West," 3:164.

59. Beckner, "Interview with Jeptha Kemper," 152; Cutler, *Life and Times of Ephriam Cutler*, 19; Nathan Ewing Statement, Draper Coll., 25S43.

60. Beckner, "Interview with Jeptha Kemper," 152; B.B. Wood, "Memoirs of Benjamin Van Cleve," 16.

61. Alexander Martin to Zachariah Johnston, 26 April 1791, Zachariah Johnston Papers, Leyburn Library, Washington and Lee University, Lexington, Va.

62. William Brown quoted in Speed, *Wilderness Road*, 62; B. B. Wood, "Memoirs of Benjamin Van Cleve," 40.

63. "Autobiography of Allen Trimble," 208; Hall, "Along the Wilderness Trail," 292. The William Christian family was probably also in this group. His wife commented in a letter that constant rain made the trip miserable. See Ann Christian to Ann Fleming, 17 August 1785, Hugh Blair Grigsby Family Papers, Virginia Historical Society, Richmond, Va.

64. "Autobiography of Allen Trimble," 211.

65. "Journal of General Butler," in *The Olden Time*, 2 vols. (Pittsburgh: J.W. Cook, 1846–1848), 2:440, entry dated 5 October 1785; Major Bean Interview, Draper Coll., 11CC105.

66. Otto A. Rothert, ed., "John D. Shane's Interview, in 1841, with Mrs. Wilson of Woodford County," *FCHQ* 16 (1942): 228; "Personal Narrative of William Lytle," 3; William W. Backus, *A Genealogical Memoir of the Backus Family with the Private Journal of James Backus* (Norwich, Conn.: William W. Backus, 1889), entry dated 7 January 1789, 40; "Autobiography of John Rowan," 94; Mrs. Charles A. Hofstetter, ed., "Journal of John Wallace, 1786 to 1802," *Kentucky Ancestors 5* (1971): 115.

67. Newton D. Mereness, "Colonel Fleming's Journal, 1779–1780," in *Travels in the American Colonies* (New York: The Macmillan Co., 1916), entry dated 25 December 1779, 626; Herman Bowman Interview, Draper Coll., 13CC170; James Masterson Interview, Draper Coll., 11CC131; Francis Ransdell Slaughter to John Ransdell, 30 January 1780, Francis Ransdell Slaughter Papers, Filson Historical Society.

68. Ann Christian to Ann Fleming, 13 September 1785, Hugh Blair Grigsby Family Papers; Cutler, *Life and Times of Ephriam Cutler*, 21.

69. Rothert,"Shane's Interview with Colonel John Graves," 239; John Thompson to John Breckinridge, 14 June 1792, Breckinridge Family Papers, Library of Congress, Washington, D.C.; Drake, *Pioneer Life in Kentucky: A Series of Reminiscential Letters from Daniel Drake, M.D., of Cincinnati to His Children* (Cincinnati, Ohio: Robert Clarke, 1870), 176; *Virginia Centinel and Gazette, Or the Winchester Repository*, 3 November 1794 and 9 November 1795; Clift, *"Second Census" of Kentucky, 1800*, iv–xiii. The two classic works on Kentucky slavery deal sparsely with the eighteenth century: Ivan E. McDougle, *Slavery in Kentucky, 1792–1865* (Lancaster, Pa.: Press of the New Era Printing Co., 1918) and J. Winston Coleman Jr., *Slavery Times in Kentucky* (Chapel Hill: The University of North Carolina Press, 1940). For

the eighteenth century, see Allan Kulikoff, "Uprooted Peoples: Black Migrants in the Age of the Revolution, 1790–1820," in Ira Berlin and Ronald Hoffman, eds., *Slavery and Freedom in the Age of the American Revolution* (Urbana and Chicago: University of Illinois Press for the United States Capitol Historical Society, 1983), 143–71; Gail S. Terry, "Sustaining the Bonds of Kinship in a Trans-Appalachian Migration, 1790–1811," *Virginia Magazine of History and Biography* 102 (1994): 455–76; Ellen Eslinger, "The Shape of Slavery on the Kentucky Frontier, 1775–1800," 92 *RKHS* (1994): 1–23. For the argument that Kentucky slavery was less oppressive than in eastern states, see Todd H. Barnett, "Virginians Moving West: The Early Evolution of Slavery in the Bluegrass," *FCHQ* 72 (1993): 221–48; and J. Blaine Hudson, "Slavery in Early Louisville and Jefferson County, Kentucky, 1780–1812," *FCHQ* 73 (1999), 249–83.

70. Hickman, "A Short Account of My Life and Travels," 18; Samuel Meredith to John Breckinridge, 6 June 1790, Breckinridge Family Papers; Elizabeth Meredith to John Breckinridge, April 1790, ibid.; "Autobiography of Gen. James Taylor," 22.

71. Marquis de Chastellux, *Travels in North-America in the Years 1780–81–82 by the Marquis de Chastellux* (New York: White, Gallaher, and White, 1827), 255; Charles Drake, ed., *Pioneer Life in Kentucky*, 26; "Autobiography of John Rowan," 97.

72. John May to Samuel Beall, 15 April 1780, Beall-Booth Family Papers, Filson Historical Society (May's experience was not entirely lacking in comfort, for he brought along a slave as body-servant); Hickman, "A Short Account of My Life," 18; John Taylor quoted in Speed, *Wilderness Road,* 54; Condict, "Journal of a Trip to Kentucky," 116.

73. Martzloff, "Reminiscences of a Pioneer,"192; "Autobiography of Gen. James Taylor," 3; "Personal Narrative of William Lytle," 3–4; "Autobiography of Allen Trimble," 206; Daniel Deron Interview, Draper Coll., 12CC239.

74. Hall, "Along the Wilderness Trail," 292; Beckner, "Interview with Mrs. Sarah Graham," 240; James Wade Interview, Draper Coll., 12CC12; Hickman, "A Short Account of My Life," 42; Otto A. Rothert, "John D. Shane's Interview with Mrs. John McKinney and Her Son Harvey, Bourbon County," *FCHQ* 13 (1939): 159; Mrs. John Arnold Interview, Draper Coll., 12CC241; "Personal Narrative of William Lytle," 4; "Autobiography of Gen. James Taylor," 3 and 6.

75. Thomas Jones Interview, Draper Coll., 12CC232; G. Yocum Interview, Draper Coll., 12CC150; Rothert, "Shane's Interview with Mrs. John McKinney," 160.

76. Hall, "Along the Wilderness Trail," 292–93; "Autobiography of Allen Trimble," 206–07.

77. "Personal Narrative of William Lytle," 4; W.P. Strickland, *The Autobiography of James B. Finley, or Pioneer Life in the West* (Cincinnati: Methodist Book Concern, for the author, 1855), 24; "Autobiography of Gen. James Taylor," 3; Rothert, "Shane's Interview with Mrs. John McKinney," 160.

78. Shane interview #47, Draper Coll., 13CC191.

79. Coffman, "Big Crosssing Station," 5; Hall, "Along the Wilderness Trail," 293; William McClellend Interview, Draper Coll., 11CC181; James Wade Interview, Draper Coll., 12CC11 (Carooth's wife was partially scalped, but she survived); Daniel Deron Interview, Draper Coll., 12CC239; James Walker Interview, Draper Coll., 12CC54, William Boyd Interview, Draper Coll., 12CC58; James Hedge Interview, Draper Coll., 13CC210; G. Yocum Interview, Draper Coll., 12CC150; Lewis Flanagan

Interview, Draper Coll., 13CC210; F.F. Jackson Interview, Draper Coll., 15CCG. McNutt's defeat occurred in October 1787 near the Little Laurel River, but Whitley numbered the dead at 21 or 22 people. McFarland's Defeat occurred in March 1793. See, Bayless Hardin, ed., "Whitley Papers, Vol. 9—Draper Manuscripts—Kentucky Papers," *RKHS* 36 (1938): 200.

80. "Autobiography of Gen. James Taylor," 5–6; Bond, "Memoirs of Benjamin Van Cleve," 17; Beckner, "Early Adverntures of William Sudduth," 45; Rothert, "Shane's Interview with Colonel John Graves," 240.

81. "Autobiography of Allen Trimble," 209–10. Children witnessed some grisly scenes. A postal carrier in Sarah Graham's company went on ahead; the group soon encountered his riderless horse and his body "cut all to pieces and stuck on the bushes." See Beckner, "Interview with Mrs. Sarah Graham," 238–40.

82. Anne Crabb, "'What Shall I Do Now?' The Story of the Indian Captivities of Margaret Paulee, Jones Hoy, and Jack Callaway, 1779–ca.1789," 70 *FCHQ* (1996): 369–70. Margaret was adopted into an Indian family and released in a prisoner exchange in 1784.

83. James Taylor Interview, Draper Coll., 9CC71. This incident became known as Moore's Defeat.

84. Hardin, "Whitley Papers," 198–99 and 203–4. Whitley stated there were four children, but other accounts indicate only three. As his advice to Mrs. McFarland reveals, Whitley possessed strong principles. In another attack, known as McClure's Defeat, a father and mother fled, leaving their eight-year-old daughter behind to be captured. Whitley went to great lengths to rescue her. He resolved to adopt the abandoned child as his own and when Mrs. Drake some time later came to reclaim her daughter, Whitley initially refused to give her over to such a careless parent. Mrs. Whitley, however, finally prevailed upon her husband to return the girl to her mother. See "Whitley Papers," 204, for this episode.

85. Drawn from the account of captive Charles Johnson as related in Frederick Drimmer, ed., *Captured by the Indians: 15 Firsthand Accounts, 1750–1820* (New York: Dover Publications, 1961), 184–94. Johnson stated that the Indians were primarily Shawnees, accompanied by several Delawares, Wyandottes, and a few Cherokees from the South. The two decoys were named Devine and Thomas, the latter appearing overly cooperative in his role of decoy. Thomas had been captured in 1790; he allegedly used his share of the money captured from May to later buy land. See George Edwards Statement, Draper Coll., 9S88. Thomas's son, Isaac, rendered an opposite account and claimed that Thomas was reluctant but Devine played his role well. Isaac Thomas described both the May attack and the subsequent attack on Marshall's boats. See Isaac Thomas Statement, Draper Coll., 7S132.

86. Drimmer, *Captured by the Indians*, 192.

87. Collins, *History of Kentucky*, 700–3; Annah Nicholson Statement, Draper Coll., 7S38. See also the report of Gen. Charles Scott to Gov. Beverley Randolph, 2 April 1791, W.F. Palmer, ed., *Calendar of Virginia State Papers and Other Manuscripts, 1652–1781, Preserved at the Capitol in Richmond*, 11 vols. (Richmond: 1875–93) 5: 282–83. Scott described other recent attacks on the river as well. As late as 1794, Indian attacks on Ohio boats remained a frequent problem. See Benjamin Briggs, Ohio County, Virginia, to Gov. Henry Lee, 13 June 1794, Draper Coll., 12S76–77. See also the recollections of Nancy Rachford, whose father's boat was captured,

Draper Coll., 19S105; and the attack on the Malotte family related by Mrs. Sarah Munger, Draper Coll., 20S204. This Greathouse was the same man who had led the attack on Logan's family in 1774.

88. Strickland, *Autobiography of James B. Finley*, 25; Hammon, *My Father, Daniel Boone*, 89.

89. "Narrative of John Heckewelder's Journey to the Wabash in 1792," *Pennsylvania Magazine of History and Biography* 12 (1888): 37; Dale Van Every, *Ark of Empire, the American Frontier, 1784–1803* (New York: Morrow, 1963),158–59; Harry Innes to John Knox, 7 July 1790, Harry Innes Papers, Manuscript Division, Library of Congress, Washington, D.C.

90. *Kentucky Gazette*, 31 July 1795. Locating relatives could be difficult. Polly Ford had an advertisement in the Cincinnati *Western Spy* dated 14 November 1801, stating that she now lived at Fort Wayne. She sought two elder brothers or other "friends yet living."

91. Smyth, *Tour of the United States*, 1:308; Ranck, "Felix Walker's Narrative," 163–64; Young, *Westward into Kentucky*, 44; Jane Stevenson Interview, Draper Coll., 13CC163; Condict, "Journal of a Trip to Kentucky," 122. See also Jakle, *Images of the Ohio Valley*, 60–61.

92. William Brown quoted in Speed, *Wilderness Road*, 61; "Journal of J. Gregg," entry dated 4–5 April 1796.

93. Martzoff, "Reminiscences of a Pioneer," 193; Robert Jones Interview, Draper Coll., 13CC180; Mrs. McFarland Interview, Draper, Coll., 11CC137.

94. "Letters from Capt. Laurence Butler," 43; Nicholas Cresswell, *Journal of Nicholas Cresswell, 1774–1777* (New York: The Dial Press, 1924), 84–85; Mereness, "Colonel Fleming's Journal," entry dated 27 December 1779, 627.

95. Isaac Thomas Statement, Draper Coll., 7S132; Mrs. J. Grady Interview, Draper Coll., 13CC132; John Hedge Interview, Draper Coll., 12CC128. See also Perkins, *Border Life*, 77.

96. Michaux, "Western Travels," 3:189; Collot, *A Journey in North America*, 1:48; "Letters from Capt. Laurence Butler," 43; "Diary of Major Erkuries Beatty," entry dated 18 May 1787, 176; Hulbert, *Waterways of Westward Expansion*, 86.

97. "Extracts from General Robert B. McAfee's Manuscript History," 14; "Thomas Hanson Journal," entry dated 12 May 1774, typescript copy, Reuben T. Durrett Collection, Regenstein Library, University of Chicago, Chicago; "Letters from Capt. Laurence Butler," 43; Cresswell, *Journal of Nicholas Cresswell*, 87–88. See also Johann David Schoepf, ed., *Travels in the Confederation*, Alfred J. Morrison, trans. (Philadelphia: William J. Campbell, 1911): 266–69.

98. Michaux, "Travels to the West," 3:178; Condict, "Journal of a Trip to Kentucky," 118–19; "Diary of Major Erkuries Beatty," entry dated 23 June 1796, 119. Modern studies attribute the large edifice at Moundsville to the Adena people (c. 500 B.C.–A.D. 200) and that at Marietta to the Hopewell. See John P. MacLean, "Ancient Works at Marietta, Ohio," *Ohio Archaeological and Historical Review* 12 (1903): 37–66; William F. Romain, *Mysteries of the Hopewell: Astronomers, Geometers, and Magicians of the Eastern Woodlands* (Akron, Ohio: University of Akron Press, 2000); Helen H. Tanner, *Atlas of Great Lakes Indian History* (Norman: published for the Newberry Library by the University of Oklahoma Press, 1987), 25–28; Jakle, *Images of the Ohio Valley*, 68–71.

99. "Thomas Hanson Journal," entry dated 15 April 1774; "Narrative of John Heckewelder," 15.

100. Joseph Herndon to Jonathan Clark, 23 October 1779, Draper Coll., 1L71; Lucien Beckner, ed., "Reverend John D. Shane's Interview with Pioneer William Clinkenbeard," *FCHQ* 2 (1928): 98; Isaac Clinkenbeard Interview, Draper Coll., 11CC1; Hickman, "A Short Account of My Life and Travels," 42; Hall, "Along the Wilderness Trail," 290.

101. *Pittsburgh Gazette*, 2 June 1787 and 24 November 1787; "Diary of Major Erkuries Beatty," entry dated 23 May 1786, 176; Smith, *Western Journals of John May*, entry dated 11 May 1788, 39; Backus, *Genealogical Memoir*, entry dated 21 April 1789, 51; James Hedge Interview, Draper Coll., 12CC117; Condict, "Journal of a Trip to Kentucky," 114.

102. *Historical Statistics of the United States*, 28, 33, and 35. On the seasonality of western migration, see Perkins, *Border Life*, 157–58.

103. Arthur Campbell to Gov. Benjamin Harrison, 27 January 1781 and 28 March 1781, *Cal. Vir. State Papers*, 1:464–65, and 602–3. See also Arthur Campbell to Gov. Benjamin Harrison, 16 January 1781, 2 February 1781, and 7 February 1781, *Cal. Vir. State Papers*, 1:438, 484, and 494; Joseph Martin to Gov. Benjamin Harrison, 31 March 1781, *Cal. Vir. State Papers*, 1:613. The Watauga Association, begun in 1775, was an unofficial government established in what is now eastern Tennessee. See John Haywood, *The Civil and Political History of the State of Tennessee from Its Earliest Settlement up to the Year 1796* (Knoxville: Heiskell and Brown, 1823), 50–61.

104. William Christian to Gov. Benjamin Harrison, 30 December 1782, *Cal. Vir. State Papers*, 3:407; Pusey, "General Joseph Martin," 57–81.

105. John Evans to Gov. Benjamin Harrison, 9 March 1782, *Cal. Vir. State Papers*, 3:89; William Christian to Gov. Benjamin Harrison, 28 September 1782, *Cal. Vir. State Papers*, 3:331–33; Benjamin Wilson to Gov. Benjamin Harrison, 9 December 1782, *Cal. Vir. State Papers*, 3:394.

106. For summaries of the Wilderness Road's development from a packhorse trail to a wagon road, see, Pusey, *Wilderness Road to Kentucky*; Jeremiah L. Krakow, *Location of the Wilderness Road at Cumberland National Historical Park* (Washington, D.C.: U.S. Department of the Interior, National Park Service, 1987); Hening, *Statutes at Large*, 10:143–44.

107. Hening, *Statutes at Large*, 13:184.

108. Speed, *Wilderness Road*, 47–51; Daniel Boone unsuccessfully sought appointment for this public work, writing to Gov. Isaac Shelby in a letter dated 11 February 1796, "I wish to inform you that I have sum intention of undertaking this New Rode that is to be Cut through the Wilderness and I think My Self intiteled to the ofer of the Bisness as I first Marked out that Rode in March 1775 and Never Rec'd anything for my trubel and Sepose I am No Statesman I am a Woodsman and think My Self as Capable of Marking and Cutting that Rode as any other man." Quoted in Archer Butler Hulbert, *Boone's Wilderness Road, Historic Highways of America*, vol. 6 (Cleveland, Ohio: The Arthur H. Clark Co., 1903), 203–04.

109. *Kentucky Gazette*, 15 October 1796.

110. Kincaid, *Wilderness Road*, 54–66 and Imlay, *Topographical Description of the Western Territory*, 38–39. The passage from Imlay is found on pages 147–48.

111. Ibid., 38–39.

112. Michaux, "Travels to the West," 3:189.

113. The literature on the Overland Trail is massive. A good place to start is Unruh, *The Plains Across.* See also Dale L. Morgan, ed., *Overland in 1846: Diaries and Letters of the California-Oregon Trail* (Georgetown, Calif.: Talisman Press, 1963); Faragher, *Women and Men on the Overland Trail*; and J.S. Holliday, *The World Rushed In: The California Gold Rush Experience* (New York: Simon and Schuster, 1981).

114. For organization and leadership on the Overland Trail, see John P. Reid, *Law for the Elephant: Property and Social Behavior on the Overland Trail* (San Marino, Calif.: Huntington Library, 1980).

Chapter 1. William Calk, 1775

1. Abraham Hanks was the uncle of Nancy Hanks, the mother of Abraham Lincoln.

2. One traditional mode of staking a frontier land claim was to sow a crop. Corn was the most common, but like corn, potatoes required a minimum of care.

3. People traveling in remote areas berift of marked trails often hired local men as pilots.

4. The Powell River Valley was narrow, but it included rich alluvial soil. Its isolation from the rest of Virginia, however, left it vulnerable to Indian raids. The settlers from whom Calk obtained "good food" would shortly be forced to evacuate. When conditions became safer, they returned, but Powell's Valley remained a frontier subject to attack, and settlers were periodically forced to evacuate the region.

5. Apparently the route blazed by Richard Henderson's Transylvania Company by Daniel Boone. Calk does not reveal how he knew it to be Henderson's trail, but his identification is suggestive of how quickly news of Kentucky spread through word of mouth.

6. Following the creek avoided the need to cross elevations, but even small creeks could involve steep and slippery banks.

7. Richard Henderson maintained a journal as well, and his entry for this date notes, "Met about forty persons returning from the Cantuckey on account of the late murder by the Indians." Henderson persuaded one to reconsider and join his company, but several members of his own party were alarmed by the eastbound travelers and headed back. The eastbound travelers were not of the Transylvania Company, but part of the many adventurers who had been exploring Kentucky during this period. See "Pioneering in the Heroic Stage, Kentucky," extracts from the journal of Richard Henderson in John R. Commons et al., eds., *A Documentary History of American Industrial Society*, 10 vols. (New York: Russell and Russell, 1958), 2: 120.

8. Nathaniel Hart was among the Transylvania Company's prime investors. The lead was for molding bullets.

9. Shortly after turning back, Drake and Hanks encountered another group headed for Kentucky and, regaining their courage, resumed their westward journey. "The Journal of William Calk, Pioneer," *Mississippi Valley Historical Review* 7 (1921): 370.

10. Richard Henderson's journal entry for this date mentions "Stewart and

ten other men" returning from Kentucky. See Commons, "Pioneering in the Heroic Stage," 221.

11. Henderson's journal entry for this date mentions meeting "James McAfee with eighteen other presons returning from Cantuckey." McAfee and his brothers, along with several friends from Pennsylvania, had prospected for land as early as 1773 in the vicinity of Harrodsburg. For a veteran pioneer like McAfee to abandon Kentucky gives a good indication of the danger of Indian attack. See Commons, "Pioneering in the Heroic Stage," 221.

12. While blazing the way to the site of future Boonesborough, Boone's group had been attacked, so they constructed a crude fortification. It was called Twetty's Fort, after one of the victims. See Felix Walker's memoir in Ranck, *Boonesborough*, 164.

13. In order to get corn planted as soon as possible, Boone had already begun erecting a fortified settlement and distributing two-acre plots of land among his group of trailblazers. To accommodate more people, Henderson relocated the main fortification and within days measured 54 additional lots. Calk, who had brought his surveying instruments, may have assisted in the survey. See Commons, "Pioneering in the Heroic Stage," 222.

Chapter 2. Nicholas Cresswell, 1775

1. *Journal of Nicholas Cresswell*, entry dated 3 April 1775, 61. For another description of western leggings in this period, see Smyth, *Tour of the United States*, 1:115; Linda R. Baumgarten, "Leatherstockings and Hunting Shirts," in Ann Smart Martin and J. Ritchie Garrison, eds., *American Material Culture: The Shape of the Field* (Knoxville: The University of Tennessee Press for the Henry du Pont Winterthur Museum, 1997), 251–76, and Linda Baumgarten, *What Clothes Reveal: The Language of Clothing in Colonial and Federal America* (New Haven, Conn.: Yale University Press and The Colonial Williamsburg Foundation, 2002), 66–69.

2. *Journal of Nicholas Cresswell*, entry dated 13 April 1775, 64.

3. How one "acted the Irishman" is not clear. Irish, or Scots-Irish immigrants were numerous in the backcountry of Pennsylvania, Virginia, and farther south because remote settlements offered cheaper land. Although they spoke English and therefore faced no language barrier, these Presbyterian immigrants from Northern Ireland remained a distinctive ethnic group in the eighteenth century. Perhaps due to their poverty more than any other single factor, Englishmen like Cresswell, as well as other privileged American people, viewed them as coarse and ignorant. See James G. Leyburn, *The Scotch-Irish: A Social History* (Chapel Hill: The University of North Carolina Press, 1962); David Hacket Fischer, *Albion's Seed: Four British Folkways in America* (New York: Oxford University Press, 1989); Malwyn A. Jones, "The Scotch-Irish in British America," in Bernard Bailyn and Philip D. Morgan, eds., *Strangers within the Realm: Cultural Margins of the First British Empire* (Chapel Hill: The University of North Carolina Press for the Institute of Early American History and Culture, 1991), 284–313; Patrick Griffin, *The People with No Name: Ireland's Ulster Scots, America's Scots Irish, and the Creation of a British Atlantic World, 1689–1764* (Princeton, N.J.: Princeton University Press, 2001).

4. Gen. Edward Braddock's defeat was a major disaster. Evidence of the battle littered the site for years. Located on a major road to the Monongahela River, numerous emigrants to Kentucky passed the scene.

5. A pipe tomahawk had a hollow but stout handle. The head had an axe blade on one side and a pipe bowl on the other. Cresswell is deducing that the pipe side was used as a hammer in the engagement.

6. Cresswell implies that his landlord suspected him, with his fresh English dialect, of Tory sympathies.

7. Connolly owed his appointment to Governor Dunmore of Virginia, part of an effort to claim this region for Virginia. Through his close association with Dunmore, Connolly was among the first to obtain a legal land claim in Kentucky. Deputy Surveyor John Floyd surveyed a 2,000-acre site at modern Louisville in 1774. During the American Revolution, Connolly joined the British as an officer, so the new Virginia legislature voided his claim in 1780. See Clarence Monroe Burton, "John Connolly: A Tory of the Revolution," *Proceedings of the American Antiquarian Society* 20 (1909): 70–78; Percy B. Caley, "The Life and Adventures of Lieutenant-Colonel John Connolly: The Story of a Tory," *Western Pennsylvania Historical Magazine* 11 (1928): 26–49, 76–111, 144–79, and 225–59.

8. The exchange with Indians of manufactured products, especially metals and cloth, for furs formed an important part of the economy for many frontier towns.

9. Pennsylvania had not yet established its western borders. Virginia exploited this lapse by laying claim to the vital headwaters of the Ohio River and appointing a rival local government. On Virginia and Pennsylvania's conflicting claims to the Fort Pitt region, see Percy B. Caley, "Lord Dunmore and the Pennsylvania-Virginia Boundary Dispute," *Western Pennsylvania Historical Magazine* 22 (1939): 87–100; Michael McConnell, *A Country Between*, 268–70.

10. Rice apparently wished to take the opportunity to claim some land in central Kentucky.

11. Flour was particularly scarce. Provisioning the troops for Lord Dunmore's War the previous year had exhausted local supplies.

12. The Virginia militia had built several small stockades on the banks of the upper Ohio River during Dunmore's War. Most were abandoned as soon as the conflict abated, yet their remains provided shelter to wayfarers and a source of firewood to nearby settlers.

13. Alexander McKey (or McKee) and John Monture (or Montour), were both of mixed Indian and European heritage, and members of their families served as prominent frontier intermediaries. See James H. Merrell, *Into the American Woods: Negotiators on the Pennsylvania Frontier* (New York: W.W. Norton and Co., 1999); Larry L. Nelson, *A Man of Distinction among Them: Alexander McKee and the Ohio Country Frontier, 1754–1799* (Kent, Ohio, and London: The Kent State University Press, 1999); Richard White, *The Middle Ground: Indians, Empires, and Republicans in the Great Lakes Region, 1650–1815* (Cambridge: Cambridge University Press, 1991), 359–63.

14. During Dunmore's War, George Rogers Clark served as a militia captain at Fort Pitt. An early inhabitant of Kentucky, Clark opposed the Transylvania Company and, as a delegate from Harrodsburg in 1776, urged the Virginia Assembly to assert its claims to the region by creating Kentucky County. Clark's military exploits

against British posts in the Illinois Country during the Revolutionary War served as a basis for American claims to the region at the end of the war. Temple Bodley, *George Rogers Clark: His Life and Public Services* (New York: Houghton Mifflin Co., 1926); and James Alton James, *The Life of George Rogers Clark* (Chicago: The University of Chicago Press, 1928).

15. A reference to the battle of Point Pleasant in 1774, the encounter that decided the outcome of Dunmore's War.

16. Better known as Big Bone Lick. Cresswell was able to visit this site on his return to Fort Pitt.

17. Cresswell and other observant travelers to the Ohio Valley were surprised to find ocean fossils in the center of the continent. The evidence of an ancient ocean so far from its current shores attested to a very different prehistoric past.

18. Early Americans fenced their crops and let their livestock forage in the underbrush. To demonstrate ownership, their ears were cut. Sometimes the pattern of marking was recorded with the local county court. Cresswell's group obviously was not establishing ownership and may have marked the buffalo calves as a sort of trophy.

19. Cresap was a trader and land speculator; his operations centered at Wheeling during this period. His aggressively violent behavior toward Ohio Indians made him a controversial figure, and he was closely associated with attacks by whites that led to Dunmore's War. John J. Jacob, *A Biographical Sketch of the Life of the Late Captain Michael Cresap* (Cincinnati: John F. Uhlhorn, Printer, 1866); Mary Louise Cresap Stevenson, "Colonel Thomas Cresap," *Ohio Archaeological and Historical Society Publications* 10 (1902): 146–64.

20. Harrodsburg was established in 1774 but abandoned during Dunmore's War. James Harrod returned with a group of settlers in March 1775.

Chapter 3. James Nourse, 1775

1. A hunting shirt was a garment of coarse linen or canvas worn over clothing and was a characteristic attire of backcountry hunters in the late eighteenth century, particularly those with rifles rather than the usual musket. During the American Revolution, the hunting shirt also became a patriotic symbol. See Rhys Isaac, *The Transformation of Virginia, 1740–1790* (Chapel Hill: The University of North Carolina Press for the Institute of Early American History and Culture, 1982), 258.

2. Whether Tom was an indentured white servant or a slave is unknown.

3. George Washington was an aggressive speculator in western lands and was one of the few to have land claims located under Governor Dunmore. Washington had also explored the potential of upper Ohio Valley lands in 1770; see George Washington, "Washington's Tour to the Ohio," *Old South Leaflets* 40 (1892): 10–12.

4. Logstown had until a short time earlier been inhabited by Indians, but it was abandoned because of its proximity to hostile whites.

5. Clark had claimed land at the mouth of Fish Creek, about twenty miles downstream from Wheeling, during a journey in the summer of 1772. He built a cabin and raised corn there, but did not remain long. In the spring of 1773 he explored farther down the Ohio and returned to his father's house in Virginia that summer. He was back at his claim when he joined Michael Cresap's controversial

campaign against neighboring Indians and then joined the Virginians in Dunmore's War. R.E. Banta, *The Ohio* (New York: Rinehart and Co., 1949), 134–35.

6. To "shirt" or "shift" oneself refers to changing the undershirt or shift.

7. This was the same William Russell who had attempted to settle in Kentucky with Boone in 1773.

8. Revolutionary War veterans had been given grants to western land in lieu of pay, but locating unclaimed land and having it surveyed and recorded was left to the claimant.

9. Nourse's letter to his wife, dated 10 May 1775 and copied into his journal, summarizes the progress of the trip to Pittsburgh. It also expresses Nourse's hestition to proceed if reports of Indian raids farther downriver proved accurate. James Nourse, "The Journal of James Nourse," *Journal of American History* 19 (1925): 127–28.

10. A greatcoat was a heavy overcoat; by this date Nourse probably found it too warm to wear.

Chapter 4. James Smith, 1783

1. Some doubt exists about the year of Smith's first journey to Kentucky. The best judgment is that it was in 1783. See Josiah Morrow, ed., "Tours into Kentucky and the Northwest Territory," *Ohio Archaeological and Historical Publications* 16 (1907): 352.

2. Morrow, "Tours into Kentucky," 353. Smith made a second journey through Kentucky in 1795 to the Northwest Territory and again in 1797. These later journeys were less fully documented, his purpose being to visit Kentucky relatives and proceed to find a good location north of the Ohio River because slavery was prohibited there.

3. James Smith's father, who had remarried after his first wife's death, named two sons George.

4. The Chickamauga were a militant contingent of Cherokees who allied with the Creeks and other southern Indian groups, and they posed the main threat to travelers on the Wilderness Road.

5. Charles English's Station was an important way station, only about two miles east from the generally acknowledged end of the Wilderness Road, Crab Orchard.

6. This was Smith's half-brother George S. to Vall Smith, who had settled in Jessamine County, Kentucky, around 1780.

Chapter 5. Peter Muhlenberg, 1784

1. Henry A. Muhlenberg, *The Life of Major-General Peter Muhlenberg of the Revolutionary Army* (Philadelphia: Carey and Hart, 1849).

2. Ibid., pp. 427–28.

3. On the topic of early American Germans, a good place to start is A.G. Roeber, "'The Origin of Whatever Is Not English among Us': The Dutch-Speaking and German-Speaking Peoples of Colonial British America," in Bailyn and Morgan, *Strangers within the Realm,* 220–83. On the German colonists in Muhlenberg's region of Virginia, see John Walter Wayland, *The German Element of the Shenandoah Valley of Virginia* (1905, reprint ed. Bridgewater, Va.: Carrier, 1964).

4. The American Revolutionary troops came from two levels. The Continental troops were funded by the Second Continental Congress. These were augmented by recruits funded by the governments of Virginia and other states. Uncontrollable wartime inflation and a crisis of cash, particularly in the later years of the War for Independence, prompted the issue of western land grants to recruits at both levels. The size of the grant, issued as a warrant or certificate, was graded according to military rank. Muhlenburg and his companions had been appointed to find an appropriate location for these grants, an extended territory that was unencumbered by previous claims. It should be added that many veterans sold their land warrants to land speculators, preferring cash in hand to the expense and trouble of a long-distance relocation to an undeveloped region.

5. Fort McIntosh was constructed in 1778 but abandoned after the Revolutionary War. It was reoccupied by Gen. Josiah Harmar in 1785.

6. Ebenezer Zane was one of the first settlers at Wheeling. See John G. Patterson, "Ebenezer Zane, Frontiersman," *West Virginia History* 12 (1950): 5-45.

7. Muhlenberg, *Life of Major-General Peter Muhlenberg*, 436.

8. *Ibid.*, 444.

Chapter 6. Samuel Shepard, 1787

1. A case bottle was a square bottle molded so that it would pack neatly with others in a crate or box. A single case bottle did not bode well for the establishment's amenities.

2. Water-powered gristmills were scarce in the early western settlements due to the exposure to Indian attack and notoriously low water levels in late summer just as grain was being harvested. Pioneers therefore often brought a pair of small grindstones that were driven by hand with a shaft. Although handmills could not produce meal on a commercial scale, they were sufficient for household and neighborhood consumption.

3. Joseph L. Stephens was from Frederick County, Virginia, and a man of substantial wealth. He brought his wife and fifty slaves to Kentucky, as well as a supply of bricks and other building materials. Stephens settled near Isaac Ruddle's gristmill in Bourbon County. See Daniel V. Stephens, *Peter Stephens and Some of His Descendants, 1690–1935* (Fremont, Nebr.: Hammond and Stephens Co., 1936).

4. Lower Blue Licks was one of Kentucky's larger salt springs and, during the pioneer period, one of the key sources of the salt needed to preserve meat. The mineral content of Kentucky's saline springs was low and required much labor to extract. The water was boiled off in large iron kettles, requiring a large amount of firewood. The only other source of salt was from across the mountains, which was impractical to obtain. At the time the Dewees family passed, a salt works was operated by owner Edmund Lyne, who also rented out rights to use the salt spring to private individuals. The Lower Blue Licks had been the site of a major American defeat in 1782. It is also prominent in the historical annals of Kentucky because, in 1778, Daniel Boone had led a group of men there to make salt for Boonesborough and were captured by Indians. See, William Dodd Brown, "Daniel Boone's Saltmakers: Fresh Perspectives from Primary Sources," *RKHS* 83 (1985): 1–18; and John Mark Faragher, *Daniel Boone: The Life and Legend of an American Pioneer* (New York: Henry Holt and Co., 1992), 153–60.

5. Isaac Ruddle had founded a fortified settlement, or station, in 1780 that had been captured by a British-led Indian army in June 1782. Ruddle and about 300 other captives were taken to Detroit and later exchanged. Ruddle returned to Kentucky soon thereafter, but two of his young sons remained with their adoptive Indian families and returned years later as adults. He came from the same area of Virginia as did Joseph Stephens, and they may have been previously acquainted. Maude Ward Lafferty, "Destruction of Ruddle's and Martin's Forts in the Revolutionary War," *RKHS* 54 (1956): 297–338.

Chapter 7. Mary Coburn Dewees, 1788

1. A version of this diary was published by John L. Blair, "Mrs. Mary Dewees's Journal from Philadelphia to Kentucky," *RKHS* 63 (1965): 195–217. The version presented here comes from a handwritten copy in the Special Collections of Regenstein Library, Reuben T. Durrett Collection, University of Chicago.

2. Wooden chimneys, lined with mud, were common in poorer dwellings. An "ordinary" was another name for a tavern.

3. Fleas, lice, ticks, and mosquitoes were a common travail encountered by travelers. Such vermin were probably more difficult for someone from a privileged background, as were the Deweeses.

4. James O'Hara was one of Pittsburgh's earliest settlers and a leading western merchant. President Washington appointed him quartermaster general of the U.S. Army in 1792, a post he held until 1796.

5. The U.S. Army erected Fort Steuben in 1786 to protect federal surveyors of Ohio's Seven Ranges (it burned down in 1790, but the fledgling settlement around it developed into modern Steubenville). Mingo Bottom, site of a former Indian habitation and a noted landmark, was a large meadow at the mouth of Yellow Creek on the north side of the Ohio River.

6. A reference to the battle of Point Pleasant in 1774, during Dunmore's War, rather than the Revolutionary War as mistakenly stated.

7. Rev. William Woods was one of the settlement's most prominent settlers and was instrumental in organizing several Baptist congregations in neighboring parts of Kentucky.

8. The tiny settlement of May's Lick was founded in 1788. See Charles Drake, ed., *Pioneer Life in Kentucky: A Series of Reminiscential Letters from Daniel Drake, M.D., of Cincinnati to His Children* (Cincinnati: Robert Clarke, 1870).

9. John Grant's Station was a small but strategic settlement on the road between Limestone and Lexington. It was established in 1780 but abandoned two years later and burned by Indians. Grant returned and rebuilt a fortified cabin at the site in 1784. Bryan's, or Bryant's Station, was among Kentucky's earliest settlements, founded in 1779 by Morgan Bryant. It survived a major siege by Indians in 1782.

10. Mr. DeWees had apparently prepared a home site before moving his family to Kentucky. This was a common practice, particularly among families of means.

Chapter 8. John May, 1788

1. The manuscript journals of May's two trips have been lost. May's grandson Richard S. Edes published versions in the nineteenth century, but apparently Edes

took editorial liberties. See *Journal and Letters of Colonel John May of Boston* (Cincinnati: Robert Clarke and Co., 1875, for the Historical and Philosophical Society of Ohio). For the publication history of the May journals, see Dwight L. Smith, ed., *The Western Journals of John May, Ohio Company Agent and Business Adventurer* (Cincinnati: Historical and Philosophical Society of Ohio, 1961), 7–12. The John May whose boat was captured on the Ohio, described in the Introduction, was a different individual.

2. John May to wife, 7 May 1788, in Richard S. Edes, ed., "Journal and Letters of Col. John May, of Boston Relative to Two Journeys to the Ohio Country in 1788 and 1789," *Historical and Philosophical Society of Ohio* 4 (1873): 35.

3. John May returned east briefly and brought a second cargo of goods in 1789. This second journey was recorded in a much more succinct record, reflecting May's lesser sense of novelty.

4. What May called a "portmant" was probably a portmanteau, a type of luggage. His arrangement with Kirkendall implies that May intended to establish a foothold at Marietta but return east within the year. This would have been a normal plan for a western merchant, although in May's case may have been in preparation for bringing his family west.

5. May was referring to Marietta, at the mouth of the Muskingum River. May was staying in quarters across the river from Pittsburgh because the city was notoriously expensive. He spent several days at this location to await the arrival of his freight wagons and to meet with several Ohio Company leaders.

6. Samuel Purviance was a prominent Baltimore merchant, apparently attempting to expand his operation into the western settlements. The attack is reported in Lexington's *Kentucky Gazette*, 4 April 1788.

7. This was the same O'Hara the Dewees family had met. Col. William Butler had been a Continental officer during the Revolution.

8. The landing at John Sumerall's ferry on the Youghiogheny River (the modern town of West Newton) was the Ohio Company's preferred point of embarkation for the Ohio. See Rowena Buell, ed., *The Memoirs of Rufus Putnam and Certain Official Papers and Correspondence* (Boston: Houghton, Mifflin and Co., 1903), 104.

9. Josiah Harmar had been a lieutenant colonel of Pennsylvania troops during the Revolution. In 1790, he would be appointed brigadier general of the federal army. He led a disastrous campaign against the Ohio Indians in 1790. Parsons was an Ohio Company director and later a territorial judge. Sargent was an agent and territorial secretary. Gen. Rufus Putnam of Massachusetts was one of the primary architects of the Ohio Company; he had led the first party of company settlers to Marietta in 1787. Putnam had served in the French and Indian War in 1757; he was an army engineer in 1776 and a brigadier general in 1783. He served on the Supreme Court of the Northwest Territory in 1792, and in 1796 he was appointed surveyor-general of the United States. He was also a member of Ohio's Constitutional Convention in 1802.

10. This would have been Fort Franklin in Verango County, built in 1787 under the command of Maj. Jonathan Heart.

11. May was residing at Hulin's, on the Monongahela River across from Fort Pitt, where he was able to avoid the higher costs of Pittsburgh while, at the same

time, be convenient to the river port town. May's interest in cures for worms and rheumatism serves as a reminder of how common these ailments once were.

12. Also present was another Ohio Company diarist, James Backus, who unfortunately neglected to record his observations of the site, but offers supporting information on this excursion. See William W. Backus, *A Genealogical Memoir of the Backus Family with the Private Journal of James Backus* (Norwich, Conn.: William W. Backus, 1889), enrty dated 11 May 1788, 18.

13. John Gibson, a veteran of Dunmore's War, was also a Revolutionary veteran and among the early settlers at Pittsburgh.

14. The rifle was still a recent innovation; the best makers were located in the western settlements of Pennsylvania, Maryland, and Virginia. It was the weapon of choice among western migrants who could afford one because the spiraled inner bore shot farther and more accurately than the standard musket.

15. Arthur St. Clair was governor of the Northwest Territory. His family resided near Pittsburgh in Westmoreland County, Pennsylvania.

16. A small fortified settlement, also known as Crawford's Landing, was founded by Isaac, George, and Friend Cox, located about one mile upstream from the fledgling town of Wellsburg. James Backus was one of the passengers, along with Gen. T.H. Parsons, Colonel Butler, Major Sargeant, Captain Rice, Wanton Chase, and others of lesser note. See Backus, *Genealogical Memoir*, entry dated 24 May 1788, 19.

17. Located about five miles from the Ohio, West Liberty was the seat of Ohio County, Virginia.

18. At this time Zane was a delegate from Ohio County to the ratifying convention in Richmond for the U.S. Constitution. See John G. Patterson, "Ebenezer Zane, Frontiersman, " *West Virginia History* 12 (1950).

19. A reference to Dr. James Hervey, author of a work entitled *Contemplations and Meditations*.

20. May here is describing a prominent ancient mound about twenty feet high on the edge of Marietta, a feature of much curiosity to early inhabitants. See also Backus, *A Genealogical Memoir*, 20.

21. Maj. John Doughty commanded Fort Harmar.

Chapter 9. Joel Watkins, 1789

1. Probably the town later known as Liberty, the seat for Botetourt County.

2. This western section of Virginia, isolated by mountains, suffered frequent Indian attacks; some settlers were driven away, at least temporarily.

3. Reaching streams ("western waters") that drained into the Mississippi River rather than the Atlantic Ocean was an important milestone for eighteenth-century travelers.

4. Rivers and creeks deposited rich alluvial soil, commonly called bottomland because it was usually located near the lower end, or bottom, of the drainage basin.

5. Limestone, a soft alluvial rock, was sometimes worn away by surface water to create steep-sided, deepwater deposits called sinks or sinkholes.

6. This unidentified boatyard was apparently at the terminus of a route known as the Lewis Trail.

7. Daniel Boone had been driven by lawsuits over land claims to relocate his family to Point Pleasant in 1788. See Faragher, *Daniel Boone*, 261–63.

8. Hewn logs that were squared represented a more refined and stable style of house building.

9. Paris, the seat of Bourbon County, was founded in 1789 and originally named Hopewell.

Chapter 10. Moses Austin, 1796

1. Stanford was named the seat of Lincoln County in 1781, tracing its origins to Logan's and St. Asaph's stations.

2. Isaac Shelby, who had settled in 1783, served as the state of Kentucky's first governor when it was admitted to the union in 1792. He was a veteran of Dunmore's War and the Revolution, in which he distinguished himself at the battle of King's Mountain. Shelby served again as governor, 1812–1816.

Chapter 11. Francis Baily, 1796

1. Andrew Ellicott, *The Journal of Andrew Ellicott, Late Comissioner on Behalf of the United States during Part of the Year 1796, the Years 1797, 1798, 1799, and Part of the Year 1800* (Philadelphia: Printed by Rudd and Bartram for Thomas Dodson, 1803).

2. William Penn laid out Philadelphia according to a widely emulated grid plan. John Reps, *Town Planning in Frontier America* (Columbia: University of Missouri Press, 1980).

3. This is a reference to popular British leader William Penn, whose determination was instrumental in Britain's victory over France in the Seven Years War.

4. Baily adds in a note here, "The boat we had was 12 feet broad, 36 feet long, and drew 18 inches of water when she had upwards of 10 tons of goods in her."

5. Auguste de la Chaise was on a covert mission. The Spanish still controlled the port of New Orleans and restricted American commerce. La Chaise was one of several agents sent by revolutionary France's emissary to the United States, Citizen Edmond Charles Genet, to exploit Kentucky's keen interest in open commerce. France hoped to involve the United States in its war with Spain. The plan called for an American military force headed by George Rogers Clark to attack New Orleans, but failed due to France's inability to provide the promised financial support and the determined opposition by President Washington. See J.W. Cooke, "Governor Shelby and Genet's Agents," *FCHQ* 37 (1963): 162–70; Stuart Seely Sprague, "Kentucky and the Navigation of the Mississippi: The Climactic Years, 1793–1795," *RKHS* 71 (1973): 364–92; Richard Lowitt, "Activities of Citizen Genet in Kentucky, 1793–1794," *FCHQ* 22 (1948): 252–67; Ellen Eslinger, *Citizens of Zion: The Social Origins of Camp Meeting Revivalism* (Knoxville: The University of Tennessee Press, 1999), 146–52.

6. Baily adds in a note here, "Contrary to what an experienced person might suppose, it is always the best way to make towards that part where the water is most violently agitated, as *there* the river is deepest, and there is no danger unless your

boat strike[s] against the rocks. By attending to this observation, a person may generally conduct his boat with safety."

7. Baily adds in a note here, "This is only the case when the river is low; at other times the water flows even with, and sometimes over the banks, so amazingly does this river rise when the floods come down."

8. Baily explains here in a note, "To *blaze* a road, is to mark the trees on each side with a tomahawk; it is done by chopping off the bark about three or four inches broad, and six or eight long; and a person well used to it will blaze as he rides along. If the bark be not completely cut through, the mark will never grow out."

9. Baily adds here in a note, "I have seen several of these ancient remains in different parts of the country near the Ohio on the two Miami rivers they are very numerous, and I have not the least doubt in my own mind but that they were built by a race of people more enlightened than the present Indians, and at some period of time very far distant; for the present Indians know nothing about their use, nor have they any tradition concerning them. I have seen some of them so small, as to induce a belief that they were intended for the defence of one family only. In other places I have seen some of them so large as to be capable of containing a great army: in this latter case, they have generally two or three or more of the burying mounds near them. Their situation is generally near some water; and if they should happen to be at some little distance from it, there is sometimes a covered way made down to it, in order to defend the garrison when they go down to fetch it."

10. Baily adds in a note here, "On the 22nd December, at 8 a.m., it was 50 below zero; and on the 23rd December, at 8 a.m., it was 7 ½ below zero; at the *mouth* of the Ohio, as observed by Mr. [Andrew] Ellicott." Ellicott's narrative of his travels in 1796 follows in the present volume.

11. Baily adds in a note here, "By accounts which I saw in several of the newspapers afterwards, I found that the breaking up of the Ohio occasioned a degree of mischief unknown in any preceding period. Out of several hundred families which descended the river this season, there were very few but experienced its ill effects in some measure or other. Some who were asleep in their boats at the time it happened had but just time to make their escape to the banks, whilst their boat (containing, perhaps, every particle of property which they possessed in the world,) was torn away by the violence of the current, and never seen more. Others were overtaken more unexpectedly, and, property and all, were hurried crying in vain to the spectators on the shore to come to their assistance. Some of these boats would happily strike the shore, where they were secured; but others, many others, would soon be staved by the floating ice, and everything on board be lost. There was an instance of this kind recorded in the Pittsburgh paper, where a man and his family; together with a number of negro slaves, all perished in this manner: they were seen from the shore in several places along the banks, but no one would venture to their assistance, for fear of sharing the same fate."

12. Baily notes here, "It is a well-known fact that the Americans judge of the quality of land when they are in the woods from the kinds of trees which grow on it. Thus maple, hiccory, buckeye, &c. indicate the richest soil."

13. Baily apparently consulted this scholarly periodical after his return.

14. Baily adds in a note here, "Imlay takes notice that the discharge of the sap might be of service in ascertaining the changes of the weather, having seen a journal

wherein it was particularly noted, together with the variations in the atmosphere. (See Imlay, p. 146, note)"

15. Baily adds a note here, "It was no small satisfaction to arrive at this place, not only that we might supply ourselves with those necessaries of which we had been so long deprived; but as we had been banished from society so long, the sight of a few people like ourselves gave us much pleasure; particularly as we recollected the names of a few persons who resided here, whom we had seen at Pittsburgh."

16. Thomas Hutchins prepared a map of the Ohio River for Bouquet's expedition in 1764. About a decade later, he prepared a more elaborate version, frequently published in the historical literature of the early Ohio Valley, titled, "A Topographical Description of Virginia, Pennsylvania Maryland, and North Carolina" (London, 1778).

17. Baily adds in a note here, "We came to the Little Kanaway about five o'clock. The Ohio makes a beautiful turn here to the right, which renders the point of land on the northern side, opposite the Little Kanaway, a beautiful situation. There are some good plantations on this spot, and we put ashore in our canoe and got some eggs and milk, which was a great treat to us. It is twelve miles from Muskingham."

18. Baily adds here, "The Great Kanaway is near 500 yards wide at its mouth, and is so considerable a branch of the Ohio that it may be mistaken for it by persons ascending this river. It rises in North Carolina, and runs a course of 400 miles before it empties itself into the Ohio. Its navigation is unfortunately obstructed by a fall not eighty miles from its mouth."

19. Baily adds, "The Sciota at its mouth is about 200 yards wide, its current gentle, and navigable for nearly 200 miles, with a portage of only five or six miles to Sandusky."

20. Drayage services for disembarking immigrants appears to have been a regular business, supplementing farm income. James Hedge recalled that in 1793, there were "A good many wagons waiting at Maysville [Limestone], . . . for loading when we got there. For loading immigrants." James Hedge Interview, Draper Coll., 12CC117.

Chapter 12. David Meade, 1796

1. For more on Meade, see David Hackett Fischer and James C. Kelly, *Bound Away: Virginia and the Westward Movement* (Charlottesville: University Press of Virginia, 2000), 159–63.

2. It was common among English-speaking Americans in the eighteenth century to term all Germans as Dutch. The region of Frederick County, Virginia, included a substantial number of German inhabitants.

3. This is apparently a reference to immigrant origins from the German province of Saxony.

4. In 1754, young George Washington led Virginia militia toward the French outpost at Pittsburgh, known then as Fort DuQuesne, but was forced to surrender. Washington's surrender occurred near the same place as General Braddock's defeat.

5. Meade apparently did not provide shelter for the boat's slaves.

6. Pioneers dealt with clearing land of large trees by first killing them by cutting through the bark all around the base, cutting off nutrition. This quickly prevented leaf development, opening the ground beneath to the sun and producing space

for crops with a minimum of labor. The more common term for this practice was *girdling*.

7. This references William Henry Harrison and the Ohio side of the river.

8. For a description of floating mills, see Andrew Ellicott's entry for November 11, on page 241 of this volume.

9. About 600 French people had been enticed to Gallipolis by an agent of the Scioto Company (a subsidiary of the Ohio Company), who grossly misrepresented the site's character, particularly its exposure to Indian raids.

10. In 1782, a large Indian force besieged Bryant's (or Bryan's) Station. Although the station withstood the siege, the contingent of Kentucky militia that pursued the invaders was ambushed at the Lower Blue Licks. Some seventy men were killed or missing, a major disaster for the fledgling settlements. See Richard H. Collins and Willard R. Jillson, "The Siege of Bryan's Station," *FCHQ* 36 (1938): 15–25.

11. The first permanent settlement at Lexington had been in 1779, as a fortified settlement. Located in the central Bluegrass region, it quickly emerged as a central place. At the time of Meade's arrival, its population exceeded that of Pittsburgh, Cincinnati, Louisville, and Kentucky's capital, Frankfort. Lexington boasted a population of approximately 1,600 people and 300 dwellings.

Chapter 13. Andrew Ellicott, 1796

1. Gen. James Wilkinson has been described as one of the Ohio Valley frontier's greatest rogues for duplicitous relations with colleagues, but especially his secret relations with Spanish authorities at New Orleans in exchange for commercial privileges. See James Riley Jacobs, *Tarnished Warrior: Major General James Wilkinson* (New York: 1938); Lowell H. Harrison, "James Wilkinson: A Leader for Kentucky?" *FCHQ* 66 (1992): 334–68; John Thornton Posey, "Rascality Revisited: In Defense of General James Wilkinson," *FCHQ* 74 (2000): 309–51, and James Wilkinson, *Memoirs of My Own Times*, 3 vols. (New York: 1941).

2. Ellicott is referring to the attacks made by Michael Cresap and Daniel Greathouse that contributed to the outbreak of Dunmore's War in 1774. McConnell, *A Country Between*, 274–75.

3. A large Indian mound lay on the edge of Marietta and later became part of the Marietta cemetery. The region included additional, smaller mounds.

4. The Ohio Company founded Belpre in 1789.

5. The Ohio Company founded Belleville in 1789.

6. Virginia militia colonel Andrew Lewis's troops had played a critical role at the battle of Point Pleasant.

7. Apparently, numerous prehistoric fossils lay near the earth surface or were exposed by water erosion.

Sources

Austin, [Moses]. "A Memorandum of M. Austin's Journey from the Lead Mines in the County of Wythe in the State of Virginia to the Lead Mines in the Province of Louisiana West of the Mississippi [1796–1797]." *The American Historical Review* 5 (1899–1900); 518–42.

Baily, F.R.S. *Journal of a Tour in Unsettled Parts of North America in 1796 and 1797 by the Late Francis Baily.* London: Baily Brothers, 1856.

Cresswell, Nicholas. *The Journal of Nicholas Cresswell, 1774–1777.* New York: The Dial Press, 1924.

Dewees, Mary Coburn. "Journal of Mary Coburn Dewees." Reuben T. Durrett Collection, Special Collections, University of Chicago Library.

Ellicott, Andrew. *The Journal of Andrew Ellicott, Late Comissioner on Behalf of the United States during Part of the Year 1796, the Years 1797, 1798, 1799, and Part of the Year 1800.* Philadelphia: Printed by Rudd and Bartram for Thomas Dodson, 1803.

Kilpatrick, Lewis L., ed. "The Journal of William Calk, Kentucky Pioneer." *Mississippi Valley Historical Review* 7 (1921): 363–77.

Morrow, Joshua, ed. "Tours into Kentucky and the Northwest Territory: Three Journals by the Rev. James Smith of Powhatan County, Va." *Ohio Archaeological and Historical Publications* 16 (1907): 348–401.

Muhlenberg, Henry A. *The Life of Major General Peter Muhlenberg of the Revolutionary Army.* Philadelphia: Carey and Hart, 1849.

Nourse, James. "Journey to Kentucky in 1775." *The Journal of American History* 29 (1925): 121–38, 251–60, and 351–64.

Shepard, Samuel. *Diary, 1787–1796.* Massachusetts Historical Society.

Smith, Dwight L. *The Western Journals of John May, Ohio Company Agent and Business Adventurer.* Cincinnati: Historical and Philosophical Society of Ohio, 1961.

Still, Bayard, ed. "The Westward Migration of a Planter Pioneer in 1796." *The William and Mary Quarterly*, ser. 2., 21 (1941): 318–43.

Index

CPSIA information can be obtained at www.ICGtesting.com
Printed in the USA
BVOW02s0058050815

411777BV00002B/132/P